Purposehood

Transform Your Life, Transform the World

by Ammar

This edition published by PHD Publishing.
For information, write to purposehood@phdpublishing.com.

First Edition

ISBN: 978-1-7344497-2-3

Library of Congress Cataloging-in-Publication Data

Charani, Ammar
Purposehood®: Transform Your Life, Transform the World
Includes index.

Summary: "Purposehood: Transform Your Life, Transform the World will challenge you to reflect on your own existence as Ammar combines his hard-won clarity of life's purpose with deep philosophy and science to help you change yourself and the world." – Provided by publisher.

ISBN: 978-1-7344497-2-3 (hardbound)
1. Philosophy 2. Inspirational

Library of Congress Control Number: 2020936373

Cover and illustration design by Catalin Serban.
Produced for PHD Publishing by Michael Roney and Sarah Clarehart, Highpoint Executive Publishing.

10 9 8 7 6 5 4 3 2 1

Contents

Dedication

I dedicate this book to iSH and to you.

You ask, "Who is iSH, and why me?"

iSH is the grand mystery that keeps us curious, asking questions, and searching for answers. iSH is the unseeable, unimaginable, and still unexplainable force that sparked existence. iSH is the grand inspiration that pulls us forward toward a better future for all.

Religious people call it "God"; Star Wars fans call it "the force"; some cosmologists and mystics call it "the universe"; some Eastern religions call it "consciousness"; some atheist scientists call it the "nothingness"; and Einstein called it "the summation of all equations." I simply call it iSH, which is a combination of the initial letters of it, She, and He, and which is like nothing imaginable or describable.

If there is a thing you can imagine or describe in a sentence, as in "iSH is …" or "iSH is not…" then that definitely is not iSH, as the boundaries of your imagination, and the limitation of your description, would render iSH a product of your perception. In this book, I sometimes use iSH interchangeably with God, the Creator, the universe, existence, or nothingness. I assign no religious labels nor dogmas to it.

You are encouraged to interpret iSH as you wish, but hopefully your understanding will be free from the influence of dogmas handed down by previous generations, as well as from the interpretations of others. As we humans discover more of the creation mechanics, and as existence reveals its secrets to our evolving humanity, our perception of iSH will change. Yet, this creating force will remain different for different people. I would even dare to say iSH is unique to each one of us. We all make iSH in our own image or for our own needs. iSH is all that and none of that. I personally view iSH as the grand mystery beyond.

It is to you, my friend; you, the young mind that is the future of existence, the hope of humanity, of life, of the universe; you, who have never stopped being curious, have never accepted dictated ideas handed down by generations of acquiescing followers; you, who always challenge the status quo, always question the past, always look toward the future; you, who desire a life of happiness, success, fulfillment, meaning, and purpose, I dedicate this book.

Acknowledgments

I am grateful for all my Five Extensions of Being.

I am grateful for having a self that is driven by endless curiosity; a self that enjoys inwardly and outwardly mindful reflections and appreciates the times alone and in silence.

I am grateful for a large family, spread around the globe, who infuse my existence with rich emotions and remind me that I'm never alone.

I am grateful to have work that brings meaningful accomplishments to my life and for working with people who positively influence my existence and give me the privilege to positively influence theirs.

I am grateful to the diverse friends, forums, groups, and communities around me. Some belong to my "Inclusion List," whom I count on to be my cheerleaders when I am feeling down. Others belong to my "Expansion List," where I receive, through their challenges to me, my inspirations and ever-expanding awareness.

I am grateful to nature with all its wonders, beauty, and magnificence for giving myself, my family, my coworkers, and my communities the most important gift of all, life. I am grateful to nature for revealing its mysteries and expanding my awareness with every mindful step I take among its amazing creatures.

And I am grateful to iSH, for being.

Introduction

My friend, we live in the jungle of life, dense and dark. We are confused, tense, stressed, anxious, full of regrets, and tired from constantly running, either after our desires or away from our fears. There's this vacuum in our lives that is never filled, no matter how many desires we acquire or goals we achieve.

We are taught in the jungle of life to climb the *Pyramid of Desires* by satisfying first our basic desires before moving to our essential ones. Then, if we are fortunate enough, we might arrive to our fundamental desires of happiness, success, and fulfillment. Hopefully, before we die, we even might satisfy our existential desire of discovering why we are on this Earth and the purpose of our lives.

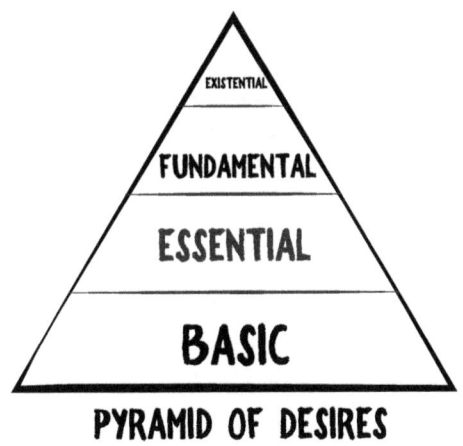

PYRAMID OF DESIRES

However, when we have no direction in our lives, that purpose all-too-easily becomes *satisfying our infinite basic desires*. Our happiness, success, and fulfillment become dependent upon fulfilling those desires better, sooner, and more often. We end up in the service of them with work we don't like, superficial relationships we don't enjoy, and lifetimes wasted without true fulfillment.

What if we flip that pyramid and first strive to satisfy our existential desire—the *why* of our existence? If we simply do that, then everything will change. We will have direction in our lives. Happiness, success, and fulfillment will become byproducts of walking the path toward our guiding star. We will seek work and relationships that are guided by our existential purpose and fulfill only the desires that take us back to the Garden of Eden.

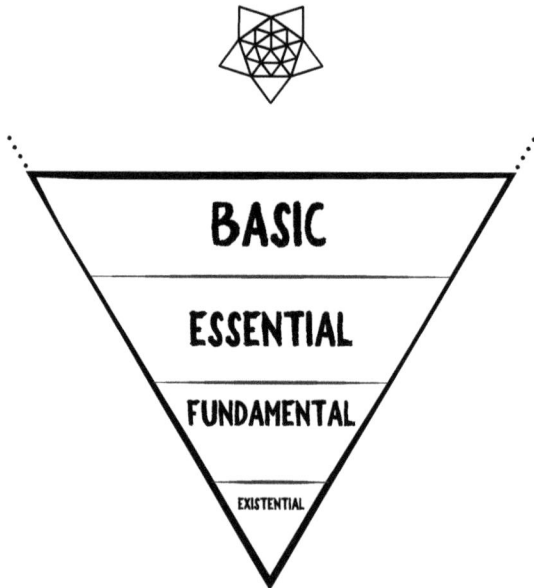

There is another life out there in the Garden of Eden, a life of clarity, a life of gratitude, a life where happiness, success, and fulfillment are filling the air, and all we need to do to receive them is just be. This book is about getting back to Eden where we were born, before we were taken away to the jungle of life and imprisoned, first by the limiting beliefs of the people around us, then by the limiting beliefs we created for ourselves. It's about unleashing our own potentiality along with that of every human on this Earth.

Humanity has accomplished what seemed impossible a mere century ago, and we're forging our way to the stars while decoding the secrets of creation. Humankind's small percentage of geniuses have paved the road for the rest to capitalize on advancements in science, technology, engineering, math, medicine, arts, music, and philosophy, among many other fields. Our future is waiting for us with inconceivable wonders not far away from today. It's said that 2 percent of humanity are geniuses. Imagine if every human is a genius. Where could we go and what would we become? My friend, this is our destiny—the unleashed potentiality of every human.

It took me a lifetime of learning and exploration to discover this simple truth, and in this book, I share what I learned with you. This book, this philosophy, is the product of my journey so far. It will continue to evolve and expand as life reveals more of its mysteries, and people like you share their experiences with me.

You ask, "How did you get here?"

PART I

Discovering Purposehood:
A Forward-Pulling Existential
Theory

How I Got Here

It's said that who we are today is a product of a child's interpretation of a story that happened in our earliest memory—the first self-directed branch point[1] in our lives. Mine is a story of misdiagnosis, specifically when I was told as a very young child that if I didn't stop playing, I would die from a heart defect. This led me to contemplate death and look for the purpose of life at a young age. At first, I thought I found it in religion, as I attended Christian Orthodox and Catholic schools, and later spent 10 years with Sufi masters and religious scholars learning, practicing, and teaching.

Life was all about fulfillment through serving others, so when I had a chance after graduating with an engineering degree from a university in the United States, I served for five years as a clergyman. Later, I sought success as an entrepreneur, starting businesses in many sectors around the world and employing thousands of people.

However, in my pursuit of success, I totally forgot about happiness. So, I redirected my life toward the pursuit of happiness through luxurious possessions and unique experiences. During this period I experienced a major existential disruption, a near-death experience, as my heart flatlined for 35 seconds. That was my **Day of Awakening**. I was not only awakened from death, I also woke up to the ultimate search for purpose. On that day, I was nudged forcefully, again, to search for the purpose of my life.

For the next 11 years, I searched for my purpose in biology, quantum mechanics, neuroscience, psychology, mathematics, religion, philosophy, and mysticism—all to no avail.

Then came my **Day of Clarity**. As I was walking by the Spanish shores of the Mediterranean Sea after 10 days of fasting on water, I realized I should be looking first for the purpose of existence, of the universe, life, and humanity, in order to extrapolate the purpose of a human's life and thus mine.

Six-and-a-half months later, as I was in deep meditation surrounded by nature on the night of my twenty-first day of fasting, I felt connected to all that existed. When I opened my eyes, I felt overwhelmed with a mixture of happiness, success, and fulfillment. I was there in Eden. It was as if the answers to all my existential questions had been downloaded, all at once. On that **Night of Destiny**, I was able to clearly see where my guiding star was pulling me. With that newfound understanding of the future, I became determined to re-examine my past to discover the times when I had experienced similar clarity.

I spent many months examining my life, from my earliest memories to present day, searching with an existential flashlight for those periods when I was growing my potential and receiving happiness, success, and fulfillment, all at the same time. The search took me way back to my early childhood. It seems this is the time when we clearly live, without reservations, our existential purpose, which I call *Purposehood*.

You ask, "But why then? What is so special about being a child?"

Are You a Creative Genius?

In 1968, Dr. George Land was contracted by the National Aeronautics and Space Administration (NASA) to develop a test to find the most creative scientists among its employees. NASA intended to allocate them to critical missions, as it was preparing to land a man on the moon. The test was designed to find exceptional people who were able to come up with creative solutions to any problem they might face. His test found that 2 percent of NASA employees were geniuses. My friend, you can understand the power of these creative geniuses on humanity's evolution. Einstein once wrote: "Imagination is more important than knowledge. For knowledge is limited, whereas imagination embraces the entire world, stimulating progress, giving birth to evolution."

NASA has a lot of very smart people, but the questions that come to mind are why are there perhaps two exceptionally creative people—geniuses—among every hundred of us? Is it genetic or is it learned? Nature or nurture? Do you think the 2 percent were born geniuses or worked hard to become the way they are?

To answer these questions, Dr. Land administered the test to 1,600 children between the ages of four and five. What he found shocked him: The percentage of children who tested at the genius level of creativity was 98 percent. Can you imagine that? *The universal odds of being born a genius are 98 percent!*

Dr. Land decided to re-test these children every five years, and again, the results were shocking. By the age of 10, the percentage of those testing at the genius level dropped by 68 points to 30 percent. By the age of 15, it was 12 percent, and for the one million adults tested afterward, it was down to 2 percent.

This means that you won the top evolutionary prize among all creatures at the time of your birth, only to have society strip it away by the age of 10. I wonder if the 98 percent of geniuses among five-year-old children could have been 100 percent at birth?

The Seed of Potentiality

Every creature is born, just like a plant, with a seed to grow into their ultimate potential. I call this the *seed of potentiality*. You can think about it as a line of code not unlike the code written for an artificial intelligence (AI) program that sets the basic capabilities of a machine to learn and grow beyond its initial code, adapting to its environment and challenges. In nature, it's meant to activate a *nature intelligence*, which enables everything in the natural world to evolve and expand.

SEED OF POTENTIALITY FOR ALL CREATURES

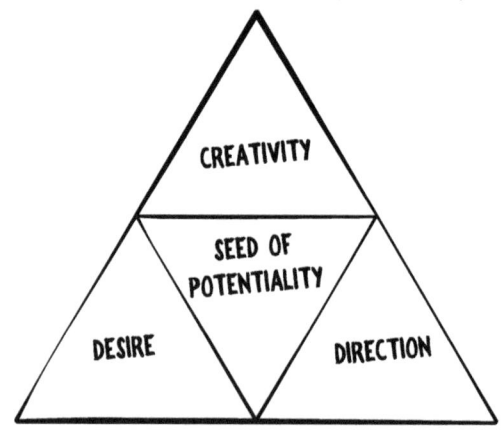

The seed of potentiality has three components: desire, creativity, and direction. Nature's creatures are born with basic desires that help them survive and reproduce. They have enough creativity to allow themselves to navigate through challenges that otherwise would prevent them from acquiring their basic desires. You can see this clearly in nature if you observe the roots of any plant as they navigate around rocks to reach water, or if you watch beavers building dams. This desire and creativity always lead them in the direction of their *existential purpose*, to become what they were meant to be.

A pine seed will use its innate desires to survive, reproduce, and direct its growth to become a beautiful pine tree as long as it's not constrained by outside forces. When challenged with threats, it uses its basic creativity to overcome those challenges and still try to grow to its full potential. However, a pine seed is never faced with the existential dilemma of choosing what to become besides a pine tree or what role to play in this existence beside the role it's meant to play. The same applies to all matter and creatures in the universe, except humans.

Your unique seed of potentiality is meant to activate *human intelligence* (HI) in order for you to grow as "creator." To do so, it's made of infinite desires, limitless creativity, and directional choice.

Your desires are different than those of other creatures. While their desires are limited to their basic needs in order to survive, reproduce, and fulfill their purpose, your human desires are infinitely fueled by wanting better, more, and sooner. You don't want food just for sustenance, you want better-tasting food with a wide variety of choices, and once it's to your taste, then one bite is not enough; you want to keep eating until you can't eat any more. When a thought of a desirable food comes to your mind, you don't want to wait until you are invited to a birthday party for that chocolate ice cream; you want it now. Obesity plagues humanity, but how many obese animals have you seen?

Your creativity is not limited to survival and reproduction like other creatures; it is spaceless, timeless, and formless. You can be sitting in a cave, but your imagination can expand across galaxies, creating worlds of strange creatures that no one has ever seen before. You are here in the present, yet your creativity is capable of not only solving the problems you are facing now, but also reimagining the stories of your past, and most importantly, imagining a possible or even an impossible future. And while you possess a realistic structural imagination, you are also capable of *imagining* new structures that don't exist in nature or haven't even been thought of before. Aren't the arts such as painting, movies, or poetry, as well as sciences such as bioengineering, robotics, or coding, all about limitless creativity?

Your destiny of who you will become is not set in stone or predetermined by genetic codes. When it comes to your existential direction, *you have the ability at any moment of your life to make a directional choice.* You can either be like a feather moving in whatever direction the wind blows, or mindfully choose a positive direction for your life.

Do you choose to continue living directionless as a product of accumulated past stories, limiting beliefs, and expectations of others, or will you choose to take charge of who you want to become? Do you want to continue trudging in the directions of scarcity, suffering, rejection, and vacuum, or live with abundance, ease, and gratitude in the direction of your Purposehood?

Do you choose to remain in the jungle of life, running away from fears and after infinite desires, suffering from stress, anxiety, and regrets—or do you choose to find your way back to Eden?

You ask, "What is Eden, and how do I find it?"

Our Garden of Eden

We are born in the land of potentiality at the center of our beautiful, fertile, circle of living, as wide as our awareness can be. It is a land filled with hopes, dreams, and potential for greatness. You may even call it the Garden of Eden. We're born carrying within us the seed of potentiality, waiting to be nourished with happiness, success, and fulfillment. These nourishments have developed over billions of years of an evolving universe, with Earth's blue skies, shiny stars, sunshine and rain, to become the hormones of incentives in our brains. We're born free to innovate and explore, to attract and want, to love and belong, to construct and beautify, to imagine and create a better world for all, to play a major role in the game of existence.

In the first years of our lives, we are like any other creature, fueled by basic desires, exponentially expanding our creativity, and living with a clear direction of what we are meant to become: *creators*.

Like all lifeforms, we receive happiness, success, and fulfillment as a reward for living our life the way we should in the direction of our Purposehood. We don't need to teach five-year-old children how to be happy—it radiates through them. We don't need to teach them to be successful—they never give up until they accomplish what's on their mind, regardless of how many tries it takes. We don't need to teach them about fulfillment—they go to sleep every evening with no regrets, knowing they have invested their day the best way possible. Children don't need to think about life's purpose—they simply live it with every breath they take, with every new skill they learn, and with every interaction. With every moment of their life they grow closer to their potentiality as they develop the skills they need to play their role in existence. They intuitively stay connected to life, to existence, to the universe—even as they exit the warmth of the womb to experience this new reality.

But alas, we don't stay in that state for long. The moment we are born, we are shackled with labels that give each one of us a name, a nationality, an ethnicity, a religious sect—none of which we choose. Then slowly, we're taken into the jungle of life to grow and become what others are expecting of us. We are fed limiting beliefs that make us doubt our self-worth and move us away from the roles we were born to play in this life. We overlook our existential purpose and true potential.

While we are growing up surrounded by tense, stressed, and anxious people who are full of regrets, we start adding new labels to ourselves. Soon we totally forget our Purposehood and our potentiality and simply become another creature of the jungle running away from fears, or constantly pursuing basic desires. Instead of becoming the creators of a better future for ourselves, humanity, and nature, we become slaves of consumption and status, conformity and obedience, rivalry and power, vanity and possessions.

When we are constantly moving away from our Purposehood, the tension of existence becomes unbearable, and if we don't adjust our direction back toward our existential purpose, we end up living a life of vacuum, filled only with scarcity, suffering, and rejection.

Negative States of Living:

LIFE OF VACUUM = NEGATIVE DIRECTION + INFINITE DESIRES + LIMITLESS CREATIVITY = > SCARCITY + SUFFERING + REJECTION

NEGATIVE STATES OF LIVING

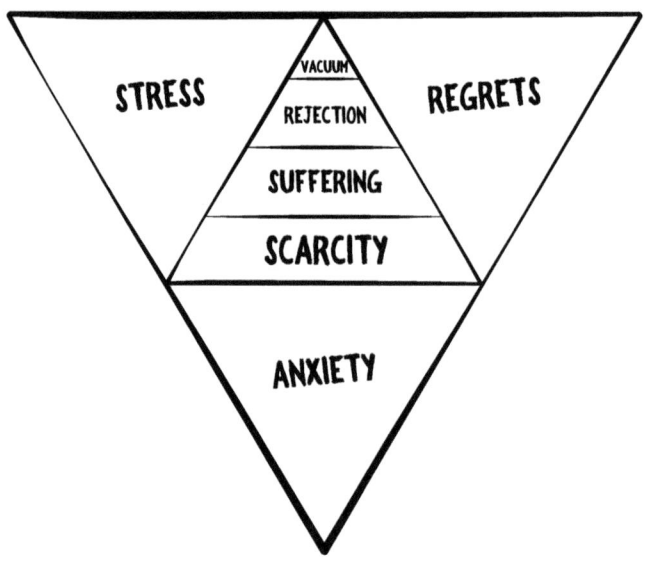

Fortunately, the seed of potentiality within us never dies, no matter how diminished it becomes. We still have the directional choice to turn around, find our Purposehood, and start moving toward it. We have the power to turn our desires into values. The power to unshackle ourselves from the limiting beliefs produced by labels, dogmas, and negative interpretations of past events. We can choose to live a life of

Purposehood with gratitude, ease, and abundance.
Positive States of Living:

LIFE OF PURPOSEHOOD = POSITIVE DIRECTION +
INFINITE DESIRES + LIMITLESS CREATIVITY
= > GRATITUDE + EASE + ABUNDANCE

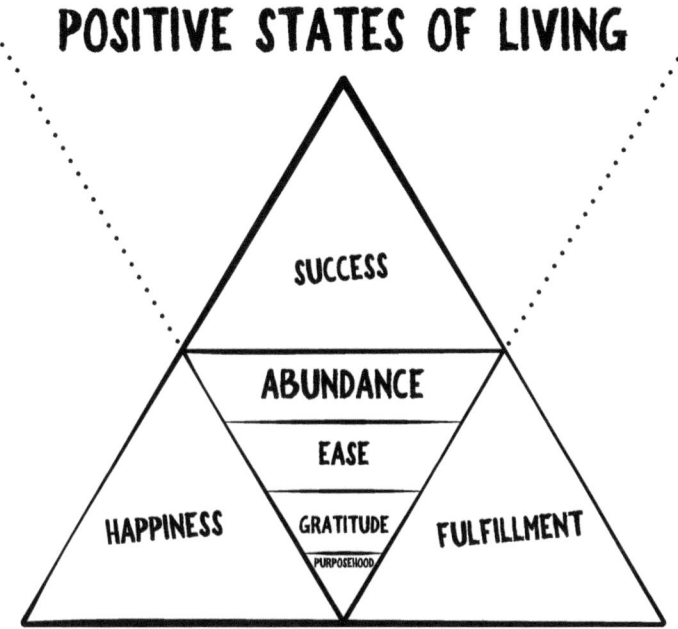

You ask, "Why is Purposehood so important for my life?"

Purposehood Is Crucial for Your Life

Viktor Frankl, an Austrian psychiatrist who developed logotherapy, the third Viennese school of psychotherapy, along with Sigmund Freud and Alfred Adler, became prisoner #119104 in a Nazi concentration camp. He realized during his ordeal that those prisoners who had a sense of purpose—oriented toward the future with something to hold on to beyond themselves, like awaiting loved ones or a life's goal they hadn't completed—were more resilient under the miserable camps' conditions.

In an interview, Frankl mentioned the case of a prisoner who wanted to commit suicide. When Frankl asked him why, the prisoner said that he had nothing to expect from his life anymore. Frankl asked the prisoner if it was conceivable that life was still expecting something from him. The prisoner told Frankl that he had started writing a collection of books, which he felt were important to share with the world, that he had not finished. Suddenly, with this simple future mind shift toward a purpose higher than himself, the prisoner's attitude toward his suffering changed. Frankl agreed with Nietzsche, who said: "Those who have a *why* to live, can bear almost any *how*."

Here's how Frankl described his formula for despair:

DESPAIR = SUFFERING - MEANING

However, adding a meaning to suffering will change the equation to:

MEANING + SUFFERING = ACCOMPLISHMENT

Frankl theorized that every human has a desire to discover the purpose of their life. Otherwise their life would feel meaningless and empty, leading to depression.[2]

Professor William Damon, one of the world's leading researchers on the development of purpose in life, later argued that having no purpose in life may not only lead to depression but also to self-absorption, addiction, physical disorders resulting from emotional factors, inability to have healthy relationships, destructive behavior, and lack of productivity.[3]

Judging from the rising number of people living a life of rejection with stress, anxiety, and regrets, it seems that loss of Purposehood may be a pandemic.

Stress

While "positive" stress, such as meeting deadlines, is essential for our advancement, negative stress is destroying our well-being and happiness. The American Psychological Association found that 75 percent of Americans reported experiencing at least one symptom of stress in the past month. This included symptoms such as being irritable, angry, nervous, unmotivated, fatigued, overwhelmed, or sad. People also reported physical symptoms of stress such as headache, upset stomach, muscle tension, teeth grinding, change of appetite, change in sex drive, and feeling dizzy.

It is no surprise that the list of worries also included items such as the future of the nation (63 percent), money (62 percent), work (61 percent), politics (57 percent), crimes (51 percent), relationships (47 percent), health (46 percent), among many others.[4] It seems people are stressed about everything!

Researchers also have determined that 8 percent of the total US population have developed the serious condition of post-traumatic stress disorder (PTSD).[5] That's over 25 million Americans who have PTSD at any given time, with women twice as likely as men to suffer from it.

Anxiety

According to the World Health Organization, more than 450 million people around the world live with mental illnesses, with anxiety disorders as the most common manifestation.[6] In fact, one in every 13 people globally suffer from anxiety. In the United States, the ratio for the disorder is much higher—possibly due to more accurate reporting—affecting 18.1 percent of people ages 18 and older. That's more than 40 million adults in America alone.

Sadly, anxiety disorders also affect 25.1 percent of American children between 13 and 18 years old, according to the Anxiety and Depression Association of America. As for depression, 16.2 million US adults had at least one case of major depressive episodes. The highest was among the 18-to-25 age group, and again, females were affected twice as often as males. Globally, more than 264 million people suffer from depression.[7]

Severe depression can be a major precursor to suicide. According to the World Health Organization, worldwide, around one million people die by suicide each year. In America, there are an average of 129 suicide deaths per day. It's estimated that for every suicide, there are 25 attempts.[8] These are people who sadly lost the why in their lives. It's a universal defeat to lose the potentiality of any human, and we all need to strive to make sure every member of our family, work, and communities has a clear Purposehood.

Regrets

Along with the power of directional choice that we were gifted as humans came regret, the most common negative emotion. "Could I have done better? What did I do wrong? How did I miss that opportunity?" We often get stuck in the past, which becomes another state of mind that generates problems and suffering. Visiting the past can be great for reflecting on a wrong decision or a missed opportunity if it leads to corrective actions and better decision-making. However, many people get stuck in a cycle of self-blame, which mainly leads to inaction.

In a University of Illinois study about what we regret most and why, researchers found that the six biggest regrets in life centered around choices in this order[9]:

- Education: "If only I had studied harder or studied something else."
- Career: "If only I were a dentist," or "I should've taken that first job offer."
- Romance: "I wish I had married John instead of Joe," or "I wish I were with Jane instead of Susan."
- Family and parenting: "If only I spent more time with my kids," or "I wish I'd called my mom more often."
- Self: "If only I had more self-control," or "I wish I could be more fit."
- Leisure: "I wish I had visited Paris when I was young," or "I should've climbed Kilimanjaro when I was healthy."

In the sample made up of college students, the list started, understandably, with romance, friends, education, leisure, self, and career. The researchers also found that the regret of missed opportunities by inaction persisted longer than a regret of acting, even if the decision was wrong.

In her book, *The Top Five Regrets of the Dying*,[10] palliative nurse Bronnie Ware recorded the top regrets of her patients. We ought to invest time reflecting on many of these, including:

- "I wish I'd had the courage to live a life true to myself, not the life others expected of me."
- "I wish I hadn't worked so hard."

- "I wish I'd had the courage to express my feelings."
- "I wish I had stayed in touch with my friends."
- "I wish that I had let myself be happier."

Basically, regret is about choices we make that waste our lives. How have you been using your lifetime? Has it been wasted on useless events and unfulfilling encounters, or has it been invested in rewarding opportunities of growth and positive relationships? Have your choices increased or reduced your potential? Are you investing your time on activities that move you closer to your Purposehood, or away from it?

In 1946, Frankl published the international bestseller, *Man's Search for Meaning*, which sparked thousands of research studies and experiments to understand the impact of having a purpose in life, a Purposehood. Since then, a number of researches have uncovered a great deal of data on its impact. Key findings from a few of these follow. I hope you will find them as fascinating as I did!

Well-Being

Several researchers found that one of the best predictors of happiness at any age is having a purpose in life.[11] These and other scientific studies found that having a purpose in life is extremely crucial to a person's well-being, physically and psychologically at any age.[12,13] For example, for older adults,[14] those who had a clearer Purposehood reported fewer chronic diseases, reduced pain, fewer physical disabilities, less dementia, were 2.4 times less likely to develop Alzheimer's disease,[15] and had fewer sleep problems.[16] In addition, people with Purposehood have a higher ability to tap into their inner strength and resiliency, which contributes to faster recovery, reduced depression, and better overall health.[17,18]

Purposehood is also essential to psychological well-being, including life satisfaction, a sense of accomplishment and enjoyment, happiness, hope, optimism, and self-esteem, in addition to reducing depression and anxiety.[19,20] Purposehood creates a future-pulling positive force that keeps us moving forward regardless of the challenges.

Some studies revealed that having a Purposehood provided higher levels of optimism and hope for people dealing with existential crises, such as cancer patients.[21] In another study, the researcher placed late-stage cancer patients in two separate groups of 8 to 10 people.[22] One group received standard supportive psychotherapy. The other received meaning-centered group psychotherapy based on Dr. Frankl's work, in which they would discuss existential purpose-related topics and share their future goals and aspirations. The meaning-centered groups were less depressed, less hopeless, experienced fewer physical symptoms, and showed more willingness to live with improved quality of life and spiritual well-being than the group receiving standard psychotherapy.

Longevity

In an article in *National Geographic Magazine*, author Dan Buettner shared his decade-long search to identify areas around the world where people lived longer and healthier.[23] He found five such small communities, which he dubbed "blue zones," since he and his team had been circling those areas on the map with a blue pen. Those areas had a higher percentage of individuals who lived to 100 years of age, while the rest lived an active and healthy life into their 80s and 90s.

The team found nine common denominators, two of which were directly related to the number of years added to a person's longevity. The first denominator—contributing to seven happier and healthier years of life—was "knowing why you wake up in the morning"—*a clarity of Purposehood*. It's not surprising that another study found that older women who were engaged in life with a clearer Purposehood started the day with a lower level of the stress hormone cortisol and maintained that level throughout the day.[24] They also had lower cholesterol and were less likely to be overweight.

In one intriguing study, the researchers followed 6,163 people between the ages of 20 and 70 for 14 years to gauge the impact of purpose on longevity.[25] They found that people with a Purposehood lived longer regardless of their age or work status and that "maintaining a strong purpose in life can be as important at younger ages as it is at much older ages."

These findings correspond with another study that has highlighted the importance of having a Purposehood as early as possible.[26] They also showed that purpose plays a unique role in longevity unrelated to other psychological and well-being factors. The researchers concluded: "Having a purpose in life appears to widely buffer against mortality risk across the adult years," and that "greater purpose predicts greater longevity in adulthood."

Relationships

The second common denominator in the Blue Zones study was "belonging," which added up to 14 happier and healthier years to centenarians' lives. In another study, Harvard researchers closely tracked the lives of 724 men for 75 years, and now their children, to determine what makes a good life.

Dr. Robert Waldinger, the current director of the Harvard Study of Adult Development said in his TED Talk, "The clearest message that we get from this 75-year study is this: Good relationships keep us happier and healthier. Period."[27] He concluded that those relationships protect our bodies and our brains.

You ask, "What makes a good relationship?"

My friend, Dr. Waldinger noted that one major takeaway from their study was that it didn't matter how many friends you have or if you're in a committed relationship; rather, it is the *quality* of the relationships that matters.

Another research study found that the presence of purpose is associated with positive social relationships, contributing to better physical and psychological well-being, since an individual without a Purposehood is more likely to suffer from depression, boredom, loneliness, and anxiety.[28, 29]

Given all this, it appears that Purposehood is an instigator for high engagement with others in life and creates a reason to take care of our well-being, either for selfish reasons like staying fit or avoiding pain, or for altruistic reasons like achieving our life's higher goal. The research concluded that a common Purposehood helps people share commitment to positive health behaviors, which leads to better health.

The bottom line: Good relationships, the ones that make us feel good about ourselves and others, are all about having a shared Purposehood and a shared direction in life!

Young People

Having a Purposehood was found to be related to optimism and hopefulness among individuals in their teens, 20s, and 30s. Those without a purpose in life were more likely to abuse drugs and suffer from anxiety, loneliness, and depression.[30,31] The importance for adolescents to have a purpose in life is even more profound as it impacts the development of their belief system and future growth.[32]

A 17-year study highlighted how having clear prosocial goals that come with clarity of Purposehood for college students predicted greater well-being.[33] When students are able to set clear goals that correspond to their Purposehood, those goals will affect the development of their personality traits.[34] Those traits will impact their genes and could be passed on to their children, as is evident in the advancing science of epigenetics.[35] Having those clear goals in life increased students' personal growth and self-awareness, commitment to share learnings and experiences with others, sense of direction, mastery and control over their daily environment, desire to pursue goals, and overall life satisfaction. The researchers concluded that investing in a social role will prepare personalities for better social integration and well-being in adulthood.[36]

In a fascinating study of over 2,000 adolescents, researchers found that students with a Purposehood linked to their learning, or what they called "self-transcendent purpose," fought temptations and distractions, stayed focused on their studies, and were less likely to drop out of school, while students who were self-oriented with no Purposehood didn't do as well.[37]

The researchers wondered if exposure to a Purposehood that

is linked to learning would improve academic performance for young students, so they ran a second study. It was found that even a one-time self-transcendent purpose intervention increased achievements, over several months, in harder courses such as STEM (science, technology, engineering, and mathematics), and contributed to a higher grade point average (GPA) in high school.

In my workshops, I found young people to be more engaged and excited as they reflected on major life issues such as the purpose of their existence and the true meaning of happiness, success, and fulfillment. Even after just that one engagement with their Purposehood, their evaluation forms at the end of the session often included statements like, "I was inspired to think about what I really want," and "This is a game changer for my life." Of course, the more engagement with Purposehood, the better the outcome. One can only imagine the results of living your Purposehood every day of your life!

However, to understand how even one intervention was able to create such positive results, the researchers mentioned earlier conducted a third study and found that Purposehooders, those who strive every day to move closer to their chosen Purposehood, spent twice as long improving their work instead of getting it over with as soon as possible.

Why did those students invest more time than others? In a fourth study, they assigned students tedious and unimportant tasks and told them they could quit at any time. In a world full of distractions, the Purposehooders showed self-discipline and completed the tasks with persistence, as they were focused on their future positive role in the world. The researchers noted that purely selfish goals such as making more money or having interesting jobs in the future "did not, on their own, consistently produce these benefits."

The big takeaway from these studies is that Purposehooders are more resilient in the face of setbacks, more persistent in pursuing their academic achievements, believe more in their abilities, produce better academic results, and find their schoolwork more meaningful, less stressful, and more exciting.[38]

Children Benefit from Purposehood

It is never too early to spark a child's interest in exploring their Purposehood. Children are already closer to true potentiality and their existential purpose. This means that parents and schools need to be careful not to misdirect children from their potentiality and Purposehood with labels, misguided expectations, and limiting beliefs. It's imperative for parents and teachers to find ways to work together in helping children pursue their Purposehood and develop their own unique intelligence. By recognizing children's aspirations and potentiality and ensuring they have access to the needed resources to grow in the direction of their Purposehood, children (like a well-nourished and unobstructed tree) can grow up experiencing better physical and psychological well-being, improved academic performance, and a greater willingness to contribute to the world.[39]

Meaningful, Successful Work

Work is a major outlet used to express our purpose in life and is a common source of purpose for many people.[40, 41] Those who find purpose in their work are more satisfied with their lives and professions.[42] Many older adults feel lost and less useful after retirement, which is a key factor contributing to the loneliness that plagues our elderly. However, when retired people re-engage in work or volunteer activities, they find a meaningful reason to continue living a healthy and hopeful life. Of course, "work" doesn't have to be limited to a formal position or job; it can also include activities at home as a full-time parent, as a student at school, or as a volunteer for a cause. It can be defined as any effort to achieve a result, and it is an integral part of our development and well-being.

One of the largest challenges to businesses is employee disengagement, which is estimated to cost the US economy more than $600 billion per year in lost productivity. Employee disengagement has been as high as 89 percent around the world and 74 percent in the U.S., but the good news in the U.S. is that recently this disengagement has dropped to 66 percent.[43] Still, that's two-thirds of employees who don't care about their work or find purpose in what they do—a shockingly large number!

More good news, if you can consider it as such, is that actively disengaged employees, those who are actively trying to hurt a business and drive customers away, has dropped from 20 percent to 13 percent. But even one such person is enough to spoil the workplace environment for all, like a worm in a box of fresh apples. Business managers need to help employees engage with their Purposehood at work in ways that advance the objectives of the business in order to create a win for all.

Nevertheless, I would like to focus here on you and your workplace. I often hear about people trying to create a work-life balance as if they have surrendered to the idea that work and life are two different things. We spend almost a third of our lives working, and if work is not life itself, then we are surely wasting one-third of our lives. Would you want to waste a third of your life suffering from tension at work, or would you rather leave at the end of the day more energized? It is your duty to make sure work is aligned with your Purposehood so that it becomes engaging, pleasurable, and even exciting.

There is no better place to grow your potentiality in the direction of your Purposehood than at work, once you make it meaningful. Now you have two options: Find work that aligns with your Purposehood, or influence your work environment to become purposeful.

There is nothing preventing you from igniting Purposehood in the lives you touch at work, be it your boss, coworkers, customers, suppliers, or shareholders. You can start by finding reasons and opportunities in your work to live your Purposehood and inspire others to live theirs.

As part of a New York University study, researchers asked 28 cleaning employees at a hospital to describe their job.[44] From the data they collected, they were able to divide the employees into two groups: People who looked at their work as a task, and others who saw the same work as a mission. The first group did the minimum possible to consider their work "finished" each day and were less willing to go beyond the job description. Those who looked at the same work as a way to help patients heal faster and assist doctors and nurses in being more effective found their job more meaningful, enjoyed it more, and stepped out of their normal tasks to interact with patients, doctors, and nurses. It was the same job just with a different purpose.

Unfortunately, the majority of people view their work as a way to make money so they can spend it on pursuing their hedonic desires or their hunger for status and power, whilst wasting a third of their lives in tension. Whereas, you, a Purposehooder, can always craft your job to become more aligned with your Purposehood, and thus make it part of your life.

People who have clarity of their existential purpose will craft their job to correspond with their Purposehood. The fact that most people are disengaged at work means that at least 66 percent of American workers—and a higher percentage globally—don't have a clarity of their Purposehood, or even worse, they are moving in a negative direction toward a vacuum like those actively disengaged employees.

When you work with people who have a shared Purposehood, you automatically feel fulfilled, successful, and happy. Furthermore, if the business itself has a clear Purposehood, those feelings will be exponential as they transfer to customers, suppliers, and shareholders.

Community

As shown by all of the research cited earlier, good relationships are the best indicators of happiness, success, fulfillment, physical and psychological well-being, and longevity. But good relationships start with clarity of your existential direction, being at ease with life, and then connecting with others who share your Purposehood—or those who are in search of theirs, so you may help them find it.

It's also clear from research that people without Purposehood are usually living a negative life and suffering from various psychological and physical challenges.

The question, therefore, is: Do you want to be surrounded by people who are injecting your life with constant negativity? You can either avoid such people so they don't infest your life with negativity, or you can choose to help them discover their Purposehood and then rebuild your relationship based on positive mutual influence and interactions. This is how you reap the benefits of connectedness and good relationships.

The Nature Surrounding You

When I sometimes mention "your nature," I don't mean human nature, nor do I mean to imply any ownership of the natural world. What I mean is the nature around you *becomes you* when you breathe its air, soak in the energy of its sun, eat the food it produces, drink the water it provides, get awed by its majesty, and become intrigued by its mysteries, inspired by its beauty, and emotional with its pet companions. Scientists have been measuring what they call *nature relatedness,* and numerous studies show that people who are more connected with nature are more socially engaged, outgoing, trusting, helpful, imaginative, creative, adventurous, and easy going.[45]

People of all ages who are more connected to nature report better social, psychological, and physical well-being.

In a specific study on undergraduate students, researchers found a higher connectedness with nature increased the six dimensions of psychological well-being: autonomy, mastery, positive relationships, self-acceptance, personal growth, and purpose in life.[46] When they tried the same study in the business environment, they found the same results on executives, in addition to increased vitality.

These researchers then decided to try yet another longitudinal experiment to see if more nature relatedness could predict future well-being, and they found that it *did* predict better than other measures. Another study showed that the more you experience nature, the more you will enjoy the positive effects on your well-being.[47] When researchers looked at the relationship between having a purpose in life and nature, they found that a purpose in life is closely related to both connectedness to nature and well-being.[48]

When a Purposehooder is in harmony with nature, they can easily find transcendence. Many religious and nonreligious people alike report spiritual experiences in nature. It makes sense: When a person is clear about their Purposehood, they are at ease with existence and feel one with Mother Nature. In return, they receive happiness as they usually do when lovingly connecting with their caring, biological mother.

However, when a person is not clear about their Purposehood, their connectedness with nature becomes superficial. Seventy-five percent of Americans, for example, report concern for the environment, yet, only 20 percent make a serious effort to live in ways that help protect it.[49]

Purpose in Life

You ask, "How is purpose in life defined?"

My friend, let's briefly explore three different approaches to expressing purpose in life before examining Purposehood's definition. One comes from psychologists, one from Japan, and one from religion.

In the first approach, psychologists initially defined purpose as a reason that compels a person to keep on living. It has been seen as a refuge from suffering, and has been studied mainly as a resilience inducer, as it did in Frankl's case of surviving concentration camps. Accordingly, many experts have conducted studies on how purpose can help patients of various ailments, both psychological and physical.

After the initial research into the healing power of meaning and purpose, a new wave of psychologists studied purpose as a source of human motivation within the branch of positive psychology as a means to deliver positive outcomes such as improved well-being, real happiness, and fulfillment for people of all ages.[50] Purpose in life proved to deliver on all fronts.

Stanford University researchers later proposed a specific definition of the purpose in life, which has been widely adopted by most researchers.[51] It defined purpose components as "a far-reaching goal with an aim beyond the self," a way to provide a personal meaning, and as an intended result that someone can progress toward and accomplish. For example, a person's purpose in life could be to raise their children to become great contributors to society. This is definitely a worthy goal that is outside the self and has a personal meaning. It also has a far-reaching aim a person can progress toward.

The second approach comes from Okinawa, Japan, home to a higher-than-average number of centenarians. It is called *ikigai*, which roughly translates to "life's worth." It's an action-oriented purpose that is the intersection among what you love to do, what you are good at, what you can be paid for, and what the world needs.

For example, if you love singing and you are good enough at it, you can go on tours where people pay to listen to your beautiful songs. Those then inspire positive feelings and actions toward making the world a better place, and this will be your ikigai. In other words, you have combined your passion, profession, hobbies, and mission into one activity in your life.

The third approach comes from religion. Unlike the first two approaches where you actually have to seriously reflect and go through a discovery process, religions offer ready-made purpose for all to follow. The basic purpose among all religions is to serve a deity in a variety of ways that will ease your suffering and bring you some type of reward in this life and the afterlife. A common thread

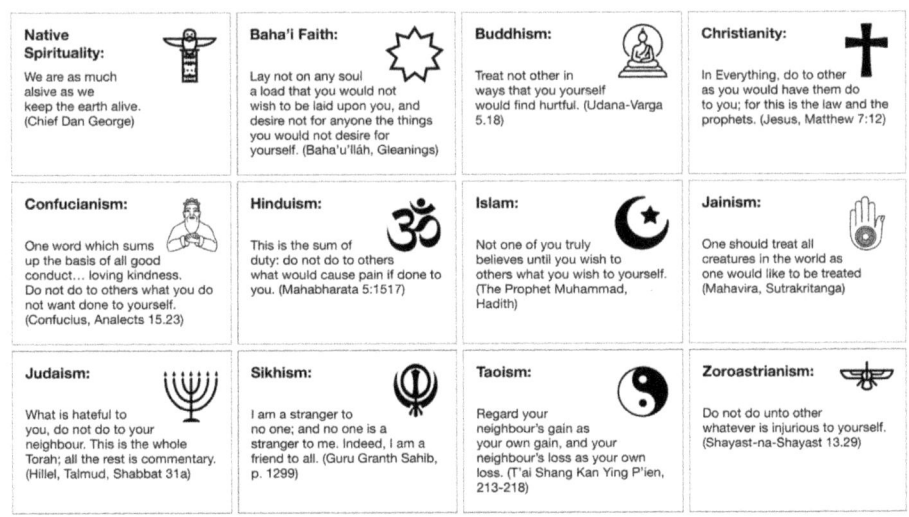

Native Spirituality:	Baha'i Faith:	Buddhism:	Christianity:
We are as much alsive as we keep the earth alive. (Chief Dan George)	Lay not on any soul a load that you would not wish to be laid upon you, and desire not for anyone the things you would not desire for yourself. (Baha'u'lláh, Gleanings)	Treat not other in ways that you yourself would find hurtful. (Udana-Varga 5.18)	In Everything, do to other as you would have them do to you; for this is the law and the prophets. (Jesus, Matthew 7:12)
Confucianism:	**Hinduism:**	**Islam:**	**Jainism:**
One word which sums up the basis of all good conduct… loving kindness. Do not do to others what you do not want done to yourself. (Confucius, Analects 15.23)	This is the sum of duty: do not do to others what would cause pain if done to you. (Mahabharata 5:1517)	Not one of you truly believes until you wish to others what you wish to yourself. (The Prophet Muhammad, Hadith)	One should treat all creatures in the world as one would like to be treated (Mahavira, Sutrakritanga)
Judaism:	**Sikhism:**	**Taoism:**	**Zoroastrianism:**
What is hateful to you, do not do to your neighbour. This is the whole Torah; all the rest is commentary. (Hillel, Talmud, Shabbat 31a)	I am a stranger to no one; and no one is a stranger to me. Indeed, I am a friend to all. (Guru Granth Sahib, p. 1299)	Regard your neighbour's gain as your own gain, and your neighbour's loss as your own loss. (T'ai Shang Kan Ying P'ien, 213-218)	Do not do unto other whatever is injurious to yourself. (Shayast-na-Shayast 13.29)

Credit: Charter for Compassion, a nonprofit organization.

of purpose among all religions is called the Golden Rule, which basically commands that you treat others the way you would like to be treated and wish for them what you would wish for yourself.

You ask, "But if there are all these ways to find one's purpose in life, why haven't the majority of people found clear purposes to their lives?"

My friend, in all three approaches, people who followed the process found some kind of a higher purpose and demonstrated better overall well-being, as illustrated in various studies. Yet, all of these approaches have challenges that limit their adoption and effectiveness.

In developing the first approach of purpose, researchers asked people what they thought their purpose was.[52] The research assumed people were already living with some type of a purpose and the question was meant to simply prompt them to reflect and identify it.

There are several major challenges with this approach:
- The majority of people are lost and confused in the jungle of life, so their answers can be misleading.
- There is no direction to the process, so it could result in either a positive or negative purpose. Extremists of all kinds believe their pursuits have personally meaningful goals that are directed beyond their self.
- A goal beyond the self could be a milestone, not an ultimate purpose. For example, caring for your sick mother could fit within this definition, but it's not likely to be your sole purpose in life.
- It focuses on the altruistic goal of a person, an approach that is inspiring but is against our selfish nature.

Maybe these challenges are the reasons why the masses haven't adopted this approach even with all the supporting research.

The ikigai approach to finding purpose also has flaws. It could be a nice tool to make your work meaningful, but the odds of matching all four elements are very slim. For example, in Japan, only 31 percent found ikigai in their work.[53] Also, the concept of developing your life's purpose based on who you are now instead of who you want to become might be good for working in an uncreative job, but it definitely limits the growth of your potentiality. Why not explore new things to love, develop new skills, and contribute to the world beyond its needs?

The concept of ikigai is actually about small daily joy that adds up to a *joyful life*, not a means to find the purpose of your life. You need to discover an overarching purpose to life to make sense of your existence. *In order to do so, you need to know the purpose of your existence. Once you understand that, then it will be easy to choose a role to play in this existence.* Unfortunately, neither the psychological definition nor ikigai provide an answer to this existential desire of knowing why you exist, and maybe this is why the pandemic of purposelessness is still spreading.

Religions have tried to address the human desire of finding an existential purpose by providing one answer to all their followers with the dogmas developed by interpreters of each faith. Obviously, this strategy has worked to some extent, as the majority of humanity follows one religion or another.

However, humanity is evolving. People are realizing that religions are made of interpretations not revelations, often obscuring, altering, or even completely losing the original teachings of the founders. Those interpretations create various competing factions within the same religion and among religions, each offering their own views of what the deity wants from you and what your purpose in life should be. Those interpretations are guarded by self-serving institutions and clergy classes that protect the dogmas.

The historical practice of grouping people together to follow a dictated purpose served humanity in its early evolution by establishing order in societies, but not anymore. People are discovering that they have the ability to interpret the scriptures for themselves directly without intermediaries, or seek answers to existential questions from a wide variety of sources. People are less willing to surrender their own minds and destinies to secondhand purposes, and increasingly are unleashing their potentiality from the limiting beliefs handed down by authority figures.

When you realize your uniqueness in this existence, then you will only be satisfied when you find your own unique destination. And when you become aware of your potentiality, you won't settle for anything less.

The best contribution anyone can make to their existence, and even to existence itself, is to help people discover their Purposehoods and unleash their potentiality. If one creative genius—a scientist, an engineer, an artist, a writer, an activist, a manager, an entrepreneur, a parent, a teacher, a thinker, a creator—could change the world and move humanity forward toward a better state of being, imagine the possibilities when every human is growing to their potentiality. When that occurs, billions of creators will be unleashed.

This is what iSH, existence, the universe, and life want from us, and we only can fulfill humanity's destiny by helping every human, if they so choose, find their Purposehood.

Toward a Purposehood Framework

You ask, "How can we unleash humanity's potentiality?"

One person at a time, starting with you, my friend. Never underestimate the power of a single human with a clear Purposehood. However, you need a practical philosophy for a life worth living, and we all need a framework that makes it easy for any person, family, business, or organization to find their Purposehood. This framework must have three components to create a transformational jump toward the better future awaiting you:

1. **A forward-pulling existential theory that provides a guiding star as we march forward.** Without first theorizing why and for what purpose humans grew from this Earth, choosing your purpose in life is like hoping to hit the center of a dartboard blindfolded. You are born facing the future with information from the past. Without a forward-pulling existential theory, you will always

be shackled with backward-pulling anchors. The ultimate joy is achieved when the existential purpose you choose for your life syncs with the purpose of existence.

2. **Empowering beliefs that inspire you to seek your Purposehood, free from the shackles of limiting beliefs instilled on you by society and self-doubts.** Beliefs are at the core of your limitations but also your potentiality. Most repeated failures are anchored in limiting beliefs. If you believe there is no purpose for life or existence, then you will never find the purpose of your life even if it hits you in the face. You need to reflect on your current beliefs to see if they are powerful enough to drive you toward your Purposehood. If they aren't, then you need to identify new empowering beliefs that can propel you forward.

3. **Practices that help you find your Purposehood Guiding Star, live your existential purpose, grow with ease, and unleash your potentiality.** If a forward-pulling theory is a guiding star toward your Purposehood and empowering beliefs are the coordinates to set you on your trajectory, then practices are the fuel that will get you there. Without practices that charge your will and resilience, widen your awareness, and turn your empowering beliefs into habits, your journey to a life of gratitude with happiness, success, and fulfillment will be short-lived.

With an existential forward-pulling theory, empowering beliefs, and practices, every human will have the ability to live a life of Purposehood with gratitude, ease, and abundance.

You ask, "What does existence want from me?"

This is the right question, my friend.

Searching for Purposehood

For 11 years, between my Day of Awakening and Day of Clarity, I focused my search for my life's purpose—on trying to understand human nature and surveying all kinds of people I met. It was odd, but fascinating, to start a conversation with, "What is the purpose of your life?" but ultimately, it gave me three profound insights.

First, the vast majority of people either have no idea or not enough clarity about the purpose of their lives. Second, when I asked my five whys[54]—a way to probe with one question leading to the next—and patiently waited for their responses, I found that all answers led to a fundamental desire, either happiness, success, or fulfillment. The third, and the most profound insight, was that their answers were based either on swift reflections on their lives up to the present point, a linear projection of a future possibility, or a borrowed purpose from a dogma.

On my Day of Clarity, I realized that in the jungle of life we are not products of the potentiality we were born with, nor are we the result of what we were meant to become. Instead, we are the products of the expectations of others. We are the results of limitations placed by society and our diminished selves on our seed of potentiality.

The purpose we will extrapolate, based on who we are today, most likely will be 98 percent wrong. Otherwise, we would be the geniuses we were meant to become in whatever we are doing today.

Actions, thoughts, emotions, and beliefs are generated from deep basic desires, and our desires are currently misdirected or at best, directionless. We are also emanating from the bad soil we were replanted in, and only if we find our way to a fertile ground will they all be rectified.

I realized that I needed to first find the purpose existence had for me in order to correctly search for the purpose of my life. If you don't know why you were grown on this Pale Blue Dot[55] in this wondrous vast universe, and you don't have a theory on how existence works and to what end, then it's highly improbable you will choose the perfect role you are meant to play in this universal theater.

This simple realization shifted my focus existentially from the exhaustive search for meaning, purpose, happiness, success, and fulfillment within my small life to the wider expanse of the universe. For the first time on this journey of discovery, I felt a sense of relief. If I were to discover a formula for my existential purpose, my Purposehood, I theorized, it would apply with some variation to every human. After all, every one of us is made up of the same stardust. Then, once we discover our existential purposes, we can extrapolate the Purposehood of humanity and, from there, life and the universe. Wouldn't it be great if humanity, collectively, had a guiding star?

You ask, "Did you find a formula to discover a human's existential purpose?"

My friend, six months into this realization I still hadn't found the answer. When I struggle, I usually fast and meditate. Fasting restricts basic desires, which frees the mind from daily concerns so it may notice the wonders of existence inside and outside the self. Silent meditation allows a person to hear the faint voice within, as well as the universal whispers that have helped seekers throughout the ages discover the laws of the universe. Those "Eureka moments" experienced by scientists are translations of the universe's whispers as it reveals itself to the seeker.

During my first week of fasting, while on my walking meditation in a park next to my house, I realized that it is much easier to discover the purpose of the tree I was gazing at if I knew the purpose of plants as a species. Plants belong to one system that has an existential purpose, and this tree was an individual player in the plant system. This tree's specific purpose is part of the existential purpose of the plant collective.

The same applies to the beautiful green parrot in that tree. Its Purposehood is part of the existential purpose of a system called *Aves class* in zoology, which is part of a higher system called *phylum Chordata*, which is part of a higher system called *kingdom Animalia*.

The existential purpose of the bee buzzing over flowers was part of the existential purpose of *family Apidae*, which is part of the Purposehood of *order Hymenoptera*, which is part of *class Insecta*, which is part of *phylum Arthropoda*, which is part of *kingdom Animalia*. Every entity is a player in a higher system serving an existential need for that system, and at the same time, the player is a system itself that creates players within to address its existential need.

The universe is a system that needed life in order to fulfill its Purposehood. While life is a player in the universe's system, it is also a system that has players in order to fulfill its Purposehood. Humanity is a player in the system of life, but is also a system of individual humans and human creations such as families, businesses, organizations, societies, and technologies. You, my friend, are a player in the system of humanity that serves a need in its Purposehood. You also are a system of thoughts, emotions, and organisms that operate to help you fulfill your Purposehood.

I realized that I didn't need to know the purpose of every human in order to find the purpose of humanity. Rather, *it's the other way around.* To know our own Purposehood, we should first know the Purposehood of humanity. Just like the purpose of a bee is tied to the existential purpose of *family Apidae*, the purpose of any human is to play a role in the Purposehood of humanity. If we were to know the existential purpose of humanity, then it becomes easier to derive our individual Purposehood, and to choose the role each of us wants to play in advancing humanity's Purposehood.

But what *is* the purpose of humanity? This is yet another question that philosophers and religions struggled with through the ages but couldn't agree on a unified answer. And history doesn't show us clear purpose beside a lot of pain and destruction, and maybe some flashes of hope.

I felt the answer was near, and all I needed to do was to apply the same logic upward. If we were to discover the purpose of humanity, then we would need to know the purpose of life/nature. Humanity is one of the species on this Earth and one of the players in the system of life. If the purpose of nature was to become clear, it would be easier to extrapolate the purpose of humanity, which would make it easier to discover the purpose of an individual human.

But what's the purpose of life itself? Here we go again. That is another question that has been asked throughout the ages with many differing answers, which are often mainly based on blind faith in someone's dogmatic interpretation. I've studied those answers for many years and found them intriguing, but not satisfying nor applicable in helping people agree on our purpose as a species.

Some biologists have observed that the purpose of life is to survive and reproduce. Other physicists have speculated that life's purpose is to increase entropy in the universe. But this couldn't be the only purpose of humanity, as we can't help but aspire for much more.

I felt the answer was even nearer. If I were to discover the purpose of life itself, then I would need to know the purpose of the universe. Earth is part of this vast universe, and if I knew the purpose of the universe, I could extrapolate the purpose of life on Earth, which would lead me to the purpose of humanity, which would help me discover the purpose of a human and my existential purpose.

You ask, "But what is the purpose of the universe?"

I was sure I would find a convincing answer beyond dogmas and prescientific philosophies since so much of science and its resources had been directed to understanding the universe. After all, we are heading to Mars soon.

To answer this existential question, I did what every seeker does: I Googled it!

The first result was a video by the renowned astrophysicist Neil deGrasse Tyson, titled "Does the Universe Have a Purpose?" I was excited to finally find the answer. As I listened, he argued that if the universe were to have a purpose, then we would have to assume a willed, desired outcome. But who would do the willing, and for what outcome? He linked the possible purpose of the universe to life on Earth and then to humanity, but found it unlikely that the universe's purpose was to make us. We humans couldn't be the purpose of the universe. He then concluded that he doubted the universe had a purpose at all.

"What?! There goes my hope of figuring it all out," I said to myself. I was frustrated. "How could something so important for our physical and psychological well-being—our happiness, success, and fulfillment, even our future—be so difficult to find?" I wondered.

You ask, "Were you about to give up?"

Sometimes you just need to let go, even if for a little bit, in order to create the space to allow the answer to come in.

In the days following my ill-fated Google search, I kept thinking, "We have billions of people who are either lost without a clear purpose or suffering from the wrong choices of purpose. Shouldn't there be one theory that makes it easy for all of them to find their existential purpose? Furthermore, if physicists believe there is one theory that could unify all of physics and explain our complicated physical existence, there must be a theory that could unify the purpose of everything. And it must be so simple that it would not be more than an inch long."

The theory of standard physics discovered by Sir Isaac Newton, which explains our mechanical view of the world, is less than an inch long: $f=ma$. Einstein's theory of relativity, which explains our universal view of the world, $e = mc^2$, is also less than an inch long. Maybe the *string theory* in quantum mechanics, which tries to explain our world in terms of its smallest particles, is a bit longer than an inch, but not by much. The Purposehood theory, if it is to be useful to the billions of humans, families, businesses, and social organizations who are in need of a clear direction—the *Purposehood of Everything Theory (PoET)*—should be like that—about an inch long! At the root of every complexity, isn't there always a divine simplicity, if you can notice it?

You ask, "Is the Purposehood discovery a spiritual experience or an intellectual one?"

My friend, is there a difference? Do you ever feel the universe is speaking to you? If you think deeply about it, I'm sure you can recall several times when the answer to a nagging question just appeared without you having to think about it; or in a moment of clarity, you became deeply aware of something that previously went unnoticed; or maybe it was a waking state of creative flow beyond your conscious experience; or a dream so revealing you didn't want to wake up or one that came true; or maybe a dream telling you to do or not to do something; or at a moment of weakness, an unexplained strength came to you; or a prayer or a wish you kept to yourself was granted unexpectedly. The universe seems to have all the answers, if you ask the right questions. All you need to do is ask big questions and leave them to the universe to reveal the answers in its due time.

Revelations come in many shapes and forms. We're so intertwined with existence in all its hardware, software, and mysteries that not having such an experience is the exception. One must be an outcast of the universe not to receive any signals. You must work hard on disconnecting yourself from existence in order to have no value, for the universe not to guide you or at least send you a hint. How unaware could a person be? Is it even possible for a human to be totally oblivious?

You ask, "Did you have such an experience?"

I will gladly share my experience, even though it really has no reflection on my conclusions, nor should it have any impact on yours. It's extremely hard to describe a transcendental experience to someone who has never experienced one. It's like trying to describe the taste of honey to someone who has never tasted anything sweet. Maybe it is similar to the "Eureka moment" that a scientist may experience when finding an answer to a vexing, years-long problem while simply walking in a forest. Flow, in everyday life, is a low intensity of a receiving state.

I was in my twenty-first day of fasting and staying up all night under the beautiful sky of the South of France. While meditating, reading, and reflecting, I watched the moon waxing, waning, and painting the sea with shimmering, silvery color right past the forest below my house. At around 3 a.m. on what I call my Night of Destiny, in a moment of meditation, I was so sure that I was connected to everything on this planet. All humans, birds, animals, trees, and every living thing I passed in my daily forest walk felt alive and connected like I'd never experienced before. Then, I felt the connectedness expand to the air, the sea, the mountains, the rocks. They all felt present in me and I in them. In what felt like an eternity, I expanded again, now connecting with the moon, the stars, and the universe. When I finally opened my eyes, I was filled with joy and it was all clear to me: To know the Purposehood of the universe, you just need to see what it has been doing for the past 13.8 billion years!

I realized: *Everything that has no directional choice will grow to become what it is meant to be if it is not obstructed by an external force. The direction of its growth toward its potentiality is its Purposehood.*

It has no choice of what role to play in existence except what it is already doing. It does exactly what its higher-order system needed it to do.

In other words, everything was created by the higher system to serve a need that system had. For example, the Purposehood of a pine seed is to become a fully-grown pine tree and to play its part in the plant system, which plays its part in a higher ecosystem, nature. Similarly, a baby squirrel is meant to grow to its full potential and do exactly what it is doing for nature. Squirrels (or any lifeform, for that matter) wouldn't have evolved to what they are today if their traits didn't serve a need of nature. You might call that "survival of the fittest players" in order to serve a specific need of their higher system.

When I look out of my home office window at a beautiful pine tree filled with living creatures, I don't need to ask what its Purposehood is. Its Purposehood is exactly what it is doing. All creatures are doing exactly what nature needs them to do. Their Purposehood is to play their part in nature's own Purposehood.

There's an old parable about a scorpion who wanted to cross a river, so he asked a frog to carry him on its back. The frog said, "No way, you will sting me and I will die."

The scorpion said to the frog: "Impossible. If I sting you, you will die and I will drown." The frog saw the logic in his words. The scorpion jumped on the frog's back and when they were in the middle of the river, the scorpion stung the frog.

As the frog started losing its strength, it asked the scorpion, "Why did you sting me? Now you will die, too."

The scorpion said: "I couldn't help it. It's my nature."

The universe created life to be a player in the universe's Purposehood, fulfilling a need the universe couldn't address with other existing players. Life created humanity to be a player in its Purposehood. Humanity is a system created by life to play a needed role in its Purposehood that other creatures couldn't fulfill.

A human's Purposehood is to play a part of humanity's Purposehood, just like a pine tree plays a role in the plant system. But for a human it is different, as you have a directional choice of what role you choose to play in existence. And when your choice is in sync with the Purposehood of humanity and life, then you will be living your Purposehood. When your choice is not in sync, you will be suffering in the vacuum of existence.

One of my best friends growing up was Hussam. I remember walking with him in the streets of Damascus more than 40 years ago, talking about what we wanted in our lives. He wanted to become a psychiatrist. He didn't need to tell me. He was already one at the age of 14. Our friends and I went to him every time we had a personal challenge. He listened, asked great questions, and gave us a few words to reflect on.

When Hussam immigrated to the U.S. a few years after I did, he had just finished medical school. He applied for several specialties in the U.S., and was accepted in some of the top programs. I remember him telling me about this great program for internal medicine that could lead to cardiology. He was debating which one he should choose and asked for my opinion. I said, "Hussam, you know exactly who you are. I am not sure why you are seriously considering anything else."

The cardiology track was probably the most lucrative of his options. I am sure he would have been a good cardiologist, but today Hussam is an amazing psychiatrist in San Diego. He loves what he does, and his patients love him. He has a wonderful family, and when I visit them, their joy rubs off on me and stays for months afterward. Hussam's purpose was to help people feel better by bringing joy back to their lives because *he* wanted to live a joyful and meaningful life. Hussam lives his Purposehood, and I have been able to see it in every day of his life for the 44 years that I've known him.

You ask, "So are you saying that in order to know the Purposehood of everything, we should first know the Purposehood of the earliest system, the universe?"

Yes, that's exactly what I'm saying. Beyond the universe there is existence itself, and beyond existence there is iSH, the grand mystery. We can only speculate about both as we don't have any related scientific information. However, we do have 13.8 billion years of information about the universe on which we can build plausible theories.

Every day, we discover something new about the universe as humanity expands its knowledge and capabilities toward unlocking all the mysteries of existence and the beyond. Humanity, through global collaboration, has photographed a black hole that is 6.5 billion times the mass of our sun and 55 million light years away.

Utilizing cosmic microwave background (CMB), an electromagnetic radiation remnant from an early stage of the universe, we can trace its history long enough to theorize how it started from nothing with a Big Bang and went through exponential expansion in a cosmic inflation. We can also theorize to a large degree of accuracy how the universe evolved from a simpler hot cosmic soup of the most basic building blocks to form hydrogen, and from there, formed all the elements in existence through the constant process of destruction and creation (0,1 states). And, in 1998, we learned that the universe is not only expanding, but doing so at an accelerated rate.

With the information we have so far, I believe we can theorize the Purposehood of the universe and from there the Purposehood of everything.

You ask, "So what is the Purposehood of the universe and everything in it?"

The Purposehood of Everything Theory (PoET)

Following are suppositions of the Purposehood of Everything Theory (PoET).

- Each element in nature plays a role in the existential purpose of the system it belongs to. The system itself plays a role in the existential purpose of a higher-order system. For example, biologists created a classification system for life that consists of three domains, six kingdoms, and six more subclassifications. In that classification, you play a role in the *Homo sapiens* species, which plays a role in the *Hominidae* family, which plays a role in the *Mammalia* class, which plays a role in the *Animalia* kingdom, which plays a role in the *Eukarya* domain, which plays a role in life's existential purpose.

- Classifications and subclassifications can be created for other aspects of existence. For example, the universe can be seen as having three domains: ordinary matter, dark matter, and dark energy. Ordinary matter could be further classified from the largest to the smallest as galaxies, nebulae, black holes, stars, solar systems, planets, dwarf planets, moons, asteroids, comets, space rocks, dust, molecules, atoms, and subatomic particles.[56]

- Physicists who are working on the string theory in quantum mechanics believe that at the core of everything that exists there is a common building block, which is a vibrating string of energy. Everything in this existence is made of vibrations, including you, me, nature, stars, and galaxies. You can think about it as musical notes, and how the combination of different notes would create different music. The universe then would be a symphony that started with a Big Bang and continues to play until it ceases to exist. Each player in every system is adding notes to this evolving and expanding universal symphony. And maybe the music will continue playing beyond this universe and others in what this theory calls the *multiverse hypothesis*.

- Some scientists speculate that on the opposite end of these basic building blocks of vibrations, there in the ultimate system beyond all, there is nothingness. Believers speculate God is the ultimate system. I see both views of nothingness and oneness as two faces of the same coin or two present states of one system

SYSTEMS AND PLAYERS

iSH

EXISTENCE

VIBRATING STRINGS

(0,1 states), which is still a grand mystery that drives our ever-lasting curiosity. It is iSH, the ultimate beyond.

- Each player is grown from a system to serve the existential purpose of that system.

- The role of a player in a system is to fulfill a system's need toward the existential purpose of that system. For example, a leaf or a seed (a player) produced by a plant has a role to play in the existential purpose of that plant (a system).

- The role a player chooses will serve all the systems preceding it and becomes a causality to forming the systems that follow it.

- Besides the core block—a vibrating string in the string theory, for example, which is a player but not a system, and the ultimate system, iSH, which is a system but not a player in a higher system—every other group is a system and a player at the same time.

- The existential purpose of the player is linked to the existential purpose of the system. For example, a leaf's existential purpose couldn't be unrelated to a need that a plant has in order to live its existential purpose.

- Everything that exists has an existential purpose. It wouldn't exist if it didn't serve a role in existence. While a player might serve many purposes in their lifetime, we call the player's reason for emergence within a system: Purposehood, the existential purpose.

- If a player fails to play its role in helping the system fulfill its Purposehood, then it will be out of sync with the system and it will perish. For example, if a species in nature is not able to serve the ecosystem, then it will have fewer chances to reproduce, and it will gradually disappear. A bird with a misfit beak that is unable to access available flowers will not be able to pollinate the plants that offer it food and will eventually perish.

- As far as we know now, all matter and creatures in existence have limited choices within the existential direction of what to become, except humans. Humans have the directional choice, with total awareness that their choices would not only impact them, but also humanity and life itself.

• For PoET, I focus on a simpler existential classification. It starts with you or me as an individual human, who belongs to humanity, which belongs to life/nature, which belongs to the universe, which belongs to existence, which is surrounded by iSH.

EXISTENTIAL CLASSIFICATION

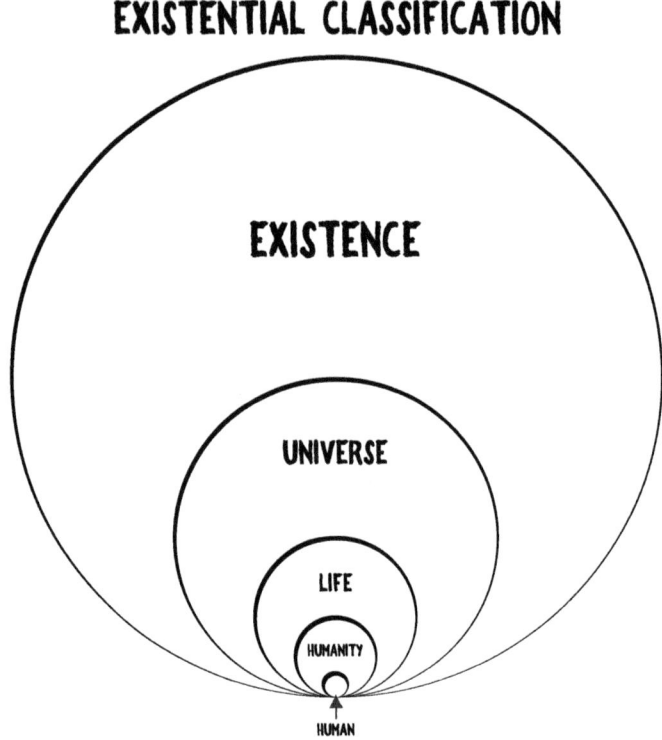

• Similar to other classifications, every circle represents a player and a system at the same time, as well as causality to the systems that emerge from it. For example, the universe is a player in existence and a causality of life, which obviously means it is also a causality of humanity. And humanity as a player in life is also a player in the universe and existence.

• In this existential classification, the Purposehood of a player is to play a role in the Purposehood of a system. For example, humanity was grown from within life through an existential selection process to play a role that fulfills a need of life. That in turn allows life to fulfill its Purposehood. A human's Purposehood is to play a role in humanity's Purposehood, which means playing a role in the Purposehood of life, the universe, and existence. Humans are creating new players and subsystems through technology, bioengineering, and artificial intelligence to address needs, as well as to fulfill their Purposehoods and play direct roles in the Purposehood of life.

- It is intellectually and maybe even spiritually interesting for us to know the Purposehood of existence, the universe, life, and humanity as a whole. However, it is essential in order for us to know our individual Purposehood. Purposehood is tremendously critical for our physical and psychological well-being, and for a life of happiness, success, and fulfillment.

- Philosophers, clergymen, some scientists, and numerous self-help experts have speculated on the purpose of human life without a convincing existential theory, which made the pursuit of purpose as elusive and confusing as the pursuit of happiness, success, and fulfillment.

- When existential purpose is evoked, it is usually viewed from a human's perspective, which produced, at one extreme, a God with superhuman abilities and desires who demands total obedience from his subjects, or at the other extreme, an existence with no purpose at all. The former makes humans servants to a list of demands by a self-serving class of clergy, whereas the latter renders human life purposeless.

- When scientists try to find a common purpose of humans' lives, they build their theories by grouping individuals' life choices as potential purposes. The problem with this approach is that humans, unlike all other creatures in this universe, are endowed with a directional choice. Even if you were to know the role you ought to play in humanity, life, or the universe, you have the choice to play that role or not. Even if iSH were to reveal your

Purposehood to you directly, you still would have the choice to follow it, ignore it, or even do the opposite. Just look at the devout followers of religions: Even though they are told specifically what their deity demands of them, many, if not most, still choose to *not* follow all those instructions.

- It's true that some people are living their Purposehood with happiness, success, and fulfillment, while others are moving away from theirs and are suffering with constant stress, anxiety, and regrets. Still, the majority are lost without a direction and are living with diminished potential. Nevertheless, our lives today are the results of our choices, which we can change at will. It's extremely hard, if not impossible, to extrapolate a formula for the purpose of a humans' life based on current choices. However, if we start by finding the purpose of a higher system such as the universe, then we can theorize the Purposehood of the system below until we arrive at our goal: finding a theory for the Purposehood of every individual human.

- A player's Purposehood has to sync with higher Purposehoods or it will perish, as the system would have no use for it or it would serve as a negative pull against the system's positive pull. And in human terms, if a person's Purposehood is not in sync and harmony with humanity, life, the universe, and existence, he or she will suffer from tension.

- When we look at the systems of humanity, life, and existence, we don't have enough conclusive information to form a theory of existential purpose. But when we look at the universe, we have two advantages. First, we have 13.8 billion years of data on the universe since its inception, and second, for the vast majority of the time since its inception from subatomic particles to galaxies, all the players in the universe have no directional choice but to do what they have been doing.

- The Purposehood of the universe can't be complicated and must be as simple as all the formulas that govern the physical universe. Those formulas, once discovered, made it easy for humanity to apply in order to reach for the stars, and similarly, a Purposehood formula should be simple enough for billions of humans to reach their guiding stars of potentiality.

- If the core building block of the universe is one in nature, vibrations of energy for example, then the Purposehood of everything should be one as well. Think about it in a programming language; if the vibrating strings of energy are the hardware, what would be the command code for the software to execute the universe program to produce everything in it?

- The Purposehood of all creatures with no directional choices are exactly what they do in their lifetime. They are all executing the same program.

- Since the Big Bang, we know that the universe has been going through evolution and accelerated expansion toward a higher and more complex state of being.

- Therefore, the Purposehood of the universe is exactly what it has been doing for the past 13.8 billion years and what it continues to do going forward, which is an *exponential evolution and expansion.*

To summarize, just like every human creation starts with a purpose that serves a desire of its creator, every creation since the start of this existence serves a function for the system it was created within. While it is becoming easier to understand the purpose of players in nature as we learn more about the intricacy of their functions in an interdependent ecosystem, it has been hard for many to see a clear purpose in a human's life, humanity, nature, or the universe. However, once we realize that the purpose of everything that has no directional choice is exactly what it has been doing, then we can theorize the existential purpose of the universe. The universe has been creating agents, systems, and forces of evolution, expansion, and exponentiality in order to evolve and expand exponentially.

The Purposehood of Everything Theory (PoET) states:

Everything in existence has an existential purpose. The existential purpose of everything is to evolve and expand exponentially.

To express it in a simple formula:

$$\textbf{Purposehood = (Evolve + Expand)}^{\text{Exponentially}}$$

or

$$PHD = (Ev + Ex)^n$$

PoET: THE PURPOSEHOOD OF EVERYTHING THEORY

$$\textbf{PHD} = \textbf{(Ev + Ex)}^n$$

PURPOSEHOOD = (EVOLVE + EXPAND)^EXPONENTIALLY

EVERYTHING IN EXISTENCE HAS AN EXISTENTIAL PURPOSE. THE EXISTENTIAL PURPOSE OF EVERYTHING IS TO EVOLVE AND EXPAND EXPONENTIALLY.

The Expo-Agent: Key to Purposehood's Exponentiality

The basic command of everything is to evolve and expand exponentially. It is the existential desire that is instilled in every player within their seed of potentiality. It's the direction of their growth.

Creatures might have varying levels of choices within that direction, but they have no choice except to evolve and expand exponentially. In order to do so, they also must survive. Once a player becomes a system of many players that help it evolve and expand exponentially, it must create a balance within the system in order to survive. That balance is created through opposing positive and negative forces that counteract each other. Every time a force arises, an opposing force is created.

However, balance doesn't accommodate accelerated evolution and expansion, and not in total sync with the exponential existential purpose of the universe. Balance has no growth, and minor imbalance leads to slower evolution and limited expansion. So, it is existentially important that within the system an *exponential agent* (expo-agent) is created in order to disrupt the balance and create a new jump in the evolution and expansion process. The expo-agent must be a more capable player, with exceptional abilities beyond the originating system, in order to help itself and the system complete their mission.

In the creation process of this expo-agent, the system passes its qualities and existential desire to the new creation so the expo-agent may develop better skills to reach the system's goal. In this process, the new creation has more complexity and more powerful capabilities, which also makes it a potential threat, if not controlled, to the survival of the system. In order to prevent the expo-agent from destroying the system that created it, the system ensures that the survival of the expo-agent is dependent on the system.

The expo-agent can only survive by consuming the energy source provided by the system. In other words, the system has to sacrifice some of its resources to make the new expo-agent dependent. We, therefore, may say the system has to become altruistic in order to make sure the expo-agent is also helping the selfish needs of the system. If an expo-agent fails to fulfill its purpose, it will simply be destroyed and replaced with an evolved version. Though an expo-agent is more complex, more capable, and has more choices and more creativity than the creating system, it is also more vulnerable as it depends on a cascade of preceding systems for its own survival. With every new system, complexity increases and resilience decreases.

LINEAR AND EXPONENTIAL GROWTH

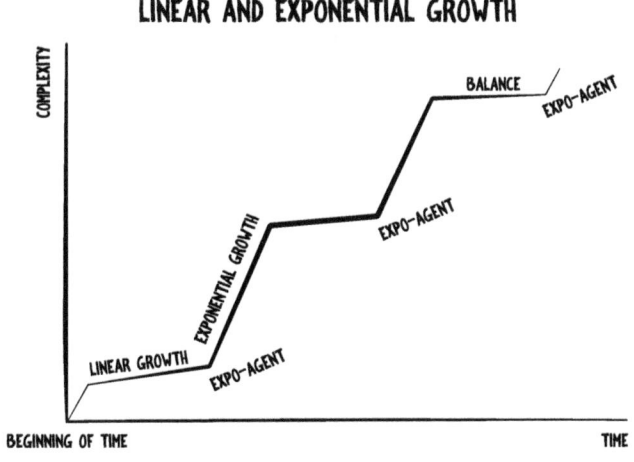

Here's a simple example of what I'm describing: Billions of years ago, the universe required an expo-agent in order to create complexity beyond matter, so it created life on Earth with dependence on the energy from the sun for life's survival. The universe's existential desire is to see life expanding all over these magnificent planets, filling the galactic landscapes with information-generating creatures. A life evolving and expanding across the galaxies is how the universe will continue its exponential evolution and expansion. It took the universe almost 10 billion years of rapid evolution and expansion to the level where it needed an expo-agent like life on this Earth.

Life was created with a mission to evolve and expand progressively faster. Indeed, life has been evolving and expanding very quickly, from simple single cells to multicellular complexity, developing more complex systems that have been expanding all over this planet. At one point, it became imperative for life to find some balance in order for it to survive, given the fact that Earth possesses finite resources. That raised a problem, since keeping a balance is not in harmony with the Purposehood of constant, accelerated evolution and expansion. Therefore, life had to create an expo-agent capable of disrupting this balance and creating new conditions to allow it to sync with the Purposehood of the universe.

The expo-agent of life is humanity. Humanity has the special capabilities of limitless creativity, infinite desires, and directional choice to help life spread across the universe beyond the confines of Earth.

For this monumental task, humanity collectively had to have limitless creativity, and to fuel such creativity, it needed to have infinite desires. Humanity had to also have a higher level of freedom to choose its direction. With such capabilities, humanity would possess the power to destroy life overall, so life made sure humanity couldn't survive without the air, water, and food it supplied.

The same existential desire that runs through life also runs through humanity; evolve and expand exponentially. *But ultimately, humanity's role in the universal system is to fulfill the Purposehood of the universe by spreading life to planets across the galaxies as quickly as possible.* This mission is becoming increasingly obvious as we unlock genetic secrets that will allow us to recreate nature and reach out to other planets for expeditions and, eventually, settlements.

Having been on Earth for a tiny fraction of time since the emergence of life and the universe, humanity has already proved to be an effective player in its own exponential evolution and expansion, taking over Earth and its resources. But like all systems, humanity collectively will look for balance for its own survival, and progress will slow down without an expo-agent.

Humanity itself needs an expo-agent that can imagine and create a better future in the direction of the Purposehood of life and the universe. In fact, this expo-agent must be so powerful that it could potentially destroy or enhance all humanity.

My friend, the expo-agent of humanity is you.

Every human can be an expo-agent of humanity. With every child born, a new possibility is created to alter the direction of all humanity positively or negatively. Your simple, daily choices influence the future, but your directional choices could shape the future for all existence.

You have a directional choice to make and you can make it right now. You can choose to:

1. Envision a positive future or subscribe to a vision of such a future and choose the role you want to play in creating it; then develop the skills and traits to play that role. This is the positive role of a **creator**.

2. Envision a negative future, or subscribe to that vision, and choose the role you want to play in creating it. This is the negative role of a **destroyer.**

3. Dedicate your life to helping others at the cost of yourself and your extensions of being. This is the altruistic role of a **martyr.**

4. Not make a choice and stay directionless in life, focused only on satisfying your basic desires. This is the selfish role of a **consumer.**

The first choice will sync you with existence and lead to a life of gratitude, ease, and abundance. The second will lead to vacuum and destruction and a life of scarcity, suffering, and rejection. The third will cause you and your extensions needless suffering while limiting your contributions to life with a contracted self. The fourth choice will keep you stuck in the jungle of life with a diminished potential and a life without meaning, true happiness, success, or fulfillment.

What will you choose?

You ask, "Is there an expo-agent emerging for a human?"

My friend, every one of us will soon be disrupted by an expo-agent of our creation, artificial intelligence (AI). When nature risked creating humans as expo-agents with the power to create and destroy Earth, it made sure that humankind depended on it for survival. Similarly, if AI were not to be totally dependent on humans for survival, then we risk the destruction of humanity itself. We need to ensure the full integration of this emerging expo-agent into humankind, just as we are integrated into nature, if we are to survive the related growing pains into universal consciousness—just as nature survived the pains we caused.

You ask, "Hasn't humanity in its pursuit of exponential evolution and expansion been destroying life? How could humanity be a positive expo-agent of life?"

My friend, humanity is still a baby who was just born into this life and the universe. As they learn, experiment, and grow, babies break things and take tremendous risks. They even sometimes cause serious damage. Ultimately, they become more learned and mature humans. Later, if they discover their Purposehood, they unleash their limitless creativity and infinite desires for a better world for themselves, their families, humanity, and life itself. Humanity will follow that same path.

Since the industrial revolution, a blink of an eye in spacetime, we have witnessed humanity become more aware of the problems it has been causing in its infancy, and already disruptors like you, social and environmental activists, concerned scientists, conscientious teachers, and social entrepreneurs are pushing major changes into the status quo. This is why the most important contribution you and I can make to ourselves, our families, our societies, humanity, and the world is to first live our own Purposehood, and then help others discover and live theirs.

Many organizations, businesses, families, and individuals might have chosen negative directions that caused them and everyone else tremendous suffering and destruction. But many are maturing to the fact that these past choices have caused pain and limited human potential in spite of the technological progress we have proudly achieved.

People are realizing that technology might give us better health but that it does not better our well-being, as our own well-being is eternally linked to the well-being of our families, work environment, communities, and nature. A link that is only realized with a clarity of Purposehood.

Families are challenged in this competitive world to unleash the potentiality of their children, and to stay happy, connected, and relevant. They are increasingly realizing that without a Purposehood they won't be able to accomplish their goals. Businesses are also realizing they will sooner or later fail and vanish without a higher purpose that syncs with the Purposehood of their stakeholders. Social organizations of all kinds are recognizing that if they don't drastically change by design, they will be disrupted out of existence.

Like all players and systems in this universe, human creations can either synchronize with the pulling force of the universe's Purposehood and grow with ease as they are pulled forward by an existential force, or they will be a dead weight, or worse—moving against the forward movement of the universe, suffering in tension before they are shattered and replaced with other expo-agents.

You ask, "How do I evolve and expand exponentially?"

My friend, you evolve every day by widening your awareness and by becoming a better version of yourself. You expand by linking the self to your other extensions of being through *selfish-altruism*— being altruistic for selfish reasons and being selfish for altruistic reasons. This is how you expand yourself: by including your family, work, communities, and nature into the self. You become exponential by making sure your evolved qualities continue influencing humanity and life throughout your lifetime and beyond, just like a star sharing its energy with orbiting planets, and when its end comes, it gifts all its treasures to the universe.

——

Now that you understand through PoET the fundamentals of your Purposehood as well as that of humanity, life, the universe, and everything else, you can start thinking about how to apply it to your life—with your family, at work, in your community, and in your relationship with nature.

In the next part of this book, you will have the opportunity to explore 27 PoET propositions to help you reflect on your beliefs, and in the process, be able to identify limiting ones that have been holding you back from finding your Purposehood and reaching your true potential.

Once you free yourself from those limiting beliefs and replace them with empowering ones, you can start the process of choosing your Purposehood by writing first your Purposehood Statement. It will guide you out of the jungle of life toward Eden—a process I will explain in Part III's practices.

By dedicating 20 minutes of your day to engage in these practices, you will grow the awareness you need for any course correction throughout your life's journey. Finally, you will explore the Five Streams of Potentiality that will propel you toward your Purposehood.

My friend, designing a purposeful life with happiness, success, fulfillment, gratitude, ease, and abundance is not a trivial process, but it's not rocket science either. Seeing the process through with patience and diligence will ultimately lead you to Eden.

You can begin the journey now by selecting empowering beliefs from the Purposehood of Everything Theory (PoET) propositions.

PART II

Empowering Beliefs:
The PoET Propositions

Know Thyself

The first set of Purposehood of Everything Theory (PoET) propositions is about knowing yourself. You are endowed by iSH with a seed of potentiality made of limitless creativity, infinite desires, and directional choice, and linked through *selfish-altruism* to your *Five Extensions of Being*—the self, family, work, communities, and nature—in order to become a *semideum*, a creator of a better future for yourself, humanity, life, and the universe.

Proposition 1:
Seed of Potentiality

"Every newborn child has a seed of potentiality with limitless creativity, infinite desires, and directional choice. As the newborn grows, their guardians either nourish it or diminish it. Your mission is to grow your own seed of potentiality, nourish the seeds of children in your care, and unleash the seeds of those in your extensions of being." – PoET Proposition 1

HUMAN SEED OF POTENTIALITY

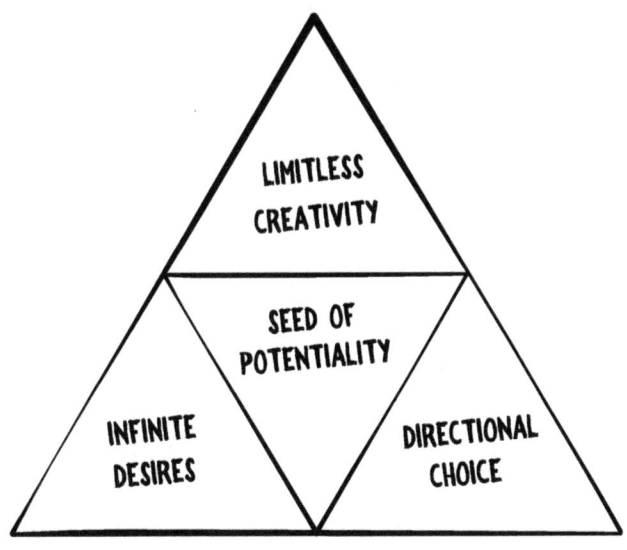

My friend, you are born with limitless creativity and infinite desires, free to choose your direction in life. You have the hope of humanity, life, the universe, existence, and iSH. You can choose to apply that to your exceptional and unique capabilities in the positive direction of your Purposehood. In the process, you will evolve and expand exponentially. And when you do, you will also help humanity evolve and expand exponentially. That, in turn, will help all of life, and the entire universe, to do the same. This is your Purposehood, and is why you were endowed with a seed of potentiality.

Your seed is not a fluke of nature; it is a necessity for a purposeful existence. Without it, the universe has no possibility of seeing life expand in barren galactic lands, adding complexity, information, and beauty to existence.

Your limitless creativity, infinite desires, and freedom of directional choice are what is needed to imagine and create new ways to expedite evolution and expansion. The seed of potentiality is what grows creators.

It's not hard to see it in every child, regardless if their behavior fits your expectations or those of society. However, to make it visible, you must remove the filters of labels, limiting beliefs, and expectations from your own eyes. Only then can you comprehend the wide spectrum of genius in children and its disruptive nature.[57]

Researchers at the Massachusetts Institute of Technology and Stanford University conducted a study in which four- and five-year-old children were given a special toy that played music only when certain beads were placed in a particular order.[58] What they found was the children followed the common principles of science by testing different hypotheses and experimenting until they found the correct solution. The research suggested that "children make decisions on the basis of the potential for gaining new information."[59]

Children are born with the existential desire to evolve and expand exponentially, growing their seed with the help of life's fundamental nourishments of happiness, success, and fulfillment. The endless supply of these nourishments is available for them as long as they are growing in the positive direction of their Purposehood.

Children are like emerging seedlings, attracted from inception to the direction of the sun and ready to receive the natural nourishments of the soil and rain. But children are born totally dependent on other humans for their initial survival and growth. Those guardians possess the power to provide these new creatures of boundless potentiality with unobstructed access to their guiding star. They can supply universal nourishments by fueling their innate curiosity and blocking social viruses that limit their choices. Those guardians also possess the power to misdirect the children and constrain their options with labels and limiting beliefs.

In short, guardians either nourish their children's seed or diminish it.

With every child born there is a new potentiality of a positive disruption or transformational contribution to humanity's growth. That potentiality is left to the parents, the caretakers, the guardians to nourish, misdirect, or stifle. The newborn starts with a clean human intelligence (HI) operating system, complete with the latest bells and whistles that have evolved throughout humanity's existence. It has been installed on an amazing machine (the human mind) that has a processing power capable of not only altering existence, but also imagining and creating a new one, with a mission to add useful information and improvements to the operating system as it installs on future generations.

The child's peripherals of the five senses are ready to accept all data input with hardly any filters. The potentiality of this child will be initially determined by the quality of filters and data provided for their processor to run on their HI operating system.

In an ideal setting, no filter is needed if the input is as pure as the fresh waters of Puerto Williams.[60] But, unfortunately, most children are born in an environment full of physical and social "viruses." These serve to limit or enslave this tremendous power of creation in order to ensure that it won't disrupt the status quo of existing power structures. In many cases, these viruses end up being transmitted by parents and guardians through labels, expectations, and limiting beliefs.

Every label placed on a child creates a limitation to their growth. With every expectation thrown at them, other possibilities are eliminated. With every limiting belief introduced, a negative force is generated, pulling them backward and away from their potentiality and Purposehood. Some of these forces are so severe that they end up crippling the operating system and killing the potentiality.

For example, aren't limiting beliefs of inferiority or superiority destructive to a human potential? For centuries, females were viewed as less capable humans, or only capable of certain roles and functions. These labels and limiting beliefs destroyed half of humanity's potential, from which we still haven't fully recovered. In many societies, this limiting belief still exists, and even in more advanced societies, women are still deprived of equal pay and equal access to opportunities. This belief was enshrined in religious and social orders and transmitted mainly by parents and guardians. It took major disruptions like world wars to open opportunities for women to grow their potentiality and for societies to accept their new roles.

Yet, there are many parents, guardians, and teachers who positively unleash the potentiality of their children. For every genius there had been at least one guardian who recognized their potential, believed in them, inspired them, and sacrificed to give them the opportunity to grow into what they were meant to become.

Take Maria Mendeleev, the mother of Dimitri Mendeleev, the inventor of the periodic table of elements. Mendeleev's family of 17 siblings became poor after his father lost his sight and then his teaching job, followed by his mother's glass factory burning down in a remote village in Siberia. Soon after, Dimitri's father passed away and his mother was left alone to take care of her children. Maria could have accepted her fate and lived a diminished existence, focusing only on providing for her family's basic needs. But Maria recognized her son's talent and wanted him to have a higher education. So, when Dimitri was 16, she took him all the way to Moscow where he was rejected by the university. Undeterred, she traveled further to the university in St. Petersburg, where Dimitri's father had graduated. Later, after Dimitri was accepted, Maria moved the whole family there to accommodate her gifted son. There, she supported her son in his studies until many years later, when he became an iconic figure in the field of chemistry.

If it wasn't for Maria Mendeleev's relentless determination and belief in her son's genius, along with her willingness to sacrifice so that her son could be who he was meant to become, Dimitri could have been another forgotten human in a distant, icy village. Humanity would have missed his genius contributions.

All major contributors to humanity's evolution were future-oriented people focused on their Purposehood, unlike the majority of humans who are lost in the jungle of life, directionless, running after their infinite basic desires or running away from their fear of failure.

Potentiality is ultimately your choice.

My friend, you are the product of your guardians, teachers, and society, but only until you become old enough to develop your own beliefs. Then, the responsibility becomes yours and yours alone. You have the power, regardless if you're aware of it or not, to drop the labels placed on you and undo past limiting beliefs bestowed upon you by diminished people and organizations bent on conformity, not innovation.

Be grateful to those who helped you survive the years of helplessness as a toddler, but don't be a prisoner of their limitations. Those limitations now only reside within you, and you have the power with a simple exercise of will to rid yourself of them all. Once you do, you will be able to develop your own empowering beliefs and see the wonders of existence without the foggy lenses of limitations.

The code of your original human intelligence operating system is still there, deep inside you. It provides a limitless creativity ready to be fueled by infinite desires in the direction of your Purposehood. Once the viruses of labels and limiting beliefs are gone, and with the right orientation toward your power source, your *Purposehood Guiding Star*, you will be able to turn your desires into values and unleash your potentiality to receive the universal incentives of happiness, success, and fulfillment.

Your limitless potentiality is only limited by the shackles you keep on yourself, and you can only truly be all you can be by freeing yourself from the expectations of others, knowing where you're heading and why, and fueling your journey with practices that harness your infinite desires. Until you do so, you either will be lost, directionless in the jungle of life, or worse…living against your Purposehood.

Your mission is to grow your seed.

My friend, you will not have a life of ease until you live in sync with the universe, and you won't be in sync with the universe until you grow your seed of potentiality. The road to unleashing your own potential starts with awareness. Once you are aware of the existence of your seed and the shackles placed on it, the road to potentiality becomes clearer. With the practices that I will introduce later, you can remove the obstacles and allow the universe to reconnect you with the resources that were meant to empower your genius, allowing you to become the intended influencer on existence itself.

Nourish the seeds of children in your care.

American football's central player is the quarterback, who at the crucial moment of play, holds the ball and initiates the actions that move the team forward toward the goal of reaching the opposite end of the field and scoring a touchdown. A quarterback has to use his limitless creativity and infinite desire to win. He must adjust to the fluid and challenging situations on the field, finding ways to utilize the talents of other players in order to create opportunities for the team toward its ultimate goal of winning the game.

This is not easy, as the objective of the players on the other side is to first tackle the quarterback before he releases the ball. If that is not possible, then the opposing team's mission is to block the ball, or at least limit the quarterback's visibility on the field of opportunities.

To allow the quarterback the time and opportunity to devise and implement a creative winning solution, he relies on an offensive line of several large players to block the attackers who aim to kill or limit his potentiality on the playing field.

Parents, guardians, families, schools, and society should play the offensive line's role of protecting the new star of their team, the advancer of the ball of hope, toward the end zone of possibilities. They must provide this unique genius among geniuses with all the space and time they need to be curious, play, try and fail, experiment, question, listen, doubt, learn, debate, experience, reflect, expand their awareness, and become the creative force and the expo-agent they are meant to be. Doing this will allow that one creative genius—potentially every young person—to create the plays that will make the whole team, the team of humanity, a winner in the game of life.

Unleash the seeds of others.

Once you are aware of your own potentiality, you will soon realize that it is closely linked to the potentiality of others. Can a tree grow to its full potential if the whole forest is blanketed with harmful gases from the nearby coal power plant? If you don't unleash the potentiality of those in your circles of influence, who in turn influence you, then your own seed will not have the needed nourishment, support, and inspiration it needs to fully bloom.

Your mission is not complicated, nor is it cumbersome. Labels and limiting beliefs are like dominoes, which can all collapse with the removal of one piece. You can play the mentor, the cheerleader, the challenger, or whatever role others need from you to remove the obstacle holding them back or to ignite the spark of awareness within them. Sometimes, you can ignite that transformational spark of awareness in others with just a positive word of support, an embrace of compassion, or even a smile of gratitude.

My friend, when you become aware of the seed of potentiality within you and those in your extensions of being, then your journey toward your Purposehood will be one of ease, happiness, success, and fulfillment.

———

I BREATHE IN PURPOSEHOOD.
I BREATHE OUT POTENTIALITY.

Proposition 2: Five Extensions of Being

"You don't exist without your Five Extensions of Being—the self, family, work, communities, and nature. The wider your awareness expands across your extensions, the more evolved you become." – PoET Proposition 2

Some psychologists argue that every human has an innate desire for self-expansion in order to enhance their effectiveness in achieving their goals. This is why we build families, forge close relationships, and create networks.[61] With such expansion, we include in our definition of self the resources, capabilities, and qualities of those with whom we are closely connected. Psychologists have studied the concept of including others in the self, which they defined as "the knowledge of who we are."[62] In doing so, they found that when we include others, we include in our self their resources, qualities, perspectives, and identities. This expands the concept of our self, and in the process, we also evolve to a better state of being.

These scientists are correct in that we humans have an existential desire to exponentially evolve and expand by building mutually beneficial relationships and strong connections. However, who you include in the self is not a matter of choice, it's a matter of awareness. There is no you without the self, your contacts, and nature. Your contacts are your family, work, and communities. You simply can't be who you are without your *Five Extensions of Being*. Think of them as a set of concentric circles with the first extension, self, at the center. The *wider* your embrace of these circles, the further along you will be on the path to your Purposehood. You are totally dependent for your own survival and growth on these extensions and their components, regardless of how you prioritize them at any given moment of your life.

FIVE EXTENSIONS OF BEING

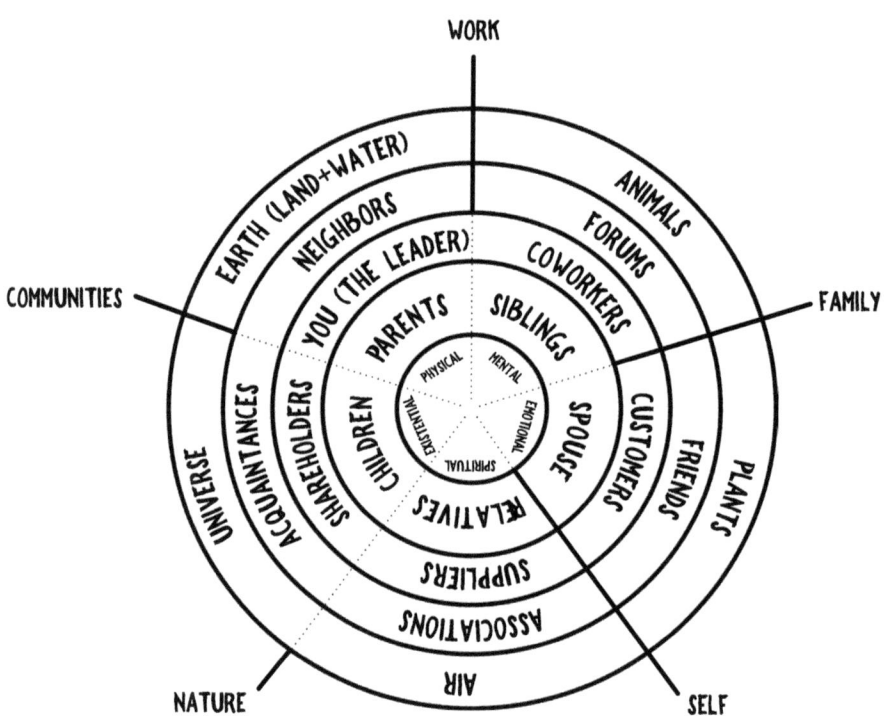

Self: The First Extension

We grow with the illusion that we are all about our self. We use terms like self-made, self-taught, self-sufficient, or self-reliant. This implies that we can be anything we wish without any support from our genetic ancestors, the people who influenced us growing up and nurtured us through our lives, or without the help of ideas and inspiration from other people and nature itself.

Of course, there is no illusion that we could have existed without being connected to our mothers in their wombs. There, in the darkness of the womb, there is no you without your mother. You are part of her, and she is your initial extension of being. But when you're born and the umbilical cord is severed, you fall under the illusion that you are on your own. You are independent.

With time, you grow thinking of the self as being just "me." If you increase your awareness beyond your physical body, you might even realize and include in your sense of self your body, thoughts, emotions, spirituality, and even your existential desire of knowing why you exist. At that point, you may fall in the trap of thinking you've reached enlightenment.

It's true that any of these notions of the self is part of who you are, but there are still four other components that are part of the self, regardless if you are aware of them or not. Without being aware of them, your existence will contract and you will not be able to discover, let alone live, your Purposehood and receive happiness, success, and fulfillment.

For example, you might not be aware of the 100 trillion bacteria that are in your body, but they are there, and they definitely are part of who you are physically. Your thoughts and emotions are created in response to the sensory input from everything around you, and your ideas are built on countless ideas of others. Your spirituality is driven by a need to connect with something beyond everything you see, and your existential desire drives you to an innate connection with the universe. You *are* the universe. There is no experience outside the self. If you are not connected to the self, there is nothing else to experience. The more you are aware and connected with all the components of the self, the wider the self extension is.

Family: The Second Extension

Our families are part of our genetic makeup, of course. Additionally, most of our identity is formed by the positive or negative values they instilled in us since we were children. That physical connection you have with your mother doesn't disappear with birth; it actually expands into an emotional and mental bond that includes your father, siblings, other relatives, and eventually a spouse and children. You grow relying on others to become who you are. You are not a sea turtle who, the moment it's born, is programmed for a long journey to its nesting ground without the help of parents. Within this second extension, you are most likely to find those who are willing to support you in spite of your many faults and be there for you when others might abandon you. Family members are great candidates to have in your inclusion list, your cheerleaders. The more you are aware of and connected with all your family components, the wider your family extension is.

Work: The Third Extension

Work is not just a job or career, but anything you do to achieve a goal. It is essential for your development. You've been working since you were born to learn new skills, study, help around the house, volunteer, develop hobbies, or hold jobs. That work is an inseparable part of who you are. Your interactions with coworkers, clients, suppliers, and shareholders can be identified in any work setting, whether business, housework, or any other goal-based pursuit. These goals and relationships form an important part of your identity and self-worth. At work, you sharpen your skills, set goals, co-create, profit, innovate, construct, achieve, and establish comradery. The more you are aware and connected with all your work components, the wider your work extension is.

Communities: The Fourth Extension

You have no choice in the physical characteristics of the family you inherit at birth, and sometimes you also feel your opportunities to choose the work you desire are limited. However, you *do* have great choice in your social relationships—based on those with whom you *choose* to spend your time. You have a wide variety of choices to be with people and organizations that can enhance your qualities, expand your understandings, and bring positive energy into your life.

Why would anyone choose to be with negative people and organizations who poison their lives with limiting beliefs and prevent them from evolving and expanding?

It's said that if you tell me who your friends are, I can tell you who you are. When you choose diverse people who support you positively while challenging and broadening your views—whether they be friends, forums, neighbors, associations, or acquaintances—they will expedite your evolution and expansion. The more you are aware and connected with all your communities' components, the wider the circle of your fourth extension is.

Nature: The Fifth Extension

Then there is nature. It's easy to see nature as something outside our human-based extensions. After all, it looks very different than us. Nevertheless, *nature is the most important of your extensions.* You simply can't live without its air, water, and nourishment. This food you eat will literally become you. Do you ever pause before devouring your meal to reflect on that? This air, water, and food are your indispensable connections with Earth, and from there to the sun and the universe. When you disconnect who you are from Earth, you disconnect from the universe, and you will be left behind suffering the tension of its forward movement.

You were grown from this Earth for the ultimate purpose of bringing nature to the rest of the universe, and if you sever your relationship with nature, you will never discover your Purposehood. You will deprive yourself of the chance of receiving happiness, success, and fulfillment.

The fact is that you can never physically disconnect from nature; you only disconnect intentionally or unintentionally through your thoughts, emotions, spirituality, and a diminished view of existence. On the other hand, when you choose to bond with nature through Earth (land and water), air, plants, animals, and the universe, you open yourself to limitless expansion. The more you are aware and connected with all your nature components, the wider your nature extension is.

Embracing All Extensions

Foregoing any of these extensions will prevent you from finding your Purposehood, leading you to a life of suffering. Mindless living is a result of the illusion that each extension circle is independent, which leads to a destiny of striving to create life-family balance, or life-work balance, only to end up with total dissatisfaction. Without any of these extensions, you will be like a car missing a wheel or an engine; there will be no chance for you to make the journey out of the jungle of life to Eden.

So many people are totally consumed with only self-pursuits, even if toward what they think is enlightenment. Others are consumed only with their families, work, or community issues such as politics, sports, religion, and environmental activism. Or, they may be focused on just two or three of these extensions, such as themselves, family, and work. Still, without embracing all five extensions, their being will not be in sync and harmony with the existential purpose of life and the universe.

You may know a person who is great to his family, work, and community, but cruel to some animals. Such a person could never find peace within himself and will always fall into negative states of living. You may also know a person who is well connected with four extensions, but their work is making them miserable. If you're in that situation, it's impossible to fully benefit from your other extensions of being. That poison from the one extension will eventually spread to the others. If any extension is toxic, then all will have some level of toxicity.

My friend, your potentiality is waiting for you in your expanded awareness of how you influence your extensions, and how they influence you, positively and negatively, and then learning how to *harvest* that connectedness for your exponential evolution and expansion toward your Purposehood Guiding Star.

The enlightened among us express who they are in every positive thought, word, or action they produce. They see themselves in one family that includes all humanity working hard as one to make life better for all, including every working individual and element of nature that makes their existence possible. They see themselves in the Earth, which is working constantly to feed the seeds that create plants; plants that work tirelessly with the pollinating bees to produce fruit; fruits that are collected by farmers and many others in the supply chain to get that food on their table. They see themselves in communities that include societies of ants, elephants, and all creatures; and in a nature that includes the whole universe, from its shining stars to its black holes.

A few mystics among us conduct their lives within only one circle, where everything is one. For these people, there is no us or them; we are all one symphony playing in this existence. For them, every being is interwoven with all other beings, as it is impossible for anything to be independent.

Every single thing that happens influences, in a small or big way, the rest of existence. A butterfly flapping its wings in Minnesota could possibly create a typhoon in Japan in what's called the *butterfly effect,* where a tiny change in a complex system can ripple out, progressively creating larger impacts. A pebble falling into a lake has a ripple effect that extends to the lake and beyond, even if the apparent effect is only the one on impact. Each being has extensions whose obvious direct impact will eventually vibrate through all existence.

Still, a few Sufi masters see no circles at all. They are consumed with divine love to the point of the annihilation of all their extensions of being. All they see is their lover, iSH, in all there is, and nothing else is real to them.

However, we are not meant to be like such people, nor should their outlook be the inspiration of humanity. Their existence is like that of other extreme achievers, such as the person who climbed steep mountains alone without ropes, or the person who walked on high-wire, attached to nothing, across an abyss between skyscrapers. These kinds of humans are meant to show the rest of us what's possible to experience and achieve, and that a human is capable of almost anything.

If you are tempted by such experiences, then make sure at some point you come down from the mountain cave and live your Purposehood by participating in that of humanity, life, and the universe.

My friend, when you expand your awareness to all your Five Extensions of Being, you become ready to live an exponentially evolving and expanding life.

———

I BREATHE IN LOVE FOR MYSELF.

I BREATHE OUT LOVE FOR MY FAMILY.

I BREATHE IN LOVE FOR MYSELF.

I BREATHE OUT LOVE FOR MY COWORKERS.

I BREATHE IN LOVE FOR MYSELF.

I BREATHE OUT LOVE FOR MY COMMUNITIES.

I BREATHE IN LOVE FOR MYSELF.

I BREATHE OUT LOVE FOR MOTHER NATURE.

I BREATHE IN LOVE.

I BREATHE OUT ISH.

Proposition 3:
Selfish–Altruism

"You expand by linking the self with your other extensions of being through selfish-altruism. Selfish-altruism is being altruistic for selfish reasons and being selfish for altruistic reasons." – PoET Proposition 3

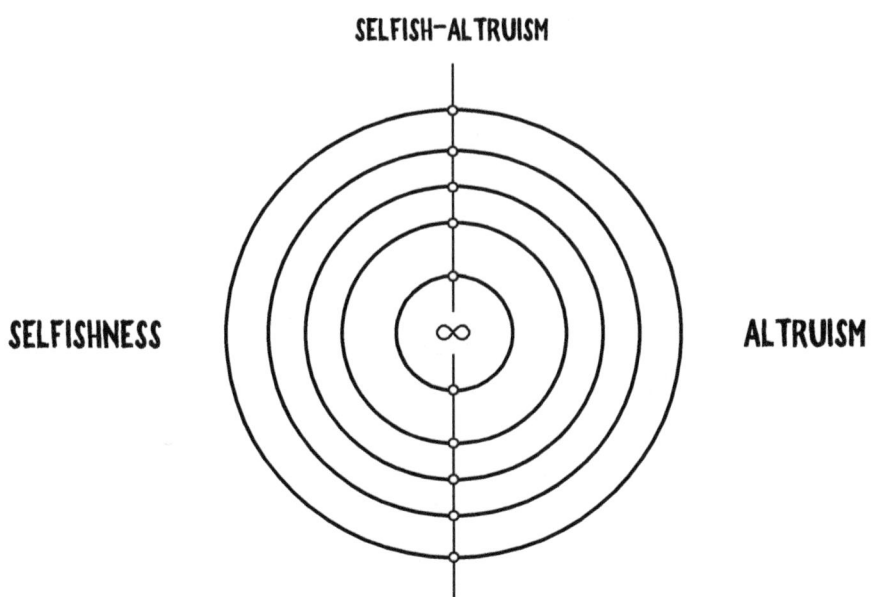

As you start your journey toward your Purposehood and unleashing your potentiality, you need to understand your true nature in order to travel the path with ease. Any choice that is against your nature will cause a constant struggle leading to tension, which could lead to suffering and destruction. If you think you are a bird and you design your life as such, the next time you jump off a cliff, you will fall down no matter how hard you flap your arms!

Your nature is a result of millions of years of genetic evolution. This development began when life was a single-celled organism. The traits that resulted gathered the wisdom of nature in its pursuit to evolve and expand exponentially, balance, and then create the expo-agent, which resulted in you!

I am not suggesting that you can't change your nature. On the contrary, the emerging science of *epigenetics* examines how changes in organisms can be caused by modification of gene expression rather than alteration of the genetic code itself. It explains how your *willed adoptions of habits and traits* could become a code in your genetic makeup that can be passed on to your offspring.

The logical approach for growth is to first expand your awareness of your human nature and the amazing tools passed on to you from the universe, life, and the collective experience of your ancestors and humanity. Without awareness of the opposing forces that are within you, you won't be able to mold them to be the creator you were meant to become.

You are a selfish being like all living organisms, and that's okay. Without the desire to self-preserve, you won't be able to survive, and if you don't survive, you won't have the chance to evolve and expand. Without the desire to self-expand, you won't be able to grow. Selfishness is a wonderful code inserted in every gene to ensure the exponential evolution and expansion of life. A person who is reluctant to passionately embrace their selfishness is a person who will struggle to reach their potentiality and find their Purposehood.

However, selfishness isn't the only basic genetic code we have. When Richard Dawkins, the evolutionary biologist published his bestseller *The Selfish Gene*, purely selfish people celebrated the fact that their negative behaviors were simply genetic. Nine years later,

Dawkins produced a BBC documentary to clarify the misunderstanding. He felt such people made a judgment based on the title and hadn't even read his book. He explained that written into our genetic code is *a need to protect our collective gene pool*, not just our individual ones. This is why most people have the innate willingness to sacrifice more for their own family, coworkers, and tribes than they would for strangers.

Altruism is also genetically coded within us to help us expand beyond our own obvious self-interests in order to help humanity evolve as a whole. While some, like psychologist Abigail Marsh, define altruism as the desire to volunteer to help others at a cost to yourself, I define it as the desire to help others in order to expedite your own evolution and expansion. There is no cost to the self in helping other extensions of being.

In the service of others, you will grow to become better and more connected while spreading your legacy exponentially. The more you're able to practice altruism further away from the self, the further you'll be able to evolve and expand.

Those who define family, coworkers, and communities as the *whole humanity* and nature as the *whole universe* are more capable of evolving and expanding exponentially than others with a narrower view.

A famous game theory experiment called "Prisoner's Dilemma,"[63] where a person has a chance to be selfish or altruistic toward their opponent, demonstrated that people who have a tendency toward being altruistic first, yet selfish if the other party doesn't reciprocate, are more likely to be winners in the game of life. As Dawkins said: "Nice guys finish first!" But what is also clear in numerous research studies is that besides those who are indifferent and totally lost in the jungle of life, there are mainly three types of people when it comes to selfishness and altruism: those who are totally selfish, those who are totally altruistic, and those who are to varying degrees what I call *selfish-altruists*.

It is like giving three hungry people each a box of wheat. One person makes bread using the whole box and devours it immediately. As soon as he becomes hungry again, he looks for wheat grown by others to pick and consume—these are selfish pickers. The second person looks around and sees other people who are suffering so they give away all their seeds expecting nothing in return—these are altruistic planters. The third person makes bread with a small portion of the wheat for herself, family, and next-door neighbors and plants the rest. For months, she patiently tends to the plants until they're grown. Once she collects the crop, she keeps a third to eat, a third to plant for the next season, and shares a third with others— these are selfish-altruist growers. The balanced selfish-altruists who are on the top of the bell curve are Purposehooders.

On one side, there are pickers who reject their altruistic nature— mindless consumers and psychopaths. On the other side, planters reject their selfish nature—martyrs and excessive givers. In between there are growers—builders and creators. Some studies show that psychopaths make up about 1 percent of the general popu- lation, and I would imagine there are about the same number of martyrs. That would leave 98 percent of humanity in the category of selfish-altruists, or growers, to varying degrees, from one end of the scale to the other.

Growers struggle with their selfish and altruistic tendencies— the urge to take and the urge to give. Once you realize there is no internal war to fight among these two innate wonderful tendencies, then you become an ultimate selfish-altruist. There's no need to feel

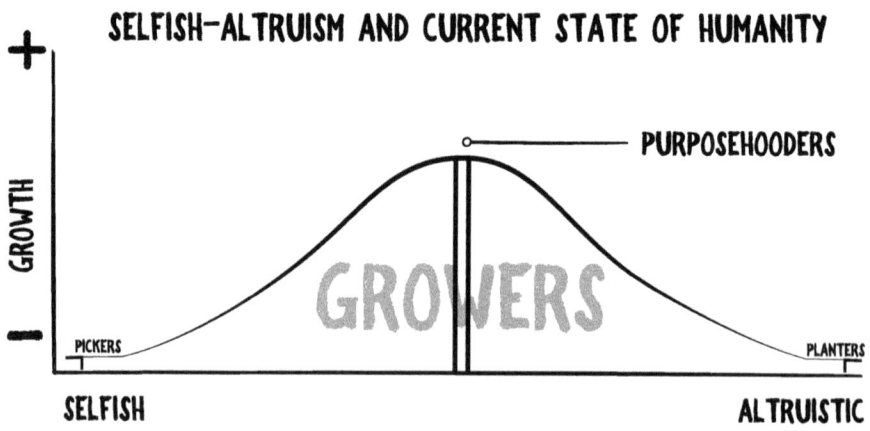

guilty for being selfish at times, nor pride for being altruistic other times; it is right to feel successful as you provide for both selfish and altruistic needs all the time.

Your circle of living is as wide as your extensions of being. At the core of your extensions is the self—the center of selfishness that demands from the other extensions selfish needs such as love and support from family, rewards and achievements from work, compassion and understanding from communities, and nourishments from nature. But if the link is *purely* selfish, it will exert a contracting negative force that pulls your extensions *toward* the self, shrinking your circle of living and turning your life into negative states of scarcity, suffering, rejection, and vacuum. The resistance force of your four extensions to your negative pull will eventually tear your life apart.

Similarly, if your link is purely altruistic, the self will be overwhelmed by the demands of your other extensions and burn out due to chronic stress. For example, the World Health Organization just recently added burnout from overwork and stress to the International Classification of Diseases that cause chronic stress and all kinds of suffering because these people fail to balance their selfish needs with the demand of work.[64] Totally giving mothers or nurses who sacrifice their personal well-being for others often suffer from burnout.

However, if you realize, just like in the Prisoner's Dilemma experiment, that there is a win-win strategy, a tit for tat, where you give when you receive but hold back if you are being used by the other party, and link all your Five Extensions of Being with selfish-altruism, then an expansion in any of your extensions will automatically expand them all. If your contributions to your work also improve your self-esteem and increase your knowledge, these improvements will positively impact your family, communities, and nature. There's no limit to how much you can expand your circle of living with the link of selfish-altruism.

You will grow with ease when you realize the selfish-altruistic nature of your existential desire, which pushes you to exponentially evolve and expand. You must become an altruist for selfish reasons. If you don't give part of yourself, you won't be able to form relationships that help you expedite your evolution and expansion. But you also must become selfish for altruistic reasons, as without ensuring self-care and self-growth, you won't be able to positively contribute to your family, work, community, and nature. By making sure you take care of your own needs—growing your seed of potentiality and moving toward the direction of your Purposehood—you will be able to offer even more help to others.

Successful growers are those who always start by being altruistic toward others but cease if others don't reciprocate. Growers are even willing to forgive and continue to give in the hope the non-reciprocator might be inspired to change their behavior, but only a couple more times. They are always looking to see if their altruism is expanding or diminishing their self, and this is how they decide consciously when to be selfish or altruistic.

The simplest way to practice selfish-altruism is to add altruistic intentions to every selfish act, and for every altruistic act, add selfish intentions. For example, if you plan to spend the day on the beach enjoying the sun and water, also pick up trash and plastic that is destroying our beautiful seas and its creatures. If you are volunteering to help build houses for the homeless, add selfish intentions such as exercising, learning new skills, and meeting new people.

If you are a parent and need time for yourself to enjoy reading a book or watching a movie, how about adding an altruistic intention to share the learning with your spouse and children? And, if you are spending time preparing food for the family, you could add a selfish intention to expand your awareness of nature by *mindfully* cooking—focusing your attention on the color, smell, texture and taste of the ingredients, learning about their nutritional components and how they got to your kitchen from the farm.

My friend, when you link your Five Extensions of Being with selfish-altruism, you pave the path to your Purposehood.

———

I BREATHE IN FOR MYSELF.
I BREATHE OUT FOR THE WORLD.

Proposition 4: Semideum

"You are a semideum, born to be a creator. While you have potentiality to become a creator, you also have a choice not to become one." – PoET Proposition 4

Have you ever looked at the night sky away from city lights to observe our crowded neighborhood of the Milky Way? It's a magnificent sight that fills you with awe. When you realize there are up to 400 billion stars like our precious sun in our galaxy alone, and there are two trillion galaxies in the universe, it's hard to see your significance on that scale of existence. But when you shift your view inward, you will see that there is a whole universe within you. And just like the galaxies in the universe, you are made of 37.2 trillion cells with maybe 100 trillion atoms in each cell, and within each atom a system of orbiting electrons around a nucleus, like planets orbiting a star.

My friend, you are a universe within a universe. You are neither a fluke of existence, nor an insignificant speck in this world. You are an inevitable product of a universe that wants to live its Purposehood—one that wants to continue evolving and expanding exponentially, and desperately needs expo-agents to expedite evolution in its accelerated expansion.

While some might see you as a product of blind chance, I see in you a product of a Purposehood entanglement, a blockchain of sorts that links the Big Bang to you, and you to the possible future that you might willfully initiate with the power of a thought, a word, or an action.

The state of humanity is like a wave function representing the probabilities for possible results of measurements on a system in quantum mechanics. It presents the probabilities of what a human can achieve from otherwise countless possible outcomes; yet, the collapse of this wave of possibilities into one outcome could easily be the action of one observer or even one belief in a desired outcome.

It's not without existential purpose that your hardware is grown from particles forged in the bellies of stars across the whole universe and brewed over 13.8 billion years of constant creation and destruction to refine and evolve the materials that would become you. Every moving part in this vast universe over that long stretch of spacetime had to be exactly as it was to produce you. It is true that anything in nature can influence existence with cause and effect, like a butterfly flapping her wings or a bat's dropping causing a pandemic across the globe. However, only you on this Earth, my friend, can start a chain reaction with the intention of causing a desired effect.

Isn't it possible that iSH, the universe, and life possess the same level of intention to cause you? The hands of your ancestors, Homo erectus, were not freed purposelessly, nor was the seed of wisdom that sprouted with human intelligence in the first Homo sapiens. You are a product of a line of heroes who, in order to bring you to life, had to overcome incredible odds of existential threats and stay alive long enough to pass the baton through your ancestors to be handed to you. Even the sperm that became you had to defeat 200 million other competitors to bring you to life. Not without merit are you here today.

The evolving human intelligence program that operates humanity and runs in you will add your uniqueness, learnings, and experiences to its core code in order to build more evolved humans. Human capabilities are exponentially expanding for a reason; one that is becoming more obvious as we become the powerful creators of the future.

It's not hard to see humanity taking life to the stars as we fulfill the universal Purposehood, but it is still a personal struggle to decide what role each one of us will want to play. Once you rid yourself of the silly notion that the world was created for you, and you realize that *you were created for the world*, your focus changes profoundly. Instead of inquiring "How do I use the world to satisfy my infinite desires?"—a question that leads most humans astray from their Purposehood and causes suffering from constant stress, anxiety, and regrets—you can instead ask the *right* question, "What does the world desire of me?" When you find the answer, you will embark on a life of ease with happiness, success, and fulfillment in every step you take.

With the right orientation, you can clearly see that regardless of what role you decide to play in this wonderful game of life, the profession you were built for is *creator*.

Born to Be a Creator

One thing for certain is that you were born a creator like every other human. Is it even possible for a human not to be one? If you are like most people, you may even struggle to keep your mind quiet for a few minutes of meditation before jumping back into creation mode, imagining the future, recreating the past, or initiating actions in the present.

It's easy to see your ability to create in the mechanical view of life, where you influence your Five Extensions of Being through your thoughts, words, and actions. Maybe soon humans will be able to create with simply a thought or a command as we integrate with an exponentially evolving and expanding AI. Still, the words you use today to inspire, teach, or share your experiences with a family member, a coworker, or a friend create (sometimes) intended and (most of the time) unintended consequences in the lives of others. Think about people you have already influenced with your words, and if you can't, then think about words that have influenced your life and you will be able to see the creation power of simple words.

It's a bit harder to see your creating power on the scale of the universal view, where spacetime stretches beyond your lifetime. But by simply looking at the biographies of people and events that occurred prior to your lifetime, you can clearly see the continued influence of individuals who shifted the entire direction of humanity, creating new expanding waves of possibilities. These were scientists who discovered the laws of physics and nature; inventors who created new technologies; engineers who constructed new structures; or entrepreneurs who advanced businesses. These also were artists who expanded our imaginations; writers and philosophers who encouraged us to think and reflect; and most importantly teachers, parents, and family members who planted the seeds of curiosity and sparked inspiration in children to become scientists, inventors, engineers, entrepreneurs, artists, writers, and philosophers.

You, my friend, have the same qualities and qualifications to become a creator like all of those who preceded you, and in turn, influence the future of humanity and life like they influenced our present.

Yet, the magic of your creating power lays in the quantum view of existence. Quantum mechanics was born out of the deep desire to understand the building blocks of everything that is in what's called *fundamental physics*. Maybe if we understood the Lego pieces that our universe, life, humanity, and ourselves are made of, we could understand what is possible in our future-oriented existence.

Almost a hundred years after the first laws of quantum mechanics were proposed, we are still no closer to explaining the weird phenomena produced by those initial equations, and later, proved by experiments and used for practical applications in modern everyday technologies like our cell phones. The most promising explanation so far is the *string theory*, which defines the building block of everything as a vibrating one-dimensional string in 11 dimensions. The mere vibrational state of the string determines the particle it manifests. As various strings interact with one another, they band together in a universal symphony to give form to the structures that exist in the universe as we know it.

If that is not strange enough, quantum particles have three

particular properties that are even stranger. These are superposition, tunneling, and entanglement.

The first property is *quantum superposition*, where a quantum, the minimum amount of any basic physical entity such as a photon, possesses all possible positions, but only one position when it's observed. In other words, the outcome among all possible outcomes is not determined until observed. The mere act of observing generates information to force a probability.

The second property is *tunneling*, where a subatomic particle passes through a barrier that seems impossible in the mechanical view of classical physics. In other words, a particle appears in a classical view to not have enough energy to pass through a barrier, yet "magically" it breaks through.

The third spooky property is *entanglement*, where a particle is connected with other particles at the time they are generated, regardless of the distances between them. In other words, a quantum state of any particle not only can't be described independently, but also a change in one state will impact the other states of the entangled particles.

With these strange properties a person can't help but wonder, "How could everything we call real be made of things we cannot regard as real?"

You ask, "This is fascinating, but what does it have to do with me?"

My friend, you are made of the same magical building blocks with the same potentiality and arranged in a unique way in order to have the ability to intentionally impact existence and the future with information you generate or rearrange through your thoughts, words, and actions.

You ask, "Is it possible that large objects like you and me could possess similar quantum effects?"

It seems unfathomable to think so, but professor Jack Harris of Yale University is exploring this exact question with experiments to show whether it is actually true on any scale.[65]

The Three Properties of Semideum

Here's how you can think about the three properties of semideum on a philosophical level:

1. **Superposition:** The possibilities of what could happen are much more than what actually happen or what you expect to happen. It's all a result of an intention: a word or an action of at least one observer. The collapse of the wave of possibilities into a specific outcome might or might not always require a conscious observer, but you are a conscious observer in this existence. With an intentional observation in the form of a thought, word, or action you become a creator or a co-creator of an outcome.

2. **Tunneling:** There are no barriers to limit potentiality. Isn't that obvious, as whatever we conceive to be an insurmountable barrier becomes no barrier at all once one human surmounts it? Take for example the 10-second barrier in the 100-meter sprint that was thought to be impossible to break until one person did. That was duplicated immediately by other runners once they realized that it wasn't impossible. All other challenges also seem impossible until one semideum changes that perception. What barriers are you willing to break through in your life? What is holding you back from being a true semideum, a creator?

3. **Entanglement:** It is easy to see the entanglement you have with your Five Extensions of Being as you influence them with every action you take. However, when you realize that every particle in existence is entangled with cause and effect since the emergence of the Big Bang, then you realize that everything is one system. Every action you take influences everything else in the universe, and you have the conscious awareness to recognize that you can intentionally exert your influence on everything there is with your choices. What an amazing power to be able to make a difference in the universe, and what a heavy responsibility!

You Have the Potential to Play Any Role You Want

My friend, as an intentional observer, a barrier-breaker, and an entangled influencer in this world, you can choose to play any role you want in life. Your Five Extensions of Being can be as narrow or as wide as you will them to be. Your thoughts, words, and actions are your tools to create a difference in this world, and they are totally under your control regardless of how others think, speak, or act. With a simple choice to direct all your tools toward your Purposehood, you can start taking the hero's journey of a semideum, where you grow through the challenges you face and work with other semideums to create a better future for yourself, your extensions of being, humanity, and nature.[66]

But You Also Have the Possibility of Becoming a Destroyer

As a semideum, you also possess the choice to become an anti-creator: a consumer, a martyr, or a destroyer. When your infinite desires fuel your limitless creativity away from your Purposehood, you will become a negative force in existence.

Humanity, life, and the universe will use a negative force to create a balance and generate opposing positive forces, as all systems do. A destroyer hardly ever grows to their full potential regardless of how destructive they become, as they are always constrained by labels, limiting beliefs, expectations, and judgments. A creator, on the other hand, is exponential in nature with no limitation. That's why positivity ultimately prevails, and life always advances to a better state of being.

This also means you will suffer with stress, anxiety, and regrets if the cord of existence that connects you to your Purposehood Guiding Star is stretched in negative tension when you move away from your existential purpose toward vacuum. Only when you pause, correct your heading, and follow your Purposehood Guiding Star, will you be able to live with ease, experiencing happiness, success, and fulfillment with every step in the beautiful journey of life regardless of the challenges.

The choice is yours. Will you choose the profession of creator, and move toward your Purposehood making positive contributions, or will you choose to be a destroyer, causing havoc and tension in people and nature as you move away from your Purposehood?

You ask, "When I choose to be a creator, do I have to become a disruptor expo-agent?"

My friend, creation is made through disruption and also with linear improvements. The choice is yours if you want to enhance or invent, as they are both positive choices in the direction of Purposehood. Your role as a creator will become clearer as you explore your essential desires later in this book. Essential desires are the molds of human creations.

I BREATHE IN CREATIVITY.
I BREATHE OUT CREATION.

Proposition 5:
Limitless Creativity

"You're endowed with limitless creativity so you may create a better future for your Five Extensions of Being, humanity, life, and the universe. You unleash your creativity by removing limitations, nourishing your seed of potentiality with practices, and collaborating with others. When you unleash the creativity of your extensions, you tap into the universal abundance of possibilities, and in the process, you expose yourself to receiving happiness, success, and fulfillment." – PoET Proposition 5

We evolved to have limitless creativity for nature to live its Purposehood. While some see the game of existence playing out through mindless accidents, I see a process toward an existential purpose. As the Purposehood of Everything Theory (PoET) states, the purpose of existence is to evolve and expand exponentially. The "how" is a process of linear growth through linear-agents, and disruptive growth through expo-agents. We diverged from other evolutionary relatives on the vast evolutionary tree through disruptive environmental conditions, DNA mutations, and natural selection filters because the system that held us needed an expo-agent.

The goal of natural selection within a system is to create the most suitable agents for growth, with the positive agents slightly more favored than negative ones in order to keep zigzagging forward toward Purposehood. But when a system creates an expo-agent to expedite its evolution and expansion, it makes sure the expo-agent is equipped with the most powerful tools to make achieving the desired goals more probable. The risk is always that this powerful agent could be a disruption in the wrong direction, but the positive balance rule will always produce a more capable expo-agent that would counter in the other direction.

The election of a political leader who opposes the forward direction of humanity is a negative linear-agent, while something like the Paris Agreement, where 197 countries agreed to combat climate change is a positive linear-agent. On the other hand, a global war or pandemic is a negative expo-agent, and an invention like the internet is a positive expo-agent. A person who is a consumer or a persistent critic could be a negative linear-agent, while a volunteer for a worthy cause is a positive linear-agent. On the other hand, a murderer is an example of a negative expo-agent, and an inventor of useful technology is a positive expo-agent. What events and people can you think of that fit this model?

Could you use this model to predict and influence possible future events? *If you can determine what state a system is currently in, you can predict the possible next occurrence to be one of the other three states.* If a system is in a linear positive direction, then you can expect the emergence of a negative linear agent or a positive or negative expo-agent. As a semideum among a group of semideums, you have the power to influence the possible outcome by intentionally creating conditions that increase one probability and reduce the probability of others.

In order to become a semideum, you had to have been born a genius and have the possibility to develop your gift to become a creator. As life evolved humanity to become the disruptive growth agent for all nature and its elements, a monumental mission, no doubt, it also provided humans with exponential powers within their seed of potentiality by removing limitations from creativity and desires, and adding choice to direction.

In what seems iSH's infinite wisdom, the potential of every agent to serve its purpose is within its innate capabilities. The human brain has evolved over millions of years to create a three-pound mass that demands 20 percent of our energy in order to generate limitless creativity unbounded by space or time. Our brains are spaceships that can imagine us traveling to realistic and unrealistic destinations, and are time-machines that can easily jump back and forth between the past and the future, sometimes resting, even for a short while, in the present. They are the analyzers of what we become aware of, the dreamers of what is impossible, and the creators of what is possible.

You ask, "But, what is the purpose of creativity?"

My friend, while the purpose of creativity itself is to evolve and expand exponentially, generating better and more ideas faster, the goal of creativity is to create. If ideas don't transform into creations, they might remain dormant in a vast ocean of a *timeless-cloud*, a storage repository for every piece of the world's possible information. You can turn them into a creation by sharing them or creating a plan or a final product. Only then will they become a reality in this existence. An idea in your head might die with you, but sharing a description of your idea might be the inspiration for someone else to make a difference in this world. This is why creativity is grown through exposure and sharing. Your limitless creativity feeds on expanded awareness, diversification of input, and challenges.

A linear biological evolution of becoming bipedal, enabling our ancestors' legs to explore further surroundings, and using their hands to create practical tools for survival, expedited the evolution of an expo-agent, the modern brain. With separate input and response areas, a prefrontal cortex for imagination, and an ability to create new connections, we became creators. This incredible machine was ready for the initial software code of human intelligence, which was able to exponentially evolve by extension-learning as it interacted with the individual's extensions of being.

As human desires evolved from those limited to survival and reproduction to infinite ones, they also grew more complex and abstract. When this happened, creativity had to be unleashed accordingly. It, in turn, evolved to become limitless, capable of creating abstract concepts like languages and art. This limitless creativity is the reason why you and every other human is born a genius, waiting to be nourished to your full-grown potential to assume a creator role in this existence.

We Are Facing Major Challenges That Limit Our Creativity

In 1958, Dr. E. Paul Torrance, a professor of educational psychology, administered a creativity test to 400 third- and fourth-grade children. The 90-minute test had questions such as, "How could you improve this stuffed toy to be more fun to play with?" He and his colleagues followed these children for 50 years, tracking all of their creative accomplishments. The data demonstrated that Torrance's creative ability score predicted creative accomplishments three times better than conventional intelligence measuring tests, with one major exception: IQ scores have been increasing generation after generation while creativity scores have been declining, especially among young children as they enter school. And as we discussed earlier with Land's findings, children younger than those tested by Torrance almost all exhibited a genius level of creativity.

At birth you were given the universe as your circle of living—a canvas to imagine the possible and impossible; to borrow from nature countless crayons of inspirations and paint the most beautiful picture of the future. Now, with the limiting beliefs you have adopted over the years, you are left with a few shades of gray and a shred of paper to express your creativity. When these are your tools, you can only do so much with them, but when you have the whole universe as your paper and nature as your crayons, there are no limits.

So, what can you do about this? When you realize the canvas and crayons are all still there, and limitations only exist in your mind, you can start by removing the obstacles to your creativity. Then, you can learn to *grow* your creativity with simple tools and practices. Finally, you can connect with others to expand both your creativity and theirs.

You ask, "Where do the limitations that constrain our creativity come from?"

My friend, they come from labels, beliefs, and expectations placed on you when you were a child by parents, guardians, and society, then from your own misinterpretations of events and the distractions of your mindless desires.

The first borders on your limitless canvas of creativity were constructed right after you were born. What seems to be a celebration of your emergence became labels constraining your potentiality; labels you hadn't chosen, like date of birth, name, nationality, ethnicity, and religious affiliation, to list some of the most restrictive. These labels enslave semideums to limiting beliefs. One limiting belief is debilitating enough, and there are countless numbers of them hidden in plain sight under an attractive label. These limitations were essential for our evolution at one point in history, but are now limitations on our exponential potentiality.

Take, for example, the "nationality" label, with which most of humanity has no choice. It was necessary at one point in history to group people who freely roamed the Earth in competing interests in order to drive innovation. But today, nation states are obstacles for the free movement of talents across borders. With a nationality label, our canvas is immediately shrunk to fit in preassigned borders. We start with the universe as our borderless playing field, then we emerge on the stage of this speck of marble to play our part in the universal game, only to be condemned to a prison cell called a country. Then we are asked by our jailers to make the world a better place right there from our assigned prison cell. Our innate sense of universality is immediately diminished to a limiting locality.

Our natural association with all living things is reduced to association, not even with humanity, but merely with the group of people who happened to live within the same prison walls we call borders. We spend the rest of our lives adopting their values, living their limitations, trying to live up to their aspirations, or struggling to break free from all their expectations. We become products of a limited exposure to cultural traditions and values of a nation, instead of soaking in humanity's with all its diversity.

The joy we get from the wide spectrum of colors in nature, which ignites our curiosity and feeds our creativity so we may add more beauty to this world, is narrowed down to a few pigments placed on a piece of cloth labeled "flag." For the rest of our lives, we are expected to gaze upon it with emotion, salute, and even kill or die to protect this flag, one we didn't choose at our birth. The oneness of humanity that we intuitively feel at birth becomes "us" and "them." Our scope of culture and history becomes limited by the language we are assigned and the stories we are told. The political borders among nations grow to become barriers of social and psychological separation. Our poetry, literature, thoughts, and emotions reinforce the differences between us and those who happen to live across the borders. The newborn star quarterback of the universal game is reduced to play in a prison cell. How sad it is to see such wasted potential.

You ask, "Could you give me an example?"

My friend, I used to visit the beautiful country of Switzerland, often driving up from the South of France. On the way there, I passed the border between France and Italy, and then between Italy and Switzerland. Since the implementation of relaxed borders in Europe, I hardly felt any difference passing from France to Italy. I only saw on the A8 highway, while cruising slightly above the speed limit, a small sign that said: "Welcome to Italy."

But Switzerland is a different story. The road into the country is a narrower one passing through several skiing villages of the magnificent Mont Blanc, but since Switzerland is not part of the European Union, you need to pass a border checkpoint under the watching eyes of Swiss officers as you're forced to make your way slowly through the border lanes.

On one winter trip, I took some time off to ski on both sides of the border. Within a few meters from each other, straddling the border, are two restaurants—one where people speak Italian and use euros to pay, and another where they speak French and use Swiss francs.

There's no natural barrier between the two sides. The borderline is merely an imaginary line across the same mountain. Yet, crazily enough, the person, family, or village on each side becomes fundamentally different. If you're born on one side, you're one kind of a person, and if you happen to be on the other side, your destiny completely changes. The way you look at yourself and people on your side of the border, and the way you look at the people on the other side, becomes very different.

This is also what happens in our lives. We conform to those imaginary walls and borders that only exist in our minds or are dictated by others. Then we design our life and create our possibilities based on those imaginary walls.

Yet, if you soar up above, free like an eagle, you will see there are no borders and no walls! Indeed, "there is no spoon!"[67] You will realize that you're free to think about yourself in whatever way you want. There's no limit to your possibilities.

We're meant to live interacting with each other for lifetime learning and idea exchange as we build, together, a better future for all, with no borders or judgments. Each one of us is a unique individual with special gifts to contribute to our collective evolution. But individuality can only function at its peak, when every individual is free to explore their full potential anywhere in the world. The Earth is one Earth and humanity is one race.

Thanks to social media, we are evolving to connect beyond artificial borders and national limitations. This connectivity will eventually, as we evolve further, bring us together as one.

Another limiting belief that is placed on us at birth without our choosing is the religious sectarian label. It's another powerful label with countless limiting beliefs, not only in regard to every aspect of our lives and how to interact with the physical world we live in, but also the mysterious beyond.

Religious and sectarian labels totally entangle this new universal gift of potentiality with parents' sets of dogmas, doctrines, and blind leaps of faith.

One might understand, but not justify, the selfish need for a parent to pass their experiences to their offspring. But the reality with most religious beliefs is that they infect children with a fake sense of certainty. Each sect claims to possess the ultimate truth, but this truth is based on someone else's manufactured interpretations. These interpretations are motivated best by the interpreter's own personal experiences, and worst by their lust for power or other selfish desires. The teachings of prophets, saints, or gurus, in most cases, were generated centuries ago. What parents end up placing their faith in is an interpretation of other interpretations. If there is an ultimate truth out there, it must be a precise equation that produces the same result, unlike the differing conclusions possessed by countless sects, even within one religion. Isn't it absurd to think that we were so lucky to be born to our parents, who happened to stumble, not by choice, on the only religious truth out of the countless sects who lay similar, but supposedly wrong, claims?

With the negative power of these beliefs, we start creating more labels and limiting beliefs for ourselves as we reach our teens. Each "I am" statement becomes a new label we create to obstruct our potential. Each "I cannot" statement becomes a limiting belief. Each projected image, as simple as posting a picture on a social network, becomes a label for others to judge us by. With each label we place on ourselves we add more expectations, more stress, and more limitations. Those external labels and internal limiting beliefs become a dense jungle around us, smothering our seed of potentiality.

And if that's not enough, our powerful brain, in the process of finding lazy answers for our misery, interprets past and present events to reinforce our limiting beliefs, thus creating more limiting beliefs.

We've lost our way in life, and whatever is left of our creativity is totally consumed by the distractions of our survival instincts, running after our infinite basic desires or running away from fears.

But all hope is not gone. All challenges could be positive if we adjust our heading toward our Purposehood, with determination to start removing the obstacles on our path and changing them into positive fuel for our journey.

For example, distractions like the internet and technology consume our precious time, preying on negative desires like vanity, and fueling mindless consumption. However, these same technologies provide us with unprecedented, faster access to wider and better knowledge, with countless resources across all humanity. They also give us the tools to expand our creativity, augmented by the many applications on our smartphones and tablets. Do you control these tools, or do they control you? How often do you look at your screens, and how many hours do you spend daily on your devices?

Ultimately, once we remove our limiting beliefs and replace them with those that are empowering, we can easily resurrect the creative genius within us and within each person in our extensions.

You ask, "How can we reclaim our genius creativity?"

My friend, the easiest way is to be a kid again. Believe that nothing is impossible, have fun exploring, and play with others. Remember that while creativity is natural, non-creative behaviors are learned. All you need to do is unlearn your limitations and revive your creative behaviors. It all starts with understanding creativity and its sparks, and choosing to unleash it through curiosity, awareness, and practices.

WE CAN EASILY CHOOSE TO UNLEASH CREATIVITY IN OUR FIVE EXTENSIONS OF BEING

When researchers started studying creativity, they focused on how it generates many unique and useful ideas. This type of creativity is called divergent thinking. Soon, they discovered another side that follows logical steps to reach a conclusion. That is called convergent thinking. I like to think about creativity as having three types, *formless creativity*, *practical creativity*, and *collaborative creativity*.

With *formless creativity*, you dream the impossible and the unimaginable regardless of practical limitations. It's a conscious dream state not unlike the dreams in your sleep, where there is no obvious purpose to your creation nor an expectation of an outcome. One of the best practices for formless creativity is simply to allow yourself to be bored. Boredom is a great tool if you allow it to push your brain into formless creativity instead of choosing pain over boredom—like half of the participants in a study who couldn't sit quietly for 15 minutes, opting for an electric shock instead.[68] You need the quiet time away from distractions or the limiting belief that being busy is what successful people do and being bored sometimes is laziness.

This formless creativity is what produces novel arts, many religious and mystic beliefs, and the ability to imagine unrealistic futures as we see in sci-fi or fantasy movies where apes take over the human world. Yet, at the core of this creativity is a quantum view of existence where some of what seems impossible is actually possible, and even probable, if it is so willed. Haven't many of humanity's ancient epic tales, religious and philosophical explanations of the beyond, and science fiction inspired useful knowledge that advanced humanity? Those ideas start with formless creativity in the mind of the creators and become structured creations as they are shaped into the constructs of language, musical notes, or scripts in movies. Some of the best theoretical mathematicians are formless thinkers, fitting their abstract theories into the construct of equations. Formless creativity is closely connected to happiness and our evolution.

Practical creativity is what we need to solve the challenges we are facing today. In our mechanical view of life, we encounter challenges that need immediate or short-term solutions, and we draw on what is possible to come up with workable fixes. It's the creativity most used by engineers, teachers, politicians, entrepreneurs, and anyone else who needs to solve a challenge toward a desired outcome. Many models have been created for developing this form of creativity, such as the IDEO process,[69] which starts with formless creativity in a rapid brainstorming session among a diverse group of people and ends with prototypes, which are narrowed down to a final choice based on three criteria of human desirability, business viability, and technological feasibility.

One of the best practices for practical creativity I found is walking in nature. Nature is on a continuous journey of practical innovation as it experiments with a wide variety of solutions until it finds optimal ones. Many of our scientific advancements have been inspired by solutions found in the natural world. Biomimicry is a field of science that derives its inspiration and practical solutions in medical techniques, robotics, and industrial materials from nature. Over billions of years, nature has developed the most practical solutions for all kinds of challenges. Those solutions are waiting for us to discover them.

Realize that nature is your outer extension of being connecting you with the whole universe. Invest the time to develop a deeper awareness of its mechanics. Consciously connect with it like you connect with your human mother. Practical creativity is closely connected to success and our expansion.

Collaborative creativity is built on the countless contributions of humanity before us and continues by interactions with other creators. This creativity progresses constantly to create a better state of being in the universal view of life, regardless of the current state. This form of creativity has fueled our exponentiality, as we have access more than ever to new ideas and research from diversified groups of people who weren't easily accessible to us just a few decades ago.

Most importantly, we can directly collaborate to solve what seems to be an impossible challenge, like taking a picture of a black hole 55 million light years away from us! This was possible through the collaboration of 200 researchers from Africa, Asia, Europe, and North and South America. Imagine what impossible challenges we can solve and impossible realities we can create when every human is a genius and we are collaborating together as equal creators.

One of the best practices of collaborative creativity is to surround yourself with widely diverse people who share your mission but not your background. These people become an extension of your creativity, expanding your awareness and your resources, as I discuss later in belonging practices within the Five Streams of Potentiality. Collaborative creativity is closely connected to fulfillment and our exponentiality.

You ask, "Which one of these creativities do we need to unleash in ourselves and people in our extensions?"

All of them, my friend. Doesn't every child have all three? Don't children always imagine the unimaginable, accomplish tasks with practical creativity, and expand their creativity by playing with other children? I found one of the best inspirations to all three types of creativity, in addition to spending time with nature, is to talk to young children and watch them create with endless curiosity, expanded awareness, and repeated practice.

You ask, "What steps can I take to resurrect my creativity?"

There is a three-step process nature uses to grow any seed of potentiality: plant the seed in a fertile ground (or remove the constraints on an existing seed), nourish it, and enlist the help of others. This is how everything in nature grows to reach its full potential.

You can use the same process to unleash your creativity:

1. Remove the constraints of labels and limiting beliefs, expectations, and judgments from yourself and all those in your extensions. For example, if you believe life is suffering, you are born a sinner, or that everyone who doesn't follow your beliefs will go to hell, how could your entire life become anything else *but* a constant struggle to free yourself from suffering, correct an existential mistake, or fit with the rest of humanity?

2. Nourish your creativity with empowering beliefs, a detachment from expectations, and by withholding judgment. Use a creativity practice such as creative boredom, nature walks, and group games. Take a normal object, like a fork, and ask each person during dinner to think about ten different ways to improve or imagine new uses for it. You can also use the streams of potentiality practices (described in the last section of this book) to unleash your creativity by controlling the impulses of your negative desires.

3. Go beyond your comfort zone and become friends with other people who don't share your nationality, ethnicity, gender, religious beliefs, political orientation, or profession and meet regularly to share ideas and views. Live like a tree in a beautiful forest consisting of all types of creatures connected through a shared Purposehood.

Expanding Creativity with the Sierpinski Triangle

You probably have noticed that I use a triangle to help illustrate many of the concepts discussed in this book. In fact, I use it to expand my creativity. Since our brains tend to optimize energy use, they want to find answers to questions quickly. Most of the time, the obvious answer is not the best one, so I need to challenge my brain to come up with more answers. In this triangle of creativity, I place the topic or question in the center of the triangle and challenge my brain to come up with at least three answers. Then, I try to connect each of the items to three other aspects and go as deep as I feel is required. This process generates what is called the *Sierpinski triangle*. If you try this, you will find that there is a deep wisdom to trinity that expands your awareness beyond the obvious.

TRIANGLE OF CREATIVITY

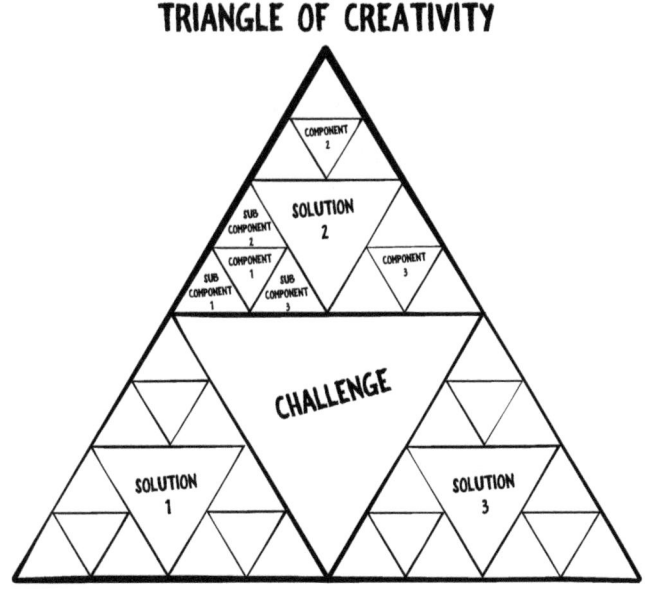

My friend, the beautiful future is ours to create. We need every human to believe in their and others' abilities as creators. We need to realize that geniuses come in every shape and form. Geniuses are artists, scientists, entrepreneurs, athletes, physicians, self-reflectors, parents and family members, workers in every aspect of life, friends and social workers, nature protectors, and most importantly, teachers.

As someone said, if we measure genius by the ability to climb trees, then all fish are stupid and all monkeys are geniuses. But if we realize that genius is contributing uniqueness to produce a better state of being, then everyone is born to become a genius, and everyone can be a genius at what they do.

We must make it our mission to treat every child as gifted, every employee as a potential growth agent, every teacher as a creator of creators, and every parent as an incubator of semideums. Likewise, we must treat every adult who's living below their potentiality as a deprived genius who needs freedom from limitations, nourishment for their seed of potentiality, and a community that supports them. My friend, this mission starts by first believing in yourself, unleashing your own creativity, and fueling it with your infinite desires in the direction of your Purposehood.

———

I BREATHE IN NATURE.
I BREATHE OUT CURIOSITY.

Proposition 6:
The Pyramid of Desires

"Every creation is born from a desire. Your infinite desires are the fuel to your limitless creativity in order to empower your role as a creator in this existence. When your desires are in the direction of your Purposehood, then they will be shaped with values that guide your journey with empowering beliefs." – PoET Proposition 6

You ask, "What is desire, and is it only a human quality?"

My friend, desire is at the core of existence.[70] It's the propellant that fuels evolution and expansion. Science can't prove or disprove, as of now, if the building blocks of the universe are conscious. There is no common agreement on a definition of consciousness as we investigate with amazement everything from subatomic particles to stars, planets, and galaxies. Still, we clearly know there are forces in the universe that drive the movement of everything. That movement brings particles together to form more evolved structures, and at the same time, pushes matter further apart to expand this universe. Some of these forces are called positive and others are called negative, which doesn't mean one is good and the other is bad—they're just labels used to identify direction and orientation.

This existential movement is in everything. It is driven by natural laws that attract positive and negative forces to form an evolved and expanded state of being. Isn't attraction a result of a desire to be attractive? Isn't attraction also an instigator of desires in others? A thing or a being must be attractive, or must become attractive, to be desired by another. Could we even dare to imagine that things "desire" to attract other things? Could desire be the fuel of consciousness? Could the desire to attract or get close to something attractive be a conscious decision?

I realize it's very hard to imagine desire when it comes to particles and the universe, but when it comes to nature, it is a bit clearer, perhaps. Isn't the desire to survive so obvious in creatures we see around us, from dogs and cats to spiders and flies? Have you stopped, before squashing a cockroach, to observe its desire to survive as it senses that you've noticed it, and runs away trying to find a hiding place where you can't reach it? The desires to survive and reproduce as a plant or an animal fuel their evolution and expansion.

In New Zealand, most native flowering plants are pollinated by animals.[71] Flowers offer nectar as a reward to the animals for helping them spread their pollen from their stamen to a different plant's stigma, producing a stronger plant through cross-pollination.

Many flowers use colors, scents, and specifically shaped landing platforms to attract particular animals. In tropical forests, various flowering plants evolved to attract specific animals and insects best suited to help them pollinate. A study led by the University of Miami biologist Nathan Muchhala found that flowers respond to the needs of the animals that are doing the best job spreading pollen.[72] Flowers develop a wider or narrower access to nectar to accommodate the beak of a particular bird that is a suitable pollinator. "Basically, the flowers are making an evolutionary decision," Muchhala said. Could that evolutionary decision be fueled by a desire to evolve and expand? Could the law of nature be to "desire" to evolve into a better version of one's self and to continue to expand beyond that?

One can debate if a need of an animal or a plant is driven by desire, or if desire exists in everything in the universe, but what we all can agree on is that *desire is at the core of being a human*. Desire is one of the three components of the seed of potentiality we possess at birth.

While the desires of animals are limited to their basic needs in order to survive and reproduce, those in humans have evolved and expanded into a complex set of desires. We desire things, emotions, thoughts, dreams, and actions. We desire what's good for us and we desire what we know is bad for us. We all have 33 desires fueling the role we are meant to play in this life. They can be organized in a pyramid, with 16 basic desires, 10 essential desires, 3 fundamental desires, 1 existential desire, and 3 *desire traits* impacting all of them.

During our early years we start with a layer of *basic desires,* and as we become aware of the abundance of options, the essence of all desires shift from finite needs to infinite wants. We start wanting better, sooner, and more of the objects of our desires. Once we also realize our power to choose and create, another layer of *essential desires* emerges to allow us to develop the role we want to play in this life. As our sophisticated bodies connect our brains with our basic and essential desires, a layer of *fundamental desires* arises to release hormones of incentives to fuel our choices. And in moments of reflections and clarity, an *existential desire* urges us to understand the purpose of our existence.

Basic Desires

When it comes to understanding human desires, researchers have focused on trying to comprehend what motivates humans to do what they do. Many concluded, as Nobel laureate Bertrand Russell did, "all human activity is prompted by desire."[73]

The understanding of desires in those cases were based mainly on a mechanical view of humanity. If humanity is only a product of biological evolution, then our desires are merely evolved ones from the basic needs still present in our biological relatives. Those needs have evolved in a human to become more complex, which prompted American psychologist Abraham Maslow to develop his Hierarchy of Needs, based on his observations of what he considered a "master race" of humans.[74] In this view, desires are progressive needs moving from one stage to another as they get fulfilled. A human starts with physiological needs, then psychological needs, then self-fulfillment needs.

Maslow realized later in his life that he missed an important need that humans have, which is transcendence—a way to reach "the very highest and most inclusive or holistic levels of consciousness"—so he placed that on the top of his hierarchy. Maslow's theory has been accepted and promoted by people and organizations that view humanity as consumers looking to satisfy their hierarchical needs, even as many scientific researchers have contested it.

Psychologist Steven Reiss studied extensive data of over 6,000 people worldwide.[75] He concluded that there was no hierarchy for what he summarized as the 16 basic desires that motivate a human. Every person is uniquely driven by the degree of intensity in those desires, and if you were to understand that intensity, you could then predict their behavior. He viewed strong and weak basic desires in a person as the sources of motivation for their actions and traits. He insisted that the many desires considered by other researchers, including those of Maslow and Murray's system of needs,[76] are represented in one of these 16 basic desires. He further felt that Maslow's hierarchy is incorrect and misleading, as there are many obvious cases where people traded safety and even some physiological needs for the pursuit of their ideals, and in some cases, were even willing to die for them.

Many researchers saw humans as products of their basic desires, and believed that the best we can do to motivate people is to feed those that are most dominant. If you view life only as a jungle and humans as its native creatures, then basic desires, with or without hierarchy, are all there is.

I found previous studies of basic desires insightful in understanding what makes a human tick in the jungle of life. They answer the "what" in the form of basic desires driven by genetic codes, but there is still a "why" that needs to be answered in order to fully understand the complexity of human desires.

If we shift our perspective and see humans as products of an existential purpose that needed them to become creators, then we can view basic desires as fuel to an essential layer of desires that enable people to become what they were meant to be. Humans are products of potentiality, born in the Garden of Eden into a nature that desires to evolve and expand exponentially. And like any new expo-agent, humans are the result of increased complexity to serve a critical function in the system that produced it. This complexity is evident not only in limitless creativity and directional choice, but also in humans' infinite desires.

Basics desires are only one layer of human desires. They are meant to provide our essential desires with adequate fuel. There are 16 desires in that basic layer: acceptance, accumulation, autonomy, curiosity, idealism, loyalty, movement, nourishment, order, parenting, power, rest, retaliation, sex, socializing, and status.

And just like the ever-deeper layers of existence become visible as we examine any object under a microscope, so too will additional layers of desires become visible under the Purposehood microscope. In fact, beneath the obvious basic desires, we will find three more layers that make a human tick. Without recognizing these layers, we can't fully understand the human motivation system, as each layer can be fueled or directed by others.

Essential Desires

The second layer is *essential desires* that are needed for a human to play their role in life as a creator and to cooperate with other humans in order for humanity to fulfill its Purposehood. I have found 10 essential desires present in every human. These are attraction, beautification, construction, domestication, exploitation, exploration, innovation, love, profiting, and want. All basic desires fuel these essential desires, where positive basic desires fuel a productive life of ease. In a life of Purposehood, essential desires mindfully guide the consumption of basic desires. But if you pursue work only to feed your basic desires, then those infinite basic desires will fuel a life of suffering.

Fundamental Desires

When you look deeper, you encounter the third layer of human desires: the *fundamental desires* of happiness, success, and fulfillment. All human activities are fundamentally driven by one of these. I find that if you ask a person to explain their actions with enough "why" questions, they will eventually arrive at either happiness, success, or fulfillment as their fundamental motivation. These desires are supported by a pain-and-pleasure apparatus, as well as hormones in our bodies—a reward and punishment system of sorts. Nature has created this to guide us to fulfill our existential role.

You ask, "What is the fourth layer of human desires?"

The Existential Desire

My friend, when you reach the fourth layer, there is only one existential desire; it is the desire to seek your Purposehood, the desire to find the reason of your existence, the desire to understand why you were put on this Earth, the desire to evolve and expand exponentially, the desire to find and play your role in life. This existential desire should be the *why* behind all our pursuits, and without it there can't be true happiness, success, and fulfillment.

Desire Traits

You ask, "How are human desires infinite, and why?"

My friend, there are three desire traits that make all desires infinite: those of betterment, excessiveness, and haste.

- **Betterment:** Whatever a human achieves or possesses, they soon become unsatisfied with it and desire something better. Isn't that the engine that drives innovations on the positive side and mindless consumerism on the negative side?

- **Excessiveness:** It was said that if a person were to have two mountains of gold, they would always wish for a third. Obesity and hoarding disorders are two negative results of wanting more. On the positive side, the desire for more resources is fueling human essential desires of exploitation and exploration in order to find new resources through scientific discoveries.

- **Haste:** When a desire emerges, its fulfillment never seems to come soon enough. Isn't it amusing to see people lining up and waiting hours to watch a new movie or buy a new product when they could easily do the same thing a few days later without waiting? How fast the connection has to be before you're satisfied with the download speed of your movie? And as soon as you're happy with the speed, the industry introduces better and larger products that need even faster connections.

These three desire traits combined become an exponential force to positively fuel a creator or negatively fuel a destroyer. Without these three, our other desires wouldn't have been sufficient to motivate our exponential evolution and expansion or drive us to play our creator role in existence.

Positive and Negative Desires

Human desires can directionally be positive or negative. As our desires grew more complex in their evolutionary journey from primitive instincts to sophisticated wants, they took on yet another complexity—a negative or positive charge. A negative desire is uncontrollable like a wild horse, whereas a positive desire is like a tamed steed. One leads you away from your Purposehood while the other carries you toward it. If your Purposehood is to become the best marathon runner because you want to inspire people to be healthy, then nourishment (a basic desire) is positive if you mindfully eat proper food that matches your sport, and negative if you eat like a weightlifter. Even your existential desire could be positive if it drives you to find meaning in your active life, and negative if it drives you to seclude yourself in a mountain cave for the rest of your life.

The same infinite desires we have could be the fuel that explodes our spaceship or propels it to higher orbits of existence. On the negative side, desires could be the fuel of destruction to all our extensions of being if they are purely selfish or purely altruistic. On the positive side, they could be the fuel of empowerment if they are rooted in selfish-altruism.

From Pyramid of Desires to Pyramid of Values

In the jungle of life, we are taught to climb the Pyramid of Desires by first focusing on fulfilling our most basic needs. Once we acquire those, we can focus on our essential ones, and as we age, we can pursue our fundamental desires. Hopefully, if we're lucky and before we die, we can pursue our existential desire and find the purpose of our lives. Maybe this could work if we were to grow in the Garden of Eden where we clearly see our existential purpose. But in the jungle of life, most people end up stuck in the pursuit of infinite basic desires that are never fulfilled. In this misdirected life of scarcity, they decide to pursue careers that provide them with more of their basic desires. As they suffer in meaningless work, they wrongfully identify happiness as pleasure, success as achievement, and fulfillment as accumulation of wealth to be able to afford all your desires, only to receive stress, anxiety, and regrets. Then they wake up one day in that life of rejection staring at a vacuum of existence lost, or on the verge of destruction.

Alas, our youth are encouraged in current educational systems and social norms to focus on making money and achieving fame. This makes basic desires the end goal, and as they grow up, they become stuck in the jungle of life, directionless. How many people live only for the purpose of satisfying their basic desires? Isn't the disengagement of the majority of employees a sign of a directionless life? Aren't those people working to satisfy their basic desires in positions that don't bring them happiness, success, or fulfillment?

You don't have to live this way! All you need to do is *flip the Pyramid of Desires and you will have the Pyramid of Values instead.* Values are consciously chosen characteristics of desires that are guided by our Purposehood. First, satisfy your existential desire by pursuing your Purposehood, and your pathway to reclaim your semideum birthright will become clearer.

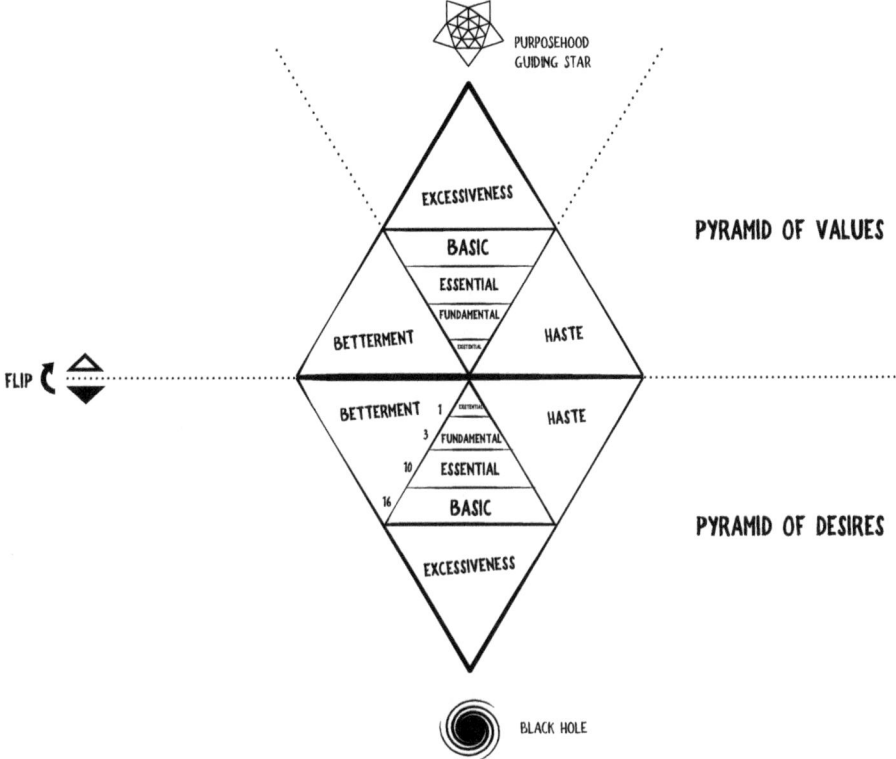

When you start by first seeking the purpose of your life, you open an expansive funnel into a life of gratitude, ease, and abundance. The three fundamental desires of happiness, success, and fulfillment become byproducts of a life of Purposehood.

Then, armed with a clear direction to your existential purpose and these fundamental nourishments, you can seek your essential desires by choosing a role in life that fulfills your Purposehood. With such a positive mindset in sync with existence, you can pursue basic desires.

When you develop positive values, you will live with ease knowing you control your desires, not the other way around. In this direction, you are looking at an expansive existence that has more than enough to satisfy all your infinite desires, as long as you are moving within the boundaries of your Purposehood.

When you're confident about your role in life, you only acquire the exact amount you need from your basic desires in order to play that role. But when your basic desires for status, power, or retribution drive you to play a role in life in order to satisfy their excessiveness, then your basic desires are in control.

Can't you see the difference in a political leader like Nelson Mandela, who became a transformational leader through his ideals and selfish-altruism, versus other selfish people who pursue leadership simply for the love of power? Isn't it easy to spot the business leader who is there to unleash the potentiality of their employees, and the one who is there only for personal achievement?

Knowing your Purposehood is the most important step you can take in your life, and the Pyramid of Values will help you develop empowering beliefs in order to reach all your goals.

You ask, "How do values shape desires?"

My friend, imagine four people: a consumer, a destroyer, a martyr, and a creator. The first is lost in the jungle of life, the second is moving toward a negative vacuum, the third is dedicating their life to ideals, and the fourth is embracing their existential role with selfish-altruism. When it comes to the basic desire of sex, for example, the consumer's value could be that sex is a natural urge that needs to be satisfied with a sexually desirable partner whenever it arises. For them, frequent casual sex is the desire they pursue. A destroyer's value is that sex is justifiable at any cost, even if it means abusing another person. These values will create sexual predators. A martyr's value could be that sex is a distraction from the pursuit of enlightenment or devotion to God. Such a person would abstain from sex and reproduction. A creator's value would be that sex is a way to express love and compassion for a special partner. Such a person will have proper control of their sexual drive and use it to create a stronger bond and emotional connection in addition to a physical one. The values a person develops will shape the desires that fuel their life. Creators will develop values for each of the 33 desires that will become empowering beliefs guiding a life of gratitude, ease, and abundance; a life fueled with positive desires.

Motivated by Values

The Pyramid of Values introduces a new theory in human motivation based on a lifetime journey motivated by the pursuit of your existential purpose. As you move in your life in the direction of your Purposehood, nature will provide you with the hormones of happiness, success, and fulfillment to further fuel your pursuit of your existential purpose. Those fundamental desires will provide direction toward the optimal roles you can play in life. These roles will fuel further happiness, success, and fulfillment. The essential desires will then provide directional controls to your basic desires, so you only get what you need to succeed in your role in life.

In this model, the existential purpose positively charges all desires *if you choose to lead your life starting from your Purposehood.* This is a crucial shift in understanding human motivation and potential.

Theories of motivation by basic desires neglect the powers of choice and purpose in motivating a person. The Hierarchy of Needs in Maslow's theory is also based on a limiting belief that you are doomed to an animal-like state and must satisfy first your basic desires before you are free to move up the hierarchy, while the Pyramid of Values is based on an empowering belief that your human awareness qualifies you to start in the other direction by first pursuing your Purposehood.

In everyday life, this model shifts basic desires from pure consumption in order to satisfy infinite wants to a fuel used only as needed in order to satisfy higher functions. This subtle shift pulls humanity forward with a vision of an abundant future instead of being anchored backward in its genetic genesis. It is the difference between a humanity driven by potentiality versus a humanity driven by instincts.

The product of the hierarchy of needs is a society filled with stress, anxiety, and regrets in the jungle of life, while the product of the Pyramid of Values is a society filled with happiness, success, and fulfillment in the Garden of Eden.

You ask, "Is there a hierarchy in the Pyramid of Values?"

There is no preset hierarchy, as all 33 desires are part of every human and there is no need to satisfy one before you move to the other. You have the choice to move in any direction and set your own priorities. However, there is an optimal order and direction placed by nature for its own Purposehood in order to help you generate values that lead to a life of gratitude, ease, and abundance. In the Pyramid of Values model, you can choose to empower your higher-order desires to dictate the intensity of your basic desires instead of responding to their urges.

Positive Values Fuel Your Journey

My friend, your power as a creator comes from knowing why you are creating regardless of what your final product is. Your "why" is embedded into your Purposehood and directed by your existential desire. This existential desire brings resilience, truthfulness, harmony with existence, selfish-altruistic giving, and corrective reflections to your progress toward your potentiality.

There is no limit to the power of a creator driven by positive values and positive desires. The process starts with awareness of your unconscious desires. When you expose these and intentionally reset them in the correct order of importance, and with the right intensity based on the Pyramid of Values, they will become part of your conscious mind. Then, when you shape those desires with your positive values, with time, those conscious values will move to your subconscious and become empowering beliefs that direct your life automatically toward your Purposehood. These empowering beliefs will guide you toward a life of Purposehood fueled by positive desires and filled with gratitude, ease, and abundance.

I BREATHE IN DESIRES.
I BREATHE OUT VALUES.

Proposition 7:
Directional Choice

"Everything moves in the direction of its existential purpose, except for humans who have a directional choice. You always have the choice to move toward your Purposehood or not. One choice takes a forward path to abundance. The others take a backward path to vacuum, a misdirected life, or a life with no direction." – PoET Proposition 7

A semideum with one directional choice is not a creator. Even the ancients realized this when they envisioned one-directional beings for their religions; angels couldn't choose bad and demons couldn't choose good. The directional choice of being good or bad, positive or negative, merciful or vengeful, a giver or taker, a creator or destroyer, was only reserved for the gods.

Don't we sometimes have to destroy some old buildings in order to create better ones? We might be able to achieve our goal by keeping the old structure, but we definitely need the choice to destroy the old one if needed. Without directional choice we have no use for our limitless creativity and infinite desires.

Choices are correlated to desires. Creatures with simple desires have simple choices, but for complex beings like humans, choice comes with complexity. With limitless creativity and infinite desires, we are faced with countless complicated choices to make every day.

These choices consume our lifetime and impact all our extensions of being and beyond.

Walking into any supermarket in a consumption-driven society, you are immediately faced with numerous products to choose from in each category, forcing you to spend precious time selecting things. As you check out, a simple choice like using a plastic bag instead of bringing a reusable bag with you might directly contribute to plastic pollution that kills 100,000 marine mammals every year,[77] ending up in the bellies of 90 percent of seabirds and in 90 percent of table salt used by you, your family, coworkers, friends, and other people around the world.[78]

The choices we have in front of us are evolving and expanding exponentially as humanity is opening new categories of options that were not even imaginable a few decades ago. These include expanded choice in education, professions, medical treatments, or even gender selection. Soon, parents will have to choose what traits among numerous characteristics they'll want for their future children. Is having so many choices positive or negative? And does our freedom of choice necessitate having more choices in every category?

Psychology professor Barry Schwartz studied what he called the *paradox of choice* in societies with ever-increasing choices.[79] He found that the overwhelming number of choices people are faced with are causing, in many cases, paralysis in decision-making and dissatisfaction with whatever they choose.

Looking on Amazon for swimming goggles gave me over 5,000 choices. Which one is the best for me? Have I chosen the right criteria to judge the best product? How would I know that I made the right choice, considering I won't have time to look at all the options? How long should I spend researching? Should I put it off till later when I have more time?

Schwartz concluded that the availability of numerous choices is making people miserable, as there is always a possibility of a better choice they might have missed, and they only have themselves to blame.

Our desire for better and faster products and services can't be met by businesses without us consuming more to fund the improvements. Businesses are driven by customer demand, and as long as we are caught in the cycle of consumption, the damage we're causing to all our extensions of being and to the environment will continue. We need to find a balance between not enough choices with too little freedom, and numerous choices with too many decision-making challenges and not enough satisfaction.

Humanity is inevitably moving toward a future with exponentially increasing choices, and these have the ability to consume our precious lifetime, causing paralysis and dissatisfaction. Without a framework for our pursuit of infinite desires, we will be stressed and anxious over the myriad of choices in front of us, and we will regret choosing wrong or missing alternatives. We need a framework to easily make positive choices that lead to happiness, success, and fulfillment.

You ask, "Do we have to always choose?"

A Theory of Choice

My friend, you choose even when you don't choose. Isn't deciding *not to choose* a choice in itself? But not all choices are equally important. Climbing the Pyramid of Values, the number of choices increases while the importance of choices decreases.

As for the number of choices, when it comes to the existential desire, you basically have one choice to make, *to pursue your Purposehood or not.* When you move up the pyramid to fundamental desires, you have three key choices of happiness or unhappiness, success or failure, and fulfillment or unfulfillment. The choices become a bit more complicated and diverse with essential desires, and exponentially more with basic desires.

Most of our lifetime is consumed with everyday decisions related to basic desires. Take eating, for example, which starts with "Should I eat or not?" Once you decide to eat, then the number of choices and decisions you have to make escalate from "What should I eat?" to "I am feeling full, should I continue eating or not?" and ending, sometimes, with regrets of what, how, and how much you ate. Having guiding values will limit choices and make navigating them easier, like the value of eating only locally farmed organic foods and mostly plants.

However, these basic decisions are not as important as essential ones like being with the person you love, choosing a career, or profiting from your investment. Still, these are less important than whether they will make you feel happy, successful, and fulfilled or not. But would happiness, success, and fulfillment even be possible to receive if you are lost in life?

When faced with choices, there are three types of decisions we make: instinctive, responsive, and directional.

- **Instinctive decisions** are unconsciously sparked by internal desires and fueled by fear of potential pain or loss of pleasure. For example, casual sex with a stranger is often driven by instinctive desire.

- **Responsive decisions** are conscious or unconscious decisions made mainly in response to outside stimuli fueled by expectations of an outcome. Shouting to catch the attention of a passerby could be a conscious or unconscious decision in expectation of a pleasant encounter.

- **Directional decisions** are conscious decisions we make, sparked by situational awareness and fueled by beliefs. When you become aware that you are lost, you might decide to stop and enter into your global positioning system (GPS) an address you believe will take you to your destination.

Your ultimate goal should be making all your decisions, if possible, responsive and directional. You do that by having a clear direction to your Purposehood, choosing empowering beliefs based on positive values, and making habits of your reactions to your positive desires.

Desires could be positive or negative. Negative desires are the ones that take you away from your Purposehood and positive desires are the ones that take you toward your Purposehood. Eating to obesity is a negative desire, while eating to health is a positive one. Forced sex is a negative desire, while consensual, loving sex is a positive one. With awareness, intention, and habitual practice we can redirect a desire from negative to positive. It is our choice to make a desire positive or negative.

The Theory of Choice states:

• Our choices increase as they climb the Pyramid of Values while their importance decreases.

• The most important choice we must make is our direction in life.

• Once a directional choice is made, then all other choices will become easier to make and will impact our journey in the direction we chose.

You ask, "What are the criteria to eliminate negative choices from our options?"

The One-Choice Process

My friend, when you compact every one of your concerns into a single one, focused on the direction of your life, the others will be automatically taken care of. There is only one choice you need to make right now: Will you be a creator as you were meant to be, continue to be lost as a consumer, become a misdirected martyr, or become a negative destroyer? The fine line between becoming a creator or any of the others is direction.

LIMITLESS CREATIVITY + INFINITE DESIRES + POSITIVE DIRECTION = CREATOR

LIMITLESS CREATIVITY + INFINITE DESIRES + NO DIRECTION = CONSUMER

LIMITLESS CREATIVITY + INFINITE DESIRES + MISDIRECTION = MARTYR

LIMITLESS CREATIVITY + INFINITE DESIRES + NEGATIVE DIRECTION = DESTROYER

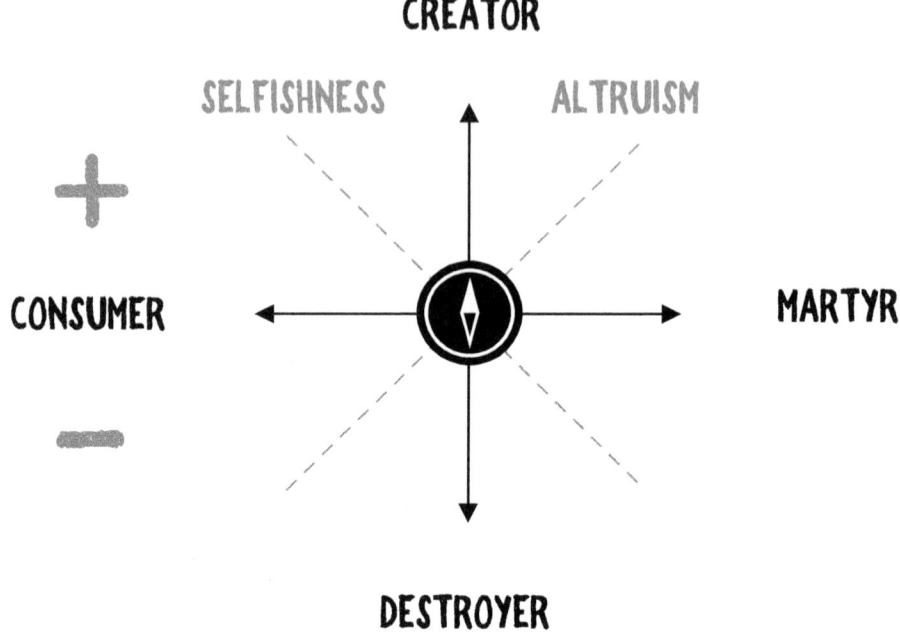

CREATOR

SELFISHNESS   ALTRUISM

CONSUMER   MARTYR

DESTROYER

A consumer oscillates between the selfish states of creation and destruction, while a martyr oscillates between the altruistic states of creation and destruction. A destroyer oscillates between the negative states of consumption and martyrdom, while a creator oscillates between the positive states of consumption and martyrdom.

Once you make that one choice, you don't need many criteria to make the right decision every time you're faced with one.

With one question you can make positive choices and decisions all the time. Just ask, "Does this choice take me toward my Purposehood or away from my Purposehood?"

The most important choice you have to make in life is to choose the direction that leads you out of this jungle to Eden, where you were born and meant to grow. Once you find the path, then all choices will have a reference point in your Purposehood Guiding Star.

When you choose to be a creator instead of giving up on your selfish needs as a martyr, remaining lost as a consumer, or worse, becoming a destroyer, then you will live a life of Purposehood with gratitude, ease, and abundance.

A life of Purposehood is a choice of creating a better future for all your extensions of being, humanity, and nature.

A life of gratitude is when happiness, success, and fulfillment come with every step forward regardless of the challenges, like Himalayan mountain climbers heading to the summit with gratitude every step of the path regardless of the cold and pain.

A life of ease is when you play your role in building a bright future for all your extensions by innovating, exploiting, exploring, beautifying, and profiting, while attracting a community you *want* to belong to; a community constructed with love and respect.

A life of abundance is when you know that there will always be enough to satisfy your positive basic desires and fuel your role in life. You will eat to have energy, move to build strength, use your power to bring justice, use your retaliation to stop aggressors, and share your possessions with those who have less. In doing so, every basic desire will become a positive desire in the direction of your Purposehood. With a positive directional choice and your seed of potentiality, your limitless creativity will always find a way to satisfy your positive desires.

Regardless of your condition today and the circumstances that led you here, you have the choice at this moment to change direction toward your Purposehood.

You ask, "Aren't people victims of their circumstances, suffering the pain of a diminished genius?

My friend, this is a legitimate question for anyone who observes the suffering of people individually and collectively. It's not hard to see how our youth are suffering from diminished potentiality as the rates of psychological illnesses steadily increase to alarming levels. But youth are not the only ones suffering. Worldwide, people of all ages are struggling with the same illnesses. These are manifesting not only in mental health issues, but also in all kinds of addictions such as alcoholism, drug abuse—prescribed or not—blind religiosity, ideological extremism, violence, discrimination against others, broken families and social structures, mindless consumerism, carelessness, and all the negative faces of infinite basic desires like acquisitiveness, rivalry, greed, vanity, lust, envy, and love of power.

I once had a discussion with a creative genius friend of mine about her life growing up with alcoholic parents. In tears, she described the neglect she and her siblings endured as they were left behind, but with their wonderful grandmother to fend for them. I encouraged her to take the opportunity to ask her ailing parents all the questions buried in her mind, and to explore their memories for mere curiosity and expanded awareness.

She insisted she wouldn't feel comfortable bringing back painful memories that would disturb her hard-acquired peace of mind. But the more she spoke about them, the more we both could clearly see a very capable couple with tremendous dedication to each other. Yet their life in the Soviet Union deprived them of being what they could have become, and they were driven to alcoholism.

In that time and place, alcoholism wasn't a political tool to pacify a restless population, rather, it was a personal reaction to the desperation of a potentiality constrained, not unlike current addictions to drugs or social media. Any social system—be it political, religious, educational, or familial—that places people in a collective direction, not permitting individual freedom of directional choice toward a future the individual wants to create, is a system that constrains one's seed of potentiality. Fueled with toxic nourishment such as alcohol, or selfish desires like consumerism, the seed will grow to spread toxicity to all its surroundings. My friend's parents were just that, the products of constrained potential, toxic nourishment, and a lack of direction that couldn't have produced anything else.

Still, that was not an excuse for them or anyone who sees themselves as victims of circumstance. Even though we might not have a choice in what happens around us, we always have a choice in how we interpret those events and circumstances, and how we respond to them. And when it comes to the direction of our lives, we always can choose the direction of our Purposehoods. Always.

You, my friend, have the choice to select what information you expose to your sensory peripherals and what to allow into your mind, such as choosing what songs to listen to. You then need to choose how to process this input with your belief processor, and what to build on the top of the outcome. If you are aware enough to recognize that your life today is not a life of Purposehood, potentiality, happiness, success, and fulfillment, and you want to change who you are, you can simply decide to redirect your lost soul in the direction of your Purposehood. Then you can adopt simple practices that will supply your seed with the right nourishment so that your journey ahead will produce a life with ease, regardless of the challenges you will face.

You ask, "Is suffering a choice?"

While pain in most cases is not a choice, suffering is. My friend, pain is a reaction to a cause. It's not a desirable choice for any creature, but it's a wonderful tool to alert you to what's going wrong. That toothache is not only a reminder to fix it before it's too late, but also an invitation to explore the causes of this pain. It's a blessing in disguise as you become aware of the harmful soft drinks and processed sugar you've been including in your nourishment. This awareness creates choices for you to either treat and/or remove the aching tooth or mask the pain with pills and continue negative habits. It also could push you to remove the cause of pain and continue on to correct your lifestyle with nourishment habits that fuel a life of ease toward your Purposehood. Pain, be it physical, psychological, or social, is always an invitation to expanded awareness and course correction. That pain you're facing with your spouse is an invitation for both of you to explore the causes and correct them together. That will lead to a better outcome for everyone involved.

However, suffering is a choice. When you choose not to correct the causes of your pain, then you have chosen suffering. Removing the aching tooth, or masking the pain with pills without changing your eating and drinking habits will not prevent the pain from resurfacing again. Likewise, removing toxic people from your life without exploring the reasons you befriended them in the first place will for sure condemn you to repeating the mistake.

My psychiatrist friend had a patient who had been through several divorces and complained to him, "Life is full of selfish people. I am always suffering because none of the partners I end up with are any good." He said to her, "Have you ever noticed that the common denominator among all of your partners is YOU?!"

Contrary to some beliefs, suffering is not the state of being. Struggling is. Struggling is the process that grows creators. Without challenges, would we even have the desire to create? And without struggling, would we have the desire to reflect, refine, and collaborate?

You ask, "If becoming a destroyer is negative and a creator is positive, is choosing to stay lost in life a neutral decision?"

My friend, inaction is a negative drag on humanity's forward movement. The seed of potentiality will not grow while you are constantly running after desires and away from fears. Humanity and life need every human to grow their potential and become a creator of the future. One less human doesn't equate to a lesser humanity, but to a *totally different* humanity. Every human creates a possible future and without that one person, the future will not be the same.

You have the power at any moment of your life to choose your direction. You can choose to stay consumed with pursuing your basic desires in the hope of one day focusing more on your essential, then your fundamental, and finally your existential desire. Or, you can flip the pyramid and start by pursuing your Purposehood for a life of gratitude, ease, and abundance.

You can choose mindful living or mindless living, an intentional life, or a fear- and desire-driven life.

You can choose to be future-oriented, past-oriented, or just live in the present like a plucked apple.

You can choose to be limited by labels and inherited beliefs, or be free of labels and limiting beliefs.

You can choose to live either selfishly or altruistically, or live as a selfish-altruist.

You can choose to limit your being to a few extensions, or expand your five extensions to all humanity and nature.

You can choose a positive direction toward your Purposehood, or a negative direction away from your Purposehood.

The directional choice, my friend, is always yours.

———

I BREATHE IN CHOICES.
I BREATHE OUT EASE.

Grow with Ease

The universe wants you for its own existential purpose to become the creator you were meant to be. Your existential reward for living your Purposehood is a life of gratitude, ease, and abundance. Your deterrent for taking the wrong path is a life of scarcity, suffering, and rejection. The pain and pleasure you feel are universal gifts to help you select the right choice.

Embodied in this next set of Purposehood of Everything Theory (PoET) propositions are empowering beliefs for growth.

Proposition 8:
Life of Purposehood

"A life of Purposehood is an intentional life, away from distractions that either lead you astray or to a negative path." – PoET Proposition 8

A day that you don't move closer to your Purposehood is a day wasted of your precious lifetime. But when you clearly see the destination and you intend to get there, moving forward is a natural way of life. It's like having an appointment that you can't afford to miss; you will make sure whatever stops you might have on the way, such as to pick up a coffee or meet a friend, will not cause you to miss your appointment. In this case, your appointment is with destiny, and a Purposehooder will not allow any distraction in life to cause them to miss it.

Distractions are inevitable because change is inevitable. Distractions are also internal, as in thoughts and emotions, or external, as in events and exposure to sensory inputs such as sights and sounds. And like everything else, distractions can be positive or negative depending on how you choose to process them. Distractions spark creativity and widen awareness, but they also can waste your precious lifetime and lead you astray. With exponentially growing possibilities, distractions are also growing exponentially, and without filters, we are distracted from living.

When you pursue your chosen existential purpose, this automatically creates a primary filter that keeps all negative distractions outside your intentional life. Whenever a distraction presents itself, your primary filter checks if this distraction will help you move forward, backward, or away from your Purposehood. A well-maintained primary filter will only let positive distractions into your living space to be considered.

For example, if your chosen Purposehood drives you to create music that inspires people to live a life of purpose, then spotting negative distractions becomes easier. You would clearly recognize those that dampen your ability to create inspiring music, such as time spent with negative people. You also will more easily spot dangerous distractions that could drag you toward a different direction in life. (These could be temptations to write lucrative music that promote violence and degrade others.) However, distractions such as an invitation to dinner with friends, or to watch an inspiring movie, might be activities that your primary filter would allow.

When you have an intentional life, focused on the pursuit of your Purposehood, every experience will become a positive one. Time you spend with your parents might be a distraction from pursuing a desire, but it could also be a source of fulfillment of domestication, love, and loyalty. A vacation is a distraction that provides the rest you need to continue your Purposehood journey. A clarity of your existential purpose, and an intention to pursue it, will bring focus to your life. You will learn to embrace positive distractions that widen your awareness and inspire you to continue living a life of Purposehood with gratitude, ease, and abundance.

You ask, "What would happen if a person doesn't have a Purposehood or lacks the intention of living it?"

My friend, the opposite of a life of Purposehood is a life of loss, where a person is led astray by mindless infinite basic desires, a life of a total devotion to selfless causes at the cost of the self, or a life of vacuum, directed toward destruction. If someone has the potentiality of being a creator of inspiring music but has no direction in life, then any distraction will move them away from being what they could have become. How many talented artists end up with misdirected lives of addictions, acquisitiveness, and vanity? How often do you meet people with wasted potential who are not doing what they are capable of? How many end up lost to addiction or distractions? And how many people choose an education, a profession, social networks, and a life based on material worth instead of existential worth?

These diminished individuals are living a life of scarcity with a constant fear of losing what they have, or fear of not being able to have what they want. This life turns into suffering as they spread negativity throughout their extensions of being.

Worse yet are those who end up using their existential gift and uniqueness for a negative purpose in the pursuit of satisfying their infinite desires. Such people will inevitably implode into the vacuum of existence, becoming black holes sucking their extensions into more destruction. Isn't a talented musician who writes songs filled with violence, despair, or materialism a black hole that fills listeners with negativity that destroys their potentiality? Aren't political leaders who spread division among people, black holes drawing countless lost souls, with their negative gravitational pull, toward a life of scarcity, suffering, rejection, and vacuum?

You ask, "What's the difference between a goal and a purpose?"

Purpose is intended by the creator. When an artist creates a painting, an artisan makes a pottery cup, a composer creates music, an author creates a book, an inventor creates a new tool, or a biochemist creates a vaccine, they have a purpose in mind for their creation.

Humanity was created within nature to play a key role in this existence, the role of a creator of the future. An expo-agent that is meant to rapidly evolve life and expand it in the landscape of the universe. You were meant to be a co-creator of that future. That's the Purposehood of every human.

Goals are specific aims you set for yourself and choose to invest your lifetime pursuing. If goals are set without having a direction, you might remain lost in the jungle of life, or they might lead you, unintentionally, to a vacuum. Goals don't give you direction, purpose does. A life without direction is a wasted life. You will live a life of Purposehood when your pursued goals are on the path toward your Purposehood Guiding Star.

My friend, having an existential purpose and living it is the most important step you can take toward an intentional life of gratitude, ease, and abundance. It will become ever more important as humanity moves toward a future where all material desires will be readily available to every human. Living our Purposehood is the existential desire that will continue throughout human existence, and without it, true happiness, success, and fulfillment will always be elusive.

I BREATHE IN PURPOSEHOOD.
I BREATHE OUT GRATITUDE.

Proposition 9: Life of Gratitude

"A life of gratitude is when you know that every being is a source of happiness, every challenge is a fuel for success, and every moment is an opportunity for fulfillment. And when you do, you will be grateful to iSH for sparking existence, to the universe for creating life, to nature for constructing humanity, to humanity for making you, and to yourself for being a creator of a better future for all." – PoET Proposition 9

Our fundamental desires for happiness, success, and fulfillment come from our existential desire to evolve and expand exponentially. When we evolve to a better version of ourselves, we feel happy, when we grow and expand into our extensions of being through selfish-altruism we feel successful, and when we invest our lifetime to create an exponential legacy with our positive impact, we feel fulfilled. These fundamental desires are life's rewards for pursuing our existential purpose; they are byproducts of living our Purposehood.

You ask, "What's the opposite of a life of gratitude?"

My friend, when a person is lost while pursuing their infinite basic desires or is moving intentionally in the direction of vacuum and destruction, they will experience a life of rejection, a rejection of nature's incentives of happiness, success, and fulfillment. The rejection of a human's Purposehood to become a creator will inevitably lead to a life of stress, anxiety, and regrets.

You ask, "How would a person express their gratitude to iSH, existence, the universe, nature, humanity, and themselves?"

You show your gratitude to a creator by being grateful for their creation. Can you truly be grateful to an artist if their masterpiece is left neglected in your attic? Gratitude is not thoughts you have nor words you say, but a life of actions that makes existence better for all. Gratitude is expressed with steps you take every day to become a better version of your current self; with actions you take to unleash the potentiality of your family, coworkers, and communities; with a helping hand extended to a nature suffering from the damage humanity caused in its careless infancy; and with an impact that inspires the exponential evolution and expansion ahead.

Your grateful thoughts and words need to be intentions of actions you plan to take in the future. For example, when you look outside your window and you feel grateful for such a beautiful day filled with sunshine and tweeting birds, you need to reflect on your own actions and of those in your extensions. Think about whether they have contributed to keeping Earth as beautiful as it was before humanity came onto the scene and if your actions are making life beautiful for those birds. If yes, then also be grateful to yourself and all who contributed to beautiful nature, and if not, then make intentions to contribute and inspire others to do so.

Gratitude is a way of life where every action contributes to your Purposehood, as well as that of humanity and nature. A life of Purposehood will automatically be a life of gratitude.

You ask, "How do I know if I'm living a grateful life?"

My friend, the existential reward for living your Purposehood is a grateful life filled with happiness, success, and fulfillment. The punishment is a life of rejection. When a person rejects their Purposehood, they live an ungrateful life. Their existential punishment is a life of stress, anxiety, and regrets. Which reward or punishment are you feeling now? And do you know the true meaning of happiness, success, and fulfillment?

———

I BREATHE IN GRATITUDE.
I BREATHE OUT EASE.

Proposition 10: Happiness

"Happiness is not pleasure, but a natural state of living. It is received, not pursued. It is a choice you can easily tune in to by living your Purpose-hood with ease." – PoET Proposition 10

You ask, "Why is happiness so elusive in an improving world?"

My friend, we live in a world that is much better than any time in history, one that keeps improving through more people accessing better health, education, opportunities, and basic needs. Yet, so many people are unhappy and psychological well-being is deteriorating. There are three misconceptions about happiness that prevent people from finding true happiness. The misconceptions are that happiness is pleasure, that happiness must be pursued, and that lasting happiness is not possible.

When you believe that happiness is pleasure, it's impossible to maintain happiness, as pleasures themselves don't last and the feelings of hormonal happiness that come with pleasure don't last either. Pleasure comes from satisfying desires, and since our human desires are infinite, it's impossible to satisfy any of them indefinitely. That's why it's impossible to be in a permanent state of happiness with impermanent states of pleasures.

As for the pursuit of happiness, psychologists are finding that this pursuit is actually causing more stress and unhappiness.[80] The belief that happiness needs to be pursued leads to the belief that happiness is hard to get, which opens the opportunity to the peddlers of happiness to sell us all kinds of products, services, and dogmas to achieve this allusive pursuit. We pursue what is not readily available.

You don't need to pursue breathing when you are always surrounded by air. When you realize that happiness is as readily available in nature as the air you breathe, you will not need to pursue it any longer—you only need to be open to receive it as you would air or sunshine. Then happiness can become a lasting state of being for as long as you keep breathing.

The Nature of Happiness

The nature of happiness is found in the happiness of nature. All creatures of nature sing happiness, day or night. Can't you hear it in the moving trees and howling winds, in the ocean waves and seagull sounds, in the buzzing bees and chirping crickets? Their happiness comes from feeling connected with nature and every other being. My friend, when you feel that connected, your brain will tune in to the signal of happiness like a receiver tunes in to the music broadcasted through a satellite.

When you know that your Purposehood is for all beings, then every step you take forward strengthens your connection with them. Your happiness will not only last, but will also evolve until you yourself become a source of happiness to all your extensions.

THE TRUE MEANING OF HAPPINESS

True happiness comes from moving closer every day to your Purposehood. This forward movement is a constant evolution toward a better version of yourself.

> You ask, "How could a person be at ease with all the challenges we face in life?"

My friend, ease comes from connectedness. Don't you feel vulnerable when you are alone in a strange land surrounded by people you don't know? How would you feel if you are on a hike in the mountains with caring friends who are experts in mountain climbing? When I did my first skydiving jump, I made sure that I was well-connected to an experienced skydiver invested in making sure that I got down all right.

Happiness and the sense of ease come from three elements: awareness, directed desires, and detachment.

1. **Awareness:** Understanding who you are, where you came from, what constitutes you, why you exist, how you fit in this world, and where you are heading is a great start to a lifetime journey of happiness. Self-reflection will allow you to further expand your awareness to your other extensions of being, just like widening a satellite receiver for a better reception with a stronger signal.

2. **Directed desires:** This is the fuel of your journey toward Purposehood. With the wrong fuel, your happiness receiver will not work; with the right fuel, you will keep moving closer to the source of happiness, your Purposehood Guiding Star. The right fuel for happiness is the positive desires that pass through your primary filter of Purposehood. Acquiring desires for the right reasons, in the right amounts, and in the right ways keep your happiness receiver powered for a lifetime of happiness.

3. **Detachment:** This is all about perfecting the process instead of the outcome. It is the will to disconnect from all the forces that have thus far held you back from growing your potentiality. When you detach from labels, you detach from limiting beliefs that anchor you in the past. When you detach from possessions, you detach from present weights that pull you down in the sea of life. And, when you also detach from expectations, you detach from future limitations of possibilities and you become free to experience life as it comes, focusing on your progress in the direction of your existential purpose.

Your state of happiness is a result of a continued journey with ease as you recognize that you are connected with everything in existence. It is the result of knowing that the universe, nature, and humanity are invested in helping you become a better version of yourself, as well as in the success of your mission. It is a result of resting assured that whatever the outcome will be, it will be the culmination of the collective will of everyone involved.

My friend, with such awareness, fueled by directed desires, and detached from expectations, there will be no limitation to the amount of happiness you can receive in your lifetime.

———

I BREATHE IN AWARENESS.
I BREATHE OUT HAPPINESS.

Proposition 11: Success

"Success is not achieving goals nor winning selfish or altruistic pursuits, but a natural state of living. Success is the process of sustaining growth with ease through selfish-altruism." – PoET Proposition 11

You ask, "What is success?"

My friend, success is another natural state of living experienced by all beings as they move toward their Purposehood. The everyday life of a fish is filled with happiness, success, and fulfillment, evident in its survival, reproduction, and playing its role in the ecosystem. This is how creatures with no directional choice live their Purposehood, evolving and expanding exponentially. Human newborns also experience success in their everyday life as they grow into directional awareness. In the pursuit of acquiring new skills and information, young children experience failure as the other face of success. Isn't failure a success in narrowing the path to a desired outcome? Isn't it an expansion of information acquired about what works and what doesn't?

As we grow older, we become contaminated by misconceptions about success when we define it as achieving goals, winning competitions, or a life of either selfish or altruistic pursuits. It's true that goals are essential for us to measure progress and set expectations, but in a world of causality where causes beyond our control impact outcomes and where immediate outcomes are merely causes in chains of universal outcomes over the long run, identifying success as achieving a defined goal is an invitation to a sense of failure sooner or later.

Aren't we reminded of this simple truth every time we hear a story about a famous achiever who was doomed by their ill-defined success? Can you think of times in your own life when goals you achieved led to undesirable consequences?

When we define success as winning, we turn life into a constant competition with others where most people are losers. How tiring is the life of a constant marathon where one person is the winner of the gold medal and everyone else is a loser?

When success is defined as a single-focused pursuit of a selfish desire, like seeking power, or an altruistic desire, like promoting a dogma, then our awareness shrinks to that pursuit, and with it, all our extensions of being. How many people cause pain to their family, friends, coworkers, and nature in the pursuit of money and power? Aren't most dangerous extremists focused on altruistic pursuits?

The Nature of Success

Success is a fundamental desire that must be easy to acquire and feel in everyday life. When you live with the limiting belief that success is at the end of a journey, or as a result of it, you postpone your feeling of that achievement until the end of the process. But when you understand that *success is actually the process itself and not the end goal*, then every step you take forward in your journey becomes a source of it.

If you start high school defining success as graduating from college, you will spend many years of your life waiting for that. And if life presents you with other opportunities or forces you onto a path that doesn't end with a college degree, then you are left feeling like a failure. But when you believe that success is daily growth in the school of life, then every day is an opportunity to be successful.

You ask, "What is growth?"

Growth is an expansion of your uniqueness in the direction of your Purposehood. You realize this expansion by simply engaging your Five Extensions of Being with selfish-altruism. You grow when you enlist others in helping you continue your journey; when you inspire your family, coworkers, communities, and nature to grow; and when you collaborate for a common purpose and walk the path together.

THE TRUE MEANING OF SUCCESS

The true meaning of success is sustained growth by oscillating between selfishness and altruism.

Just like the growth of your muscles is in the oscillation between exertion and resting, or the birth of innovation is in the oscillation between learning and boredom, or the flourishing of love is in the oscillation between being close and being apart, the growth toward your Purposehood is in intentionally oscillating between your selfish and altruistic desires.

You ask, "Isn't selfishness always negative?"

My friend, a label is what you want it to be. I don't see selfishness as positive or negative until you attach it to a positive or negative behavior. Selfishness is positive when it leads to your well-being, self-growth, and building a positive legacy. It is negative when it leads to the demise of others, a contraction of your other extensions of being, and negative legacies that last beyond your lifetime. Isn't a selfish pursuit of a Nobel Prize by a scientist positive if it doesn't come at the cost of depriving other contributors of their recognition?

You ask, "Isn't altruism always positive?"

I've seen caretakers who give to the point where they end up destroying their own lives and having no more energy to give. In the end, everyone loses, including the ones they cared for. How many mothers are like that?

Only when you realize that you grow by helping others, and they also grow when you help yourself, will you be able to grow with ease every day of your life. A true successful leader realizes that when they have more selfish time to learn, rest, and reflect, they are better able to contribute value to their family, their work and coworkers, their friends and communities, and to nature and all its beings. They also realize that without those altruistic contributions, their awareness will never grow and they will be consumed with selfishness.

You ask, "How does this apply to business?"

A business' success is a sustained growth by oscillating between growing profit and unleashing the potentiality of all its stakeholders.

My friend, the constant oscillation between intentional selfishness and altruism is the best way to sustain growth with ease toward a life of success regardless of the challenges.

———

I BREATHE IN SUCCESS.
I BREATHE OUT GROWTH.

Proposition 12: Fulfillment

"Fulfillment is a natural state of living. It is not instant gratification, a life without regrets, nor accumulation of wealth. Fulfillment is having a positive return on lifetime." – PoET Proposition 12

Fulfillment is the deepest of our three fundamental desires. It goes beyond happiness and success deep into our desire to transcend. It's how we feel when we are happy and successful but lack a sense of completeness. It's that unexplainable feeling when happiness stays longer than we expected or success expands wider than we anticipated, and so engulfs those around us, too. It's the feeling we have when we see the positive results of our actions spread beyond just one of our extensions of being.

When we define fulfillment as instant satisfaction, absence of regrets, or accumulation of wealth, then we misdirect our life toward nonfulfillment. Accumulation of material wealth is no way to measure fulfillment. The only valuable currency in our lives is time and the only true wealth we have is a lifetime, not what we own. Do we actually even own *anything*, or are we just leasing what we have for the duration of our lives? Isn't ownership a link between two dependents? Do you own your house or does your house own you? Who is on a leash, your dog or you? Isn't material wealth consuming your most precious possession, the only possession that is irreplaceable: your lifetime? Doesn't anything that consumes time without a positive return convert a true asset into a liability?

The Nature of Fulfillment

My friend, the universe's movement toward its Purposehood seems orderly in a mechanical view, uniform in a quantum view, and intentional in a universal view. The intentionality of the persistent movement of the universe toward its existential purpose also seems to drive all of its elements to fulfill the roles they are meant to play. Every action contributes to the universe's orderly chaos, uniformity, and intentionality at the same time. Fulfillment is a natural state of living experienced by every being as they play their role in the theatre of existence.

A plant, for example, is not there only to survive and grow by spreading its seeds. It also plays a role in providing other creatures with oxygen and nourishment. All lifeforms maximize the return on their days and lifetime, and when the end comes, they are fulfilled knowing that by simply being they have done the best and most they could, and the impact they left on existence will continue beyond their brief time on Earth. But a human, as a creature of directional choice, could choose to play a villainous role in the play of life, and with that could easily live an unfulfilled life.

When we live daily like other lifeforms, with a maximum possible return on our time, then we can experience the fulfillment they experience. When the end comes, we will pass to another existence knowing that our positive impact will reverberate exponentially through all the lifeforms we touched in our lifetime. My friend, the nature of fulfillment is a positive return on lifetime.

THE TRUE MEANING OF FULFILLMENT

When you live your Purposehood, grow to your potentiality, and maximize the return on your lifetime, fulfillment will be another natural state of your living.

There are three elements to fulfillment that make it easy for you to have a positive return on your lifetime: impact, intention, and legacy.

Impact leads to evolution, intention leads to expansion, and legacy leads to exponentiality, the three elements of any Purposehood.

You ask, "How do we evolve with impact?"

My friend, it's true that our impact is felt by others, but it always starts from within. What we think, say, or do will impact others regardless if we intend to or not. When you are aware of that, you will naturally ensure that your impact stays positive by having positive thoughts, words, and actions. That inner mindfulness will lead to your evolution into a better state of being.

You ask, "I understand the impact of words and actions, but how do thoughts impact others?"

Thoughts are produced by electrical activities of neurons as they move from one area in the brain to another. These interactions can be measured by electroencephalography (EEG) or functional magnetic resonance imaging (fMRI). Is it really unimaginable that those electrical activities also influence an existence that is woven together in the fabric of the universe?

You ask, "How do I expand with intention?"

All positive deeds start with positive intentions. Intention is the laser pointer for focus and the multiplier of returns on time. When you state your intention, you ensure that your focus will follow. Intentions are like the agenda of a meeting—without a clear agenda, most meetings are a waste of time. But intentions also are multipliers; you can easily attach many intentions to the same action and reap multiple benefits.

Going to the movies could be only for entertainment, but you could also add intentions of well-being, learning, reflecting, inspiring, and connecting. With these simple added intentions, you'd park at the far end of the parking lot so you can walk, take the stairs instead of the escalator, and avoid junk food. You'd look for moments in the movie to reflect on your life or to learn and research something new. You'd go with friends and family and share any inspirations you might have found. You would greet strangers you pass with warm smiles. And just like that, by simply adding intentions to everything you do, you multiply the return on your time. Prayers are another form of intentions and you can always include others and nature in them.

You ask, "How do I add exponentiality with legacy?"

My friend, while your positive and negative impact is an unintentional consequence of your inner quality, legacy is what you do intentionally. The legacies of lifeforms are interwoven in the inevitable impact they have on their extensions of being. A butterfly that flaps its wings in Indonesia might unintentionally cause a hurricane in Florida, or it might not. You, on the other hand, have the ability to "flap your wings" with a thought, word, or action with the intention to cause something positive or negative in this world, regardless if it ends up actually happening. Your intentional flap adds a tiny probability to the possibility you desired and that is the legacy you create either positively or negatively.

You can create your legacy by intentionally passing your uniqueness to others to carry on beyond your lifetime. You can do that directly by mentoring and being a positive example to those in your extensions of being, by leaving behind learnings that others can build on, and by volunteering, working, and contributing to institutions and causes that make the world a better place.

Legacy is not about being remembered, as you are never truly forgotten in an existence of causality, but about knowing that you intentionally made a difference and extended your existence beyond your brief appearance in this life. Fulfillment is the force that extends your life's outcome beyond your lifetime.

Your positive impact, intentions, and legacy are the drivers of a positive return on your lifetime and your true sources of fulfillment.

———

I BREATHE IN FULFILLMENT.
I BREATHE OUT IMPACT.

I BREATHE IN FULFILLMENT.
I BREATHE OUT INTENTIONS.

I BREATHE IN FULFILLMENT.
I BREATHE OUT LEGACY.

Proposition 13:
Life of Ease

"Life of ease is a life lived together in gratitude with shared Purposehood. When you prioritize your essential desires over basic desires, you become a conduit of happiness, success, and fulfillment to all your extensions of being." – PoET Proposition 13

As modern humans emerged from the animal kingdom to fulfill nature's existential desire to evolve and expand exponentially, their basic desires and creativity were unleashed. What nature needed, though, was a humanity capable of creating a future for life across the landscape of the universe.

It was essential for humans to evolve new communal desires that were selfish-altruistic in nature in order to build a very capable humanity. The 10 essential desires evolved to become the selfish-altruistic thread that weaves a human into humanity. They are there to build a better humanity in which each person can realize their individual self. They allow each person to become a creator, not a destroyer, and as a result, experience a life of ease.

You ask, "How do essential desires drive our interactions?"

My friend, let's briefly explore these 10 essential desires:

1. Attraction: The desire to attract and be attracted. Isn't this the most basic essential desire that brings together the forces of existence to form a higher system? You want to attract a spouse to have a family, attract coworkers to get work done, and attract interesting people to form friendships. You even want to attract birds and butterflies to your beautiful and lively backyard. But to attract you need to be attractive in your attributes and ideas. You also want to be attracted to others. How miserable life will be if you're not attracted to anything? Isn't it amazing how even an extreme oddity still finds someone to attract?

2. **Love:** The desire to love and be loved. Love is a mysterious dimension beyond attraction. It's the force that pushes us past logic, and sometimes even drives us willingly to make fools of ourselves. But it is also the force that makes us sacrifice willingly for those we love, and expand our altruism to new frontiers that can only be explored with love. *The measurement of love is the willingness to sacrifice.* When you only love yourself, you sacrifice all for your selfish pursuits, but when you truly love someone else, then you are even willing to sacrifice yourself for them. Isn't that what most mothers do for their babies? As we become a more evolved humanity, our love will eventually expand from our immediate extensions to the love of every being, and finally to the most abstract love of all, the love of iSH, the mystery beyond. That love will drive us to keep evolving and expanding exponentially and to become the creators we are meant to be.

3. **Want:** The desire to have desires. Desires are the fuel of life. Some Buddhists say, "Liberate yourself from desires and you will find that you have all you need." The challenge is that those with altruistic desires to help others don't have the ego and selfishness to lead the world. And those with the selfish desire to have all the power don't want to help others. But having both is the true power that will change the world.

When you learn to control your desires and learn to want enough of only what you need, you will fuel your journey toward your Purposehood. When you know your direction and the role you are meant to play in this life, then you can learn to mix, at the right time, the right amounts of the right desires for the right journey. In a life of abundance, which is the future of humanity, every person would have all their needs available at their finger-tips. Basic needs will be basic human rights that are provided by society to every human without having to work for them as we do today. If you find this idea strange, just think about how human life evolved in a short time from working hard all day to satisfy the most basic needs, to having enough time and money to pursue hobbies. Peasants spent 50 percent of their income on bread alone around the time of the French revolution. Someday you, or maybe your children, will have a lifetime to pursue essential, fundamental, and existential desires. We need to want better, more, and faster achievement of higher-order desires in order to keep moving forward to a better state of being. *My friend, if you woke up tomorrow and all your basic desires were provided for, what would you want to do with your life?* Without the desire to want beyond basic needs, humanity will cease to evolve and expand.

4. **Innovation:** The desire to create or use something new or unique. The desire for innovation and novelty keeps your life fresh with new creations and keeps humanity working together to advance society. The desire for novelty is a form of innovation in your lifestyle. The creative genius within each one of us is the infinite fuel of innovation. This desire, on the negative side, leads to mindless consumerism as we disregard the older version of our still-working phone to get the latest model. On the positive side, it drives innovations to find a balance with recycling and utilizing new resources that don't deplete the environment.

5. **Construction:** The desire to build a useful structure from various elements. When we construct something, we build an emotional attachment to it as we invest our time, thoughts, and hopes in creating something meaningful. Even a table you put together is more meaningful to you than a ready-assembled table you buy. We also have to rely most of the time on others as we construct,

which creates a stronger bond as we build together toward a common desire.

6. **Beautification:** The desire to be beautiful and create beautiful objects. We don't only admire the beauty in creation, but also learn from it in order to create beautiful objects, symmetry, and fractal structures in our surroundings. We want to be beautiful and we want our surroundings to be beautiful. In a misguided desire for beautification, humans have destroyed nature away from home to make our immediate surroundings more beautiful. As we each become more aware that our home is Earth, we will make sure that any place anywhere on Earth stays beautiful.

7. **Exploitation:** The desire to exploit resources by making full use of them and deriving benefits from them. On the positive side, this desire creates efficient systems and optimal utilization of resources. It also reduces waste and consumption as you try to find other uses for the same resources. Have you exploited all of what you have in your closet before going out to buy new clothes? On the negative side, mindless exploitations are depleting our seas of fish, our lands of water, and our Earth of minerals.

8. **Exploration:** The desire to explore beyond your comfort zone. Isn't it the desire that drove humanity out of Africa and now is driving us to Mars and beyond? Haven't we domesticated horses to take us further inland, just as we now are creating rocket ships to take us further in space? This is the desire that pushes us to go beyond our comfort zone to explore the beyond. It's the desire that drives our scientific discoveries and our rebellion against dogmas and old belief systems.

9. **Domestication:** The desire to have an anchor in a community of other humans. One thing travelers always long for is home. We have a desire deep within us to settle in, to plant roots, and to belong. We want to have a spouse, a family, friends, a community, pets, and a familiar place we call home. This anchor keeps the restless traveler from wandering aimlessly. The desire to lay

roots and belong is what makes us build societies and, together, advance humanity.

10. **Profiting:** The desire to create and capture value from our creations. What is the use of planting a crop if not for harvesting it and selling the excess? What's the use of spending years in schooling if it doesn't provide us better opportunities once we graduate? What's the use of innovating, constructing, beautifying, exploiting, and exploring if we don't produce extra value to improve our lives and those around us? What's the use of volunteering if not to see the fruits of our efforts in the lives of those we help or see our impact on the issues we support? One of the key motivators in business is for the employee to see the impact they have on the success of the company. We have an infinite desire to see the fruits of our labor, the results of our efforts, and the impact of our actions.

The 10 essential desires don't only drive forward individual humans, but also humanity as a whole. Most of the basic forces in our societies are results of those essential desires. For example, attraction fuels connectivity and creates marketing, love adds depth to our attraction and creates new expressions like in poetry and literature, want creates all kinds of demands that fuel production and trade, innovation creates novelty and expedites social and material evolution, construction creates engineering, beautification creates art, exploitation creates efficiencies, exploration creates science, and profiting creates economies and businesses.

You ask, "What's the opposite of a life of ease?"

When you are consumed with selfish pursuits of infinite basic desires, you will feel lonely, even in a crowd, as you become disconnected from their extensions of being, and as a consequence, you will suffer alone while facing the challenges of life. And when you are consumed by a negative direction toward a life of vacuum and destruction, all your extensions will contract, causing tremendous suffering. The opposite of a life of ease is a life of suffering. If that suffering persists for a long period of time, it could turn to a life of rejection with consistent stress, anxiety, and regret.

But when you live connected to others and work with them as co-creators to fulfill common goals, your life will be one of ease regardless of the challenges you face. *Struggling is inevitable; suffering is optional*. May you struggle with ease, my friend.

———

I BREATHE IN EASE.
I BREATHE OUT ABUNDANCE.

Proposition 14:
Life of Abundance

"Life of abundance is desiring what you need instead of needing what you desire." – PoET Proposition 14

It's intriguing to see the evolution of desires transpiring across the lifetime of a human being as we all start as babies desiring our most basic needs like eating and sleeping; then, as we get a bit older, we desire more basic desires such as socializing and status. At one point in our lives, essential desires become prominent as we select professions to make a living; then in our 50s, we recognize the importance of our fundamental desires and look for happiness, fulfillment, and a new definition for success; and at some point, when we face existential crises, hopefully before our death, we realize that we need to find a meaning and purpose to our lives.

We evolved from basic desires to higher-order desires to become semideums. That means we don't have to continue living like the cave people we used to be, or even expand our awareness gradually, as most humans do during their lifetimes. *We have the choice as awakened beings to start from the top of the evolutionary stairs of desires and use our power of creation to create a better life for our Five Extensions of Being, humanity, and nature.*

We can choose to become Purposehooders *now* and direct our basic desires in the positive direction of our existential purpose. We can choose right away to live a life of belonging and connectedness, a life of direction and guidance, and a life of abundance, in order to care for the abandoned, to provide for the deprived, and to share our blessings with others.

You ask, "Why do infinite basic desires become abundant for a Purposehooder?"

My friend, it's very simple. If you know that all you need for your journey is a dollar, then with two, you will live with abundance. How are you supposed to know what you need for a journey if you don't even know where you're going? Without a destination you will always live with scarcity.

As a Purposehooder, you know your destination and what you need for your journey. And you also know that packing too much will weigh you down instead of making the journey easier. You pack with the confidence that on the way you will find what you need to restock. You are also confident that you will always find other Purposehooders on the path to offer assistance. Those who are excessive in pursuing their desires are lost in the jungle of life without direction or not knowing what to prepare for, nor do they have people who willingly share their journey.

A pilot calculates how much fuel is needed for a flight based on the distance between where they begin and where they need to reach, accounting for the solid weight of the plane and crew. The weight of the fuel added to the solid weight can't exceed the maximum allowed for the plane to fly and land safely. Having fuel beyond the allowed total weight is not only inefficient for the journey ahead but also dangerous.

You are the pilot of your life's journey to your Purposehood. Your plane is your life, your Purposehood is your destination, your lifetime is the distance, your crew are your extensions of being, your engines are your essential desires, and your fuel is your basic desires. With the right amount of fuel, you will fly with ease and gratitude, feeling happiness, success, and fulfillment all throughout the journey. But if you over-fuel, even if you can take off, you will be too heavy and will always suffer from stress, anxiety, and regrets.

Only when you know your final objective can you get what is needed and never what misdirects you. Our basic desires are merely fuels to empower our essential desires, which in turn fuel our fundamental desires that fuel our one existential desire. The destination is your aim and the journey is your joy, not the desires themselves. When you live a life of Purposehood, gratitude, and ease, you will only want positive basic desires that keep you safe on your journey.

Take, for example, the basic desire for retaliation. When a person is directionless, retaliation is an instinctive response to any misunderstanding, as we see in most petty fights that take place among drivers on everyday roads.

When a person is misdirected toward vacuum and destruction, their retaliation is always disproportionate to any harm that was done. How many warring nations, politicians, business competitors, and even neighbors stop at nothing but utter destruction of their rivals, and with that their extensions? But when a person is guided by their Purposehood, the desire for retaliation is directed at creating a deterrent at the least cost possible to any party involved. A Purposehooder seeks retaliation for justice, not for rage, and while they respond, they might even pray for their nemeses to be guided to the path of Purposehood so they may become friends and collaborators in advancing humanity and life toward a better state of being.

A Purposehooder pauses, breathes, and smiles before responding to aggression, reflecting on the desired end to the conflict and making sure that the conflict won't derail them from their journey. Such a measured response turns retaliation into a positive desire, clearing the way forward for a safer journey toward Purposehood.

You ask, "Is knowing my Purposehood enough to direct my desires in the positive direction?"

My friend, this is a very wise question, and the simple answer is no. Knowing your Purposehood is not enough to control your desires, but living your Purposehood includes practices to do so.

The genetic pull of basic desires is so strong that you need to always be aware of their tendencies, and you need to develop practices to build enough strength in order to resist them, just like you build muscles and endurance for physical challenges.

One of the most intriguing stories told by Abrahamic traditions is that of the first humans who were endowed with a self-learning human intelligence (HI), Adam and Eve. They were told to avoid a desirable fruit in order to train them to free themselves from the constant pull of the newly unleashed infinite basic desires. Obviously, the fruit identified was randomly selected to instigate, in the simplest manner, the self-learning HI, specifically, how to control the most basic desire of eating. Eating was a simple need for other humanoids, which became a complex desire for Homo sapiens.

In the subsequent stories of human development, we read in scriptures about more restrictions placed on the evolving humanity from adding other foods to the restriction list, regulating how to exact vengeance, how to couple, how to form communities, how to better treat animals in the quest for food, and other edicts.

All those rules and regulations were merely instigators to the self-learning HI. They led to a higher awareness of the need to control the infinite basic desires in the direction of a dictated religious Purposehood in those cases. This self-learning HI program is what created a higher order of desires as humans moved to higher levels of awareness. Humans will ultimately be driven by a personalized Purposehood chosen by each person in the service of humanity's role as the expo-agent of life.

Some of the practices developed over millennia are still relevant and useful to adapt to your own needs as in the Five Streams of Potentiality. These include fasting, meditation, controlled diets that eliminate certain foods, charitable giving, and even sometimes turning the other cheek can be important for learning to control basic desires.

These and other practices also teach patience and delayed gratification instead of diving into indulgences. This learned developmental behavior is one of the best indicators of future orientation that creates capabilities such as confidence, optimism, and self-reliance.

You ask, "How do the Five Streams of Potentiality help me control my desires?"

My friend, the Five Streams of Potentiality are your nourishments for happiness, success, and fulfillment. In addition to helping you expand your awareness, detach from labels and expectations, grow with ease, and positively impact all your extensions with a lasting legacy, they also help you direct your desires toward your Purposehood.

With belief practices, you eliminate limiting beliefs and acquire empowering ones that create positive values to direct all your desires toward your Purposehood. Mindfulness frees you from the negative impulses of the desire traits of excessiveness, haste, and betterment. Giving tames the selfishness of your desires and stretches your self to all your extensions. Wellness balances the altruistic tendencies of your desires with a reminder of the need to practice self-care. Belonging ensures you stay in control of your desires with the help of people who care about you and your mission.

The more you utilize the various practices in the last part of the book, the more control you will have, and the easier it will be to live a life of abundance with ease and gratitude.

———

I BREATHE IN ABUNDANCE.
I BREATHE OUT GRATITUDE.

Proposition 15:
The Modes of Time

"In the beyond, you are a timeless, complete being who is gifted with the currency of a lifetime to invest as you wish in this existence. You are meant to be the creator of the future, the editor of the past, and the observer of the present." – PoET Proposition 15

My friend, time is a measuring unit of the forward mechanical movement of the universe, and it only ticks in the direction of the future. But if you view time on a universal scale, then it is merely a component of a block of *spacetime*: Whatever was, is, and will be is already there. Time, in this view, is a representation of existence that already happened. Yet, in the quantum view, everything is timeless, and time will only reveal observed possibilities in the present.

Think about a movie you just watched on your computer that was saved on a data storage service in the cloud. The actors in the movie lived a mechanical existence while filming the different scenes, where time always moved forward and was clearly defined in past, present, and future. The same movie, when viewed by the editor on a movie reel, becomes one block of sequential events that already happened. For existence, the movie is merely a collection of timeless data constructed from ones and zeros in a digital existence.

Only when you observe a scene does it pop into your present

and the possibility of its existence becomes obvious. Isn't your act of loading the data, selecting the position on the movie reel, and pushing the play button what brings that scene into your existence? Or is it maybe your intention to watch that causes the scene to emerge? Or maybe the cause of emergence is your belief that once the scene is selected it will appear?

You are a lead actor, an editor, and an observer of the movie of this existence, and you play these roles in its different modes. But even before that you were, still are, and will always be part of the equation that created the ones and zeros. This equation formed this time-bound universe, which emerged from an ocean of possibilities in the timeless-cloud, where all existential data is stored. You're a timeless presence in the beyond with tremendous possibilities in the block of existence, which you have been painting with your choices in this mechanical presence.

Without a three-dimensional view of time, it's very hard to understand its nature, in which each mode—past, present and future—is correct on its own, but incomplete. However, since you exist in those three modes, be aware that you are a creator oriented toward the future, an editor reshaping the past, and a timeless being witnessing the present.

Have you ever reflected on the germination process of a seed, like that of a sunflower? The seed exists in a dormant state until it's activated by environmental elements—mainly, water, oxygen, and temperature. Then, as the fruit wall splits and falls off, three parts emerge: a radicle that moves downward to become roots, cotyledons that move upward to become the first leaves, and a hypocotyl that becomes the stem connecting the two parts and lifts up the cotyledons. As the seedling grows, the three parts become obvious in roots, stem, and new branches with leaves and fruits rising in the direction of the sun. Germination is the process of expanding into significance from an insignificant existence and a plant is not whole without all of these three parts, and neither are you.

You are only complete with the roots of your past, the stem of your present, and the new branches with leaves and fruits of your future. All are growing in the direction of your forward-pulling energy, your Purposehood Guiding Star. With every step forward, the seedling needs the roots to push nourishment from the ground upward, the stem to transport the nourishment, and the leaves to transform the energy from the sun. This all happens in the service of the future-pulling existential purpose of producing fruits, which will spread new seeds for continued existence while feeding other lifeforms at the same time; selfish-altruism at its best.

Like a plant, you need to move forward toward the future with a clear existential purpose that lights your way, positive nourishment from your past that pushes you forward, and a present that is a conduit, channeling the fuel from your past toward your future with ease. You have emerged from a dormant state in the timeless-cloud to become a creator of the future, but without having positive nourishment from your past and a healthy conduit in your present, you would be like a rootless plant that is blown away by the slightest wind, or worse, a negative weed that spreads toxicity and destruction.

You need to live forward toward a clear vision of the positive future you'd like to create. You need to make sure that your past only provides you with positive nourishment, and you need to clear your present from distractions that prevent the flow of energy to your future. A positive life is lived with a positive vision of the future, a positive view of the past, and positive actions in the present. Living with a negative mode of any one of them will always lead to a negative life.

You ask, "What are the modes of time?"

My friend, time has three simultaneous modes: timelessness in the beyond where the source equation of all existences resides, completeness in the timeless-cloud where all possibilities reside, and progressiveness in this universe where probabilities are created. You are part of the timeless formula in the beyond, your individual history from the Big Bang to the end of this existence is stored in the timeless-cloud, and the impact of your thoughts, words, and actions are influencing the future of the universe as it unfolds in the progressive mode of time. Even though you only experience the progressive mode of time in this existence, you are able to transcend and experience them all in a moment of meditative clarity. But you can also experience your timelessness and completeness every day with empowering beliefs, such as those in these propositions, and by mastering your progressive three time zones of the future, past, and present, as you orient your lifetime toward a positive future, feed on the positive past, and use the present to reflect, plan, and recharge.

The root of all suffering is being stuck in one time zone. When you are stuck in the past, you live with regrets; when you are stuck in the present, you live with stress; and when you are stuck in the future, you live with anxiety. But when you visit the past for learning, pause in the present for resting, all while continuously stepping with positive confidence into the future, then you will live with abundance, ease, and gratitude. Investing your lifetime correctly among the three time zones is not only your ticket to a positive existence, but also to completeness and timelessness. *It all starts by knowing that you're made to live in and for the future.*

———

I BREATHE IN THE PAST.
I BREATHE OUT THE FUTURE.

Proposition 16:
The Future

"You're here to co-author, with other creators, a more positive future for all." – PoET Proposition 16

The future is a product of awareness, as awareness creates anticipation, anticipation creates intentions, intentions create actions, actions create probabilities, and probabilities create the future. The future is simply possibilities made more probable by your actions. When your actions are intentional, the result is an intentional future.

There is a positive correlation between the future and awareness, as the more awareness expands, the more future-oriented you are, and in turn, more future orientation equals more awareness. The reason for such a correlation is that awareness of the past is limited by the available data, memories, and new input that might help us edit the past; awareness of the present is constrained by our sensory input, the mechanical short-term predictability of cause and effect, and the need for a reactive, immediate outcome.

When you recall an event from your past, like an argument you had with a friend, you can only expand your awareness to the limits of how much detail you can recall, details you can collect from other witnesses, and various thoughts and emotions you can consider the argument through. And when you are faced with a fast-moving car as you cross the road, your awareness is driven by your immediate need to get to safety. But when you contemplate the future, all possibilities are there, regardless of how probable or improbable they are. It's like looking through an outward funnel; the further you look, the wider the opening is and the more possibilities there are. And the more awareness we have, the further we would want to look, as human curiosity is endless.

Consider humanity's evolution from limited awareness of its surroundings, which helped hunter-gatherers plan for the immediate future, to expanded awareness of the seasons that extended planning to a year, which created agricultural societies. As awareness magnified planning for the future, it also supported the creation of new future regulating systems such as dams, storage, and transportation. At some point, maybe around the emergence of religions, there was a shift from being pushed to plan for the future by basic desires to also being pulled by a vision and a belief toward the future.

Perhaps the best contribution religious beliefs have had on early human evolution was expanding the future horizon beyond a lifetime. These beliefs pushed humans to consider the future consequences of their actions and to plan further ahead. They also bolstered the belief that you will have a tremendous delayed reward for doing the right things in this life, which tempered the urgency of desires for instant gratification, a great contributor to success and well-being, as the Stanford marshmallow experiment on delayed gratification showed.[81] Those who learn to resist temptations as children will most likely be happier, as well as more successful and fulfilled in their adult lives.

Was that shift a result of an innate drive to timelessness and completeness beyond this progressive existence? Or, was it the awareness of enlightened prophets of our existential purpose? Or maybe it was the awareness of the progressive and expansive nature of possibilities that lay in the future that propelled us to imagine, plan, and create. Regardless, at some point, humanity realized a crucial fact about the future—it always comes with more advancements. We are coming to understand that it is also created through our actions today.

My friend, there are three characteristics to consider of the future: unpredictability, "createability," and positivity.

The larger and more complex a system is, the harder it is to predict its future, as any small change could alter the outcome. It's much easier to predict the future of your dog than of your children. But a person's future is easier to predict than the future of humanity and life. In all cases, the future is created through countless causes, and their effects, that are beyond any certain predictability in our progressive universe. It's simply not possible, with our limited knowledge, to predict the future with certainty. This is why attachment to expectations is a sure recipe for disappointment.

However, even if the future can't be predicted, it can still be created! Even if we can't control every cause, we are still intentional beings with an expansive view of the future. We are able to imagine a future with a desired outcome, anticipate other causes and effects, plan accordingly, and intentionally add or subtract actions to influence the outcome.

It's like playing chess. Your desired outcome is to win the match. The probability of you accomplishing that increases the more you consider the possibilities of the moves you can make with what you control, the contingencies you can plan to counter your opponent's moves, and your skill at thinking ahead. Isn't that what makes the probability of a chess master beating a novice much higher, even though they both start with the same potentiality? The chess master understands that with a clear vision of the final outcome, an expansive awareness of possible moves, the intentional actions they make to create that desired outcome, and the steps they will take to limit the opponent's options, they would probably win.

Yet, even in a simple game like chess, there's a chance that the outcome will be different than your expectations. You will never be disappointed, though, if your expectation is a better state of being.

If you are the person who lost the match, could that unanticipated outcome serve as a lesson to become humbler? Or, maybe it is a push to practice more and become even better. How could this loss impact your family and friends positively? What lessons might they learn from your loss? Could the loss be a sign to pursue other interests that can be more satisfying to all your extensions of being? Maybe it is a sign to spend more time with the family, friends, and work you've neglected, instead of playing chess. Or, maybe you can look wider and see the influence this win may have on your opponent, and how positively it will impact their extensions.

Your expansive view of the future allows you to look further in spacetime, include your extensions, and consider more possibilities and contingencies as you plan for a desired future. Yet, you should hold the belief that whatever the outcome is, *it is always toward a better state of being,* as the future always unfolds toward an optimal outcome for higher systems.

Consider the history of humanity in 500-year blocks. Regardless of the pain and suffering of individual humans, we are collectively better off today than 500 years ago, and they were better off than 500 years earlier, and so on, to the earliest humans.

The future always moves toward a better state of being, and that advancement is becoming exponential, as we can see improvements nowadays in decades, and soon in years, months, and days. The progression in the system of humanity will, in turn, extend vast enhancements in the future of every human. We already see the improvement in access to education, health care, and basic necessities evident by an increasing average lifespan. And the further we look into the future, the more aware we become and the faster we evolve in harmony with universal existential purpose toward a better state of being.

You ask, "The future is getting better for humans, but is it better for ailing nature?"

My friend, it definitely will be. Nature is hurting now due to humanity's misdirected actions, but it will soon have the opportunity to be genetically preserved, and later revived, cultivated, and improved on Earth and across the universe, as humanity matures.

Sustainability for a future-oriented humanity is not an ideal; it is a necessity for our survival.

You ask, "Is future orientation good for our minds? Isn't anxiety a sickness of future anticipation?"

My friend, all creatures are oriented toward the future. Everything in the past is a lesson learned, and the present is a preparation for the future. Even simple needs such as eating and reproducing are meant to help us live another day and plant seeds for the future. There is only one direction in progressive time, always toward the future and always toward a better state of being.

With the forward movement of time comes advancement toward a better future, as progress zigzags up and down but always forward, pulled by the universal Purposehood. A creature that doesn't match this forward movement won't be suitable for life, just as a tree that stopped growing toward the future is more suitable for firewood than being an active participant in the progress of life. The good news is that you are built to be future-oriented as a creator should be. A creator dreams a future and then builds toward it.

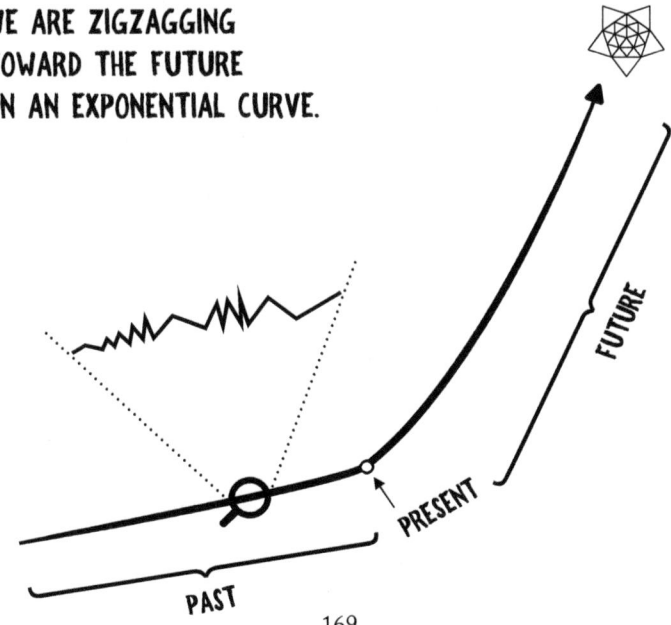

WE ARE ZIGZAGGING TOWARD THE FUTURE ON AN EXPONENTIAL CURVE.

PAST

PRESENT

FUTURE

All the tension, stress, anxiety, regrets, and depression that cause human suffering are rooted in resisting the movement toward the inevitable, better future. People and societies that want to relive a positive past or can't escape the negative experiences of days gone by are doomed to be torn apart in the tension created by the forward-moving time. Similarly, those who want to remain in the present and be detached from past and future, either to pursue their hedonistic desires or to escape the constant stress, will be also torn apart by the forward-moving time if they remain too long in the present. Additionally, those who are moving anxiously toward an anticipated future of doom will be torn apart by the time that is moving in the other direction, toward a better state of being. Having the correct orientation toward a positive future is what makes your life harmonious with progressive time as you move forward with ease.

The most important correction you can make in your life is to reorient yourself toward a positive future. With such orientation, you can't help but view all past and present experiences as preparations for the journey forward in this lifetime and beyond. This positive future pull turns regrets into reflections, stress into a positive pulling tension, and anxiety into excitement. You will also realize with a positive future orientation that the past and present are made of the future. Isn't the past merely unfolded future, and isn't the present a future unfolding? Is there even a "now" when the seconds never stop ticking forward? By the time you think of the "now," isn't it already in the past? And when you anticipate a "now" event, aren't you actually anticipating the future?

It's not the positives or negatives of the past and present that are holding you back, it's being stuck there away from your waiting, positive future. When your vision of the future is positive and you are taking the steps forward, all the net outcome of the past and present is positive and you will live with ease free from anxiety, stress, and regrets.

You ask, "How do I create the future?"

My friend, the future is created by the collective actions of all creatures. But only humanity has the capability of collectively pushing existence into a possible future. We already collectively can increase or decrease the probability of a future for life itself with our weapons of mass destruction. Today, we can create and destroy on a global level, and in the future, with genetic engineering infused with artificial intelligence and robotics, our capabilities will expand exponentially beyond our planet.

What you can do is become a positive force in the creation of a better future for all, knowing that everything in existence is either entangled or linked through the genesis block, the Big Bang. If a flap of a butterfly wing can increase a probability, imagine what your lifetime of positive actions can do for the future of your extensions, humanity, and nature.

You become a positive, future-creating force by doing the following:

First, select your Purposehood Guiding Star, unleash your potentiality, and become an influencer in your extensions of being.

Second, subscribe with others to a positive vision of the future of humanity, life, and the universe—a shared Purposehood.

Finally, every day do a simple action that makes that possible future more probable, or the opposite future less probable, as you move toward your Purposehood. You can easily do that by unleashing the potentiality of others, contributing knowledge to the collective experiences, and supporting institutions that improve life for all.

Once you contribute an action, you can observe the changes and adjust accordingly by repeating the process. Imagine the future, then accept it as it comes, knowing that, ultimately, it will be the best possible. Without imagining it and laying the stepping-stones, that possible future is less probable.

You can use the same process to deal with any anxiety, stress, or regrets. When you are faced with such an internal reaction to a situation, pause, breathe, smile, and turn your attention to the future and imagine the best possible outcome. That outcome, regardless of how improbable, is still possible.

Ask yourself, "What one simple action can I do right now to make this possibility a tiny bit more probable?" Come up with one simple action, as simple as a butterfly flap, and do it right away. Congratulations! You just increased the probability of a better outcome. You can keep increasing the probability by simply adding intentional actions.

You can also imagine the worst possible outcome and come up with an action that makes it less probable and simply do it. Start with the simplest action that you can do immediately like a text, a phone call, an email, or even a silent prayer. A prayer is a future-oriented, focused intention.

For example, if you just had a serious argument with your spouse and now you feel stressed, anxious, and full of regrets, try first to pause, breathe, smile, and then imagine the best possible outcome, such as a scenario where, because of this argument, you both realize you need a vacation in your favorite place where you will feel relaxed and connected. The worst possible outcome is that you might get a divorce. What is the one action you can do imme- diately to increase the first possibility and reduce the second one? Maybe it's to say, "I'm sorry," or reaffirm your love, appreciation, and understanding. Whatever it is, do it right away. This first action will lay the foundation for more actions that increase the probability of your desired outcome toward rekindling your love and commit- ment to each other.

You ask, "Isn't our seed of potentiality a product of our past?"

My friend, you are the seed of the future that will be. Your seed and its three components are for nothing less than the purpose of existence and its future. Creativity is there to make you dream and imagine the future. Desire is there to drive you to activate your dreams and create the future. Directional choice gives your creativity an orientation, your activities a focus, and your connections with others a meaning in order to create, with others, the best possible future.

You are not living today only as a result of your past events, your memories, or your evolution from what you were. Instead, you are living as a spark of your possible future, your imagination, and your evolution toward what you will become.

We all are moving from the age of the herd, connecting through birth labels to the age of the individuality, connecting through shared Purposehood. This move will change everything and unleash the exponential nature of human potential.

It's true we started from a point in the past and we arrived here due to trillions of past events, but all that spectacular past, today, is just a dot on the exponential curve of existence. We are at the turning point of the linear existence of our past and the unavoidable exponential existence of our future. Humanity has to play its role as the exponential agent of nature, and you are here to make sure it does.

You are not meant to be only a product of the past or an observer of the present; you are the creator of the future.

The message is so clear within you! Can't you hear it? Your destiny is to unleash limitless creativity, powered with positive infinite desires, directed toward a clear Purposehood, in order to create with others the best possible future for all.

In the multidimensional game of life, you are the center and the outlier, your roles in your extensions of being are essential for humanity, life, the universe, and existence to reach their Purposehood. When all beings grow to their potentiality, ease and harmony are present in the world. When they don't, suffering and tension are there, instead. Only on the road to your Purposehood will your potentiality be unleashed so you may co-author the future.

You will author your own destiny when Purposehood is your destination. Start by developing your vision of your future, sharing it with those around you, and contributing to theirs as they will undoubtedly contribute to yours.

———

I BREATHE IN POSSIBILITIES.
I BREATHE OUT PROBABILITIES.

Proposition 17:
The Past

"Whatever happened could not have happened any other way, and it happened for a better state of being." – PoET Proposition 17

The past is as wide as your awareness and as flexible as your imagination. It's not written in stone but constantly edited by prospective and perspective. Our view of the past is impacted by our view of the future and the amount of information we discover about what happened. When a person believes that the future is bright, they see the past, both its positives and negatives as a prerequisite to that future. However, when an individual expects a gloomy future, they see the past as net negative and the moments of past joy as hard to repeat, let alone improve on. Additionally, a person who sees the past as a closed book is shackled by finished stories they tell themselves, while an unshackled person will see the past as a story that is still being written and requires additional editing.

Take the tragic accident of the Apollo 1 crew, who lost their lives during a launch rehearsal. The story of what happened is based on the amount of information collected from investigating various aspects of the story, not only related to the time of the accident, but even further back to manufacturing the equipment, and even before, to the decision process that drove those manufacturing and design errors. The further and wider the collection of information, the more accurate and involved the assessment. Depending on who is collecting the information, the focus could be on engineering, strategy, management, or training, among other factors. Any new revelation could alter the conclusions of the investigators.

Additionally, the values of an investigator will impact their views of events of the past. If someone deemed space exploration a useless endeavor, their view would have been very different from another individual who believed the mission to be an inevitable step toward humanity's future. The first person would see the sacrifice as a waste of resources and look for reasons to stop trying, while the second would see it as a tragic but necessary step toward a better future design of the spaceship and a better future for humanity.

You ask, "Couldn't what happened in the past have happened another way?"

My friend, the fact that it happened as it did means it couldn't have happened any other way. If another way was more probable, a different present would've emerged and you might not be in it. The events of our past are the result of a chain of causes and effects that stretch as far back as you'd like to take them, starting as far as we scientifically know at the genesis block of the Big Bang.[82] What seems like a result of chaos or a simple result of a direct cause was actually caused by an incredible combination of causes that had to happen exactly as they did to produce that event. Going forward, we could intentionally inject a cause with the objective of altering a result. But looking backward, the event happened as the only possible result from all possibilities based on all the causes involved. No one can change that one simple fact.

You ask, "How could a tragic event occur for a better state of being?"

My friend, it's not enough to consider one aspect of a past event to fully understand its impact. You need to look at any past event with a three-dimensional view, a quantum view where you consider the not-so-obvious consequences, a mechanical view where you view direct causality, and a universal view where you look at the impact of events over a long period of time.

For the Apollo 1 event, in the quantum view, you could study the impact it had on the thousands of individual staff, engineers, and family members of those involved in the accident, in addition to countless people who were discouraged or encouraged to dream about space, and then weigh the positive and negative impacts.

In the mechanical view, you could study the immediate impact Apollo 1 had on the progress of the Apollo program, resulting in successfully landing a man on the moon two and a half years later.

In the universal view, you can see the impact it had on advancing humanity toward its existential purpose.

When you carefully examine any event in the past with these three views, regardless of how tragic it seemed, you will always find that it had net positive results on advancing humanity, life, and the universe toward their Purposehoods.

Since the universe is constantly pulled forward by the existential purpose, everything that happened was a cause to that advancement. That is obvious when we look at humanity's progress all through history, regardless of tragic wars, famines, or pandemics. In fact, those wars were the cause of many technological and social advancements, such as inspiring the women's empowerment movement, since women were needed to work outside homes during the first World War; the strengthening of international bodies of cooperation, such as the United Nations; as well as the development of advanced aircrafts, metals, fuels, and other technologies.

As for the individuals who lost their lives, as tragic as it was, the positive legacy they left continues to add value to their extended existence in the beyond. When you consider someone's life in return on lifetime (ROLT), you see that their life continues to produce positive returns. In that context, their tragedy will make more sense than viewing it from the pain they suffered at the time. Maybe the perspective of "That which does not kill us, makes us stronger," can be expanded to the understanding, "That which kills us, makes our extensions of being somehow stronger."

Ultimately, the past is always a net positive experience, as life always moves toward a better state of being, and the future will always be better if you're patient enough to wait. I don't consider this view to be an optimistic view of life, but a *realistic* view. All you need to do is reflect on the past to see with clarity the net positive outcome in all dimensional views.

You ask, "How do I deal with past regrets and negative experiences?"

My friend, our memories of the past are like the roots of a tree: As long as there are leaves to photosynthesize energy from the sunlight, the roots will keep growing in search for food for the leaves. Regrets are great if they lead to repentance and corrective actions, but if you are stuck repeating a negative story in your mind, your roots will only feed your future with toxicity. When you have a Purposehood Guiding Star, your memories will expand in search of positive lessons from your past.

Make sure that you have a clear Purposehood that shines the light on your future and journey forward, then allow your memories to recognize, reflect, and reframe past events to feed your Purposehood pursuit. When you recognize past events, you can identify the sources of your current nourishment and intentionally examine your memories of them. When you reflect on those memories, you can extract invaluable learnings, and you widen your views of the events themselves beyond your initial experience.

Finally, you can reframe your past experience correctly, as you realize that although the duality in existence dictates that every experience would necessarily have both positive and negative impacts, as long as you extract the lessons, then those events will always be a net positive for your future. Past events always produce net positive, so look for it. With this simple process, you can edit and re-edit past events as you move toward a better state of being. I call this crucial process of positively reframing past events: *the Purpose-*

hood Life Graph, which is part of the extended "Life Design" course and a subsequent book.

The past is your connection to all that was, from the Big Bang to the trillion of magnificent cosmic events that led to you. When you will look at the block universe standing in the presence of iSH in the beyond, you will see that you are the past that created the future of humanity, and your intentional actions today determined that future. The past is a wonderful web of roots, so use it to nourish your growth.

Remember, the past is not fixed, it is memories written with interpretations and expectations, so keep writing your story and feel free to edit it as needed. The past is not written in ink, but scribbled with a pencil. It is not printed in a book, but drafted in a journal, so write and rewrite it to fit your future view.

I BREATHE IN THE PAST.
I BREATHE OUT THE FUTURE.

Proposition 18:
The Present

"Your present is the realized future of your past; use it to reflect on how you got here, plan the present of tomorrow, and recharge for your forward Purposehood journey." – PoET Proposition 18

The present in the universal view is a snapshot of what was, is, and will be. People who subscribe only to this view become helpless, as whatever will be will be, or careless, as whatever they do is already predetermined. In the quantum view, the present is the result of the collective observation, or will, of humanity, and some people who subscribe only to this view wonder if their personal little actions, such as voting in an election, would truly impact an outcome where millions vote. In the mechanical view, the present is a fleeting moment that is best captured with pleasures, or frozen with meditations for those who believe only in this view.

However, a Purposehooder who is future-oriented yet rooted in the past, would clearly see that the present is merely a moving transitional point between the past and the future. The conduit between the roots and the leaves. The present is the future of yesterday and the past of tomorrow. With such crucial understanding, the present becomes a stepping-stone in a moving river in order to reflect on the past, plan for the future, and recharge for the journey ahead.

This fact was described beautifully by the ancient philosopher Heraclitus of Ephesus who said, "No person ever steps in the same river twice, for it's not the same river and they are not the same person." The present is nothing but the illusion of suspending the flux of spacetime.

Imagine your lifetime as a line on a two-dimensional graph where space is the x-axis and time is the y-axis. The start on the x-axis is where you were born, and the end is where you will die. On the y-axis, the time you were born is the past and the time you will die is the future. If you point to the present on the graph, you will clearly see that the whole graph, which is composed of countless points, represents the summation of the future and the past, except for this one tiny point. Yet, this tiny point in spacetime is not even a real point on your lifetime graph, but simply an accounting reference—one that is always moving forward, increasing your past lifetime account and reducing your future lifetime account.

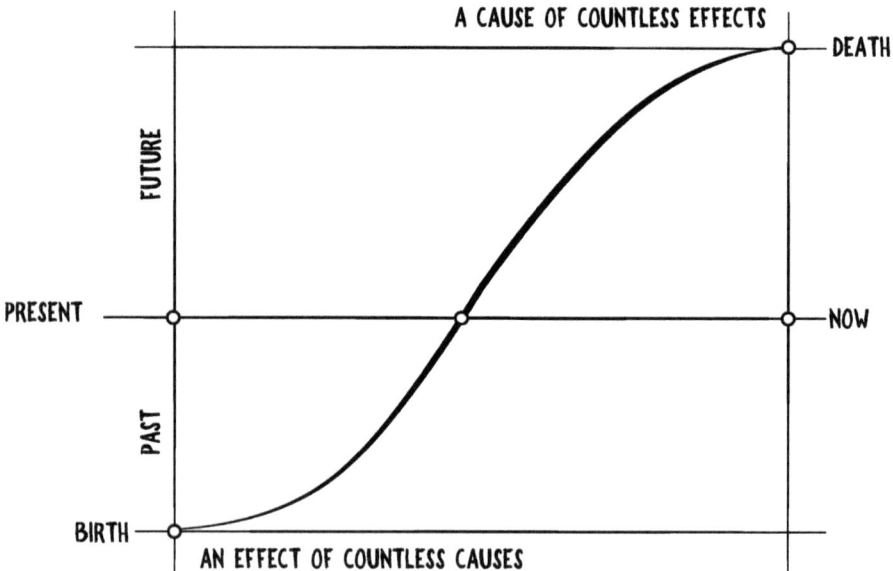

LIFETIME

How could anyone actually suspend a constantly moving reference point between the future and the past? Between what is still possible and what was inevitable? And between being a cause of future effects and being the effect of past causes? The moment you were born, your entire lifetime was made of your future, and the moment you die, your entire lifetime will be made of your past. Isn't it amazing how toddlers are so at ease with existence as they are free of the heavy weight of the past? They are so full of life; they have all their future ahead of them with no attachment to expectations.

Yet, even when your present reference point ceases to exist, your past (in this lifetime) and future (in the beyond) stay active. Your lifetime that started as an effect of countless causes will end as a cause to countless effects. Your legacy and impact that you left behind will continue influencing events until the end of time, writing your future in the beyond.

You ask, "Should we then disregard the now?"

My friend, this present moment is a gift of awareness between two states that needs to be correctly utilized. Those who use it correctly will master their positive return on lifetime (ROLT). When you realize the present for what it is—a moving transitional point between two states—it will add a new depth to your existence. It's like mastering the transition of your breath between breathing in and breathing out. You breathe in the future, you breathe out the past, and in between lies your present. When you are able to notice that point in the flux of life, then you will always be at a higher state of awareness. You need to learn to pause to separate the future from the past, and to use that moment as a stepping-stone toward an intended future.

One of the best practices for doing this is to pause, breathe, and smile randomly, often allowing yourself to interrupt the flow of time and pay attention to your present reference point.

You ask, "How do I utilize the present?"

There are three things you can do in that moment of transition: reflect on the past, plan for the future, or recharge for the journey ahead. When you intentionally pause to reflect on the past, you allow yourself to capture the lessons that will increase the return on your lifetime. As Socrates said, "The unexamined life is not worth living." You want to take the time to reflect on your past in order to design a life worth living for your future. You also can pause to plan the future by imagining, planning, and initiating with intention the actions that make it more probable. Finally, you can use the present to mindfully recharge all your extensions of being for your forward journey by taking the time to connect deeper with others, consume the right nourishment, and expand your awareness with meditation and other potentiality practices.

Just be mindful that a Purposehooder doesn't stop for long to reflect, plan, and recharge before moving forward. Those who are stuck in the present will always be stressed by the mechanical tension of life.

There are people who want to live constantly in the "now," as they want to escape the past and the future. For some, that lifestyle is as necessary as a hospital is for an ill person—though a hospital is only meant for an urgent visit, not as a place to reside. If they stay there too long, they will become like addicts who are not able to function outside this unnatural comfort zone.

If it was natural to live always in the "now," then nature would have produced mostly monks. But life needs creators and creators are always future-oriented. Still, it is important for the rest of humanity to have such experts who have mastered control over their basic desires and can teach others how to do so.

The present moment is a goodbye to a beautiful past and a hello to a wonderful future, which is constantly whispered through a life of gratitude. Live it to the fullest with awareness and ease!

———

I BREATHE IN A PAUSE.
I BREATHE OUT A SMILE.

Proposition 19:
Principled-Flexibility

"Principled-flexibility is how progress is made in a life built with constant change. Absolutism is a rigidity that constrains creativity and growth." – PoET Proposition 19

When professor Clay Christensen of Harvard Business School was a college student in England playing on the varsity basketball team, he learned that the championship game was scheduled to be played on a Sunday. This was a problem for Clay because, as a devout Mormon, he had made a personal commitment to God to only perform religious activities on the Sabbath. When he told his coach, the response was, "I believe that God will understand." Later, everyone on the team came to Clay and said, "You've got to play. Can't you break the rule, just this one time?"

It was a difficult decision for Clay to make, as the team would undoubtedly suffer without him. The guys on the team were his best friends, and everyone dreamed of winning the final. He contemplated the decision for a long time, but finally decided not to play. The team lost the championship by a few points, which he could have easily made.

He concluded, "It is easier to hold to your principles 100 percent of the time than 98 percent of the time." He believed that once a person justifies crossing the boundary of their moral principles, there will always be other reasons to cross them again. He concluded that prioritizing the immediate and tangible rewards of breaking his principles just once would end up diverting him from his end goal in life.

My friend, what would you have done in that situation? Would you have played?

I struggled with this question for eight years, from the time I heard the professor tell his story. I knew there was a time in my youth when I wouldn't have hesitated in answering that principles are too important to break, especially religious ones. And it wasn't because religious interpreters promised hell to those who break them, but because I believed in the absolute truism of those principles. In those days, I wouldn't have played, but today I would.

You ask, "Why would you play?"

My friend, I would have played, not to please my teammates, coach, or the fans, nor to avoid living under the pressure of expectations or regrets; I would have played because I don't think that life's decisions are meant to be easy.

We don't grow by taking the easy road and, sometimes, we need to struggle with decisions in order to expand our awareness. That's how we reflect—how we learn about ourselves. It's how we examine beliefs, set intentions, and feel gratitude. It's how we decide to give and to belong. Mainly, that's how we evolve and expand.

I want to struggle with a decision every now and then as I'm offered a drink I don't like, a meat dish I'd rather not eat, a cigar I used to enjoy, and an invitation I'm inclined to reject. I want to think about it and decide one way or another, and then reflect on my decision and learn why I decided that way. I want to struggle with my principles every now and then. I want to challenge them and my beliefs in them. *I want to choose to have a choice in every decision I face*, as any creator should. Absolutism is rigidity and rigidity is a constraint on creativity and growth.

In the journey of life, you are not on a rocket ship traveling to the moon, where a two-degree diversion from your course would change your destination. You are on a sailboat through the sea of life, and you need to zigzag your course forward using, and sometimes even challenging, the forces of the wind to reach your destination. How uninteresting life would be without choices to make, challenges to overcome, and mistakes to repent from.

Principles are beliefs, and beliefs can be empowering or limiting. But absolute beliefs are always limiting, regardless of how positive they might seem. Without doubt there is no curiosity, without curiosity there is no creativity, and without creativity there is no potentiality. Yet, we still need core beliefs on which to build our lives, as it's hard to build stable structures on flowing water.

We need principles based on empowering beliefs to help us navigate toward our Purposehood in the sea of distractions with mindless fears and desires, but we should always be grateful to be proven wrong so we may adjust our headings accordingly. It's the true scientific process of believing in your theory and praying for someone to prove it wrong. There is no better gift than discovering an alternative choice, and no better blessing than a person who presents this gift.

Clay was right; it's easier to hold on to your principles 100 percent of the time rather than 98 percent of the time. But, if you want to grow to your full potential, it's better to hold on to your principles 98 percent of the time and struggle with decisions 2 percent of the time.

My friend, you need not be so soft as to be easily bent with a whisper of a wind, nor so hard that you can be easily broken with the force of a storm. Principled-flexibility is how you navigate the sea of change with ease and gratitude and how you create a better future for your Five Extensions of Being.

———

I BREATHE IN PRINCIPLES.
I BREATHE OUT FLEXIBILITY.

Proposition 20:
Leadership

"Everyone is a leader, and their responsibility is to unleash the potentiality of those they influence." – PoET Proposition 20

Humanity has been entrusted by iSH, the universe, and life to lead the exponential evolution and expansion of nature. To prepare it for this leadership position, humans were granted the power of choice. Giving humans this power and burden was risky, but without it, humanity's leadership couldn't have been developed. It was a selfish-altruistic decision that had to be made. During the learning process of humanity's development, life patiently endured the destruction caused to nature as humanity expanded its understanding of nature's laws and fluidity as it constantly changes toward a better state of being.

Now it's becoming clearer that humanity is the expo-agent in charge of spreading life across the universe. As human awareness is expanding, humanity needs to consider how much suffering is acceptable for other creatures to endure in the process. We are the only force in nature that can intentionally create or destroy for all. Our many failed experiments with growth threatened life itself and almost destroyed our precious planet during our years of early learning. But the knowledge we have acquired will give us the ability to repair the damage we carelessly caused and to soon terra-form barren planets in our solar system and beyond.

When you reflect on the process nature used to unleash human-ity's rapidly growing leadership—one that would help life progress toward its Purposehood—you can see three main steps in its own leadership role.

First, nature has been the role model for humanity to learn from and be inspired by as it revealed its secrets and formulas for us to use.

Second, nature provided humans with all the tools they needed to overcome obstacles and grow their own potential, and in doing so, accepted their failing experiments and the suffering caused during development as part of the growth process.

Third, it entangled humanity in nature's Purposehood, which is to rapidly evolve to a better state of being across the expanse of the universe.

The potentiality of everything is to become what they are meant to be, and leave their impact on their extensions in the direction of their Purposehood. The potentiality of *humanity* is to be what it could become and leave its positive impact on life in the direction of the collective Purposehood.

The role of every human is to become a leader of leaders; your leadership role is realized in your extensions of being. It's a selfish-altruistic pursuit as you unleash your own potentiality and receive happiness, success, and fulfillment by becoming a conduit for others to do the same, learning from nature's leadership that produced this amazing humanity. Here's how you can become the best leader humanity needs:

- Become a role model to all your extensions in how you im-prove your physical, mental, emotional, spiritual, and existen-tial well-being and how you conduct yourself with others and nature. What's important in this role is your persistence and the journey itself regardless of success or failure. By sharing with others how you pursue your Purposehood and how you deal with the challenges you face, you share the merits of authenticity, humility, and vulnerability; at the same time, you become an inspiration for others in their journey toward their Purposehood.

- Enable others to unleash their potentiality and pursue their Purposehood by blocking obstacles in their way and giving them the tools they need for their own journeys. Leadership is not a title nor a position; it is a privilege to influence others to become a better version of themselves. In the process, they will positively impact their extensions directly, and the rest of humanity and nature indirectly. Regardless of the position or title you have in your extensions, you can always step up to take a leadership role by inspiring and assisting those around you to find their Purposehood, unleash their potentiality, and embrace practices that help them grow with ease. The least anyone can do is be an essential part of their lives, positively influencing and inspiring in thoughts, words, and actions. People don't need to be told what to do; they need to be *shown* that they can become what they want to be. When you are part of their inclusion or expansion lists, you can become a cheerleader or an eye-opener for their growth.

- Involve everyone in your extensions in the big picture so you all may share a common purpose. Nature freed our ancestors from walking on all fours and constantly looking for food so that we now may look up to the stars and dream of a universe full of life. Similarly, you need to help those in your spheres of influence to free themselves from the distractions of mindless desires and look up at a vision of a better future for all. This should be the mission of any enterprise on this starship Earth. The success of this mission depends on every crew member playing their leadership role in the best possible way and toward the best possible outcome as we, together, increase the probability of that bright possible future.

You ask, "What is the primary role of a business leader?"

The Purposehood of a business is to evolve and expand exponentially. This Purposehood can only be realized by one thing—not strategy, not market conditions, not value propositions, not even capital—only people. Workers with unleashed potentiality will create a winning strategy, develop resilience to market conditions, improve value propositions, and generate capital. Simply put, if one person can change the course of history and the future of humanity, one person can also change the future of a business positively or negatively. Your job as a business leader or as a leader of any kind of organization is to:

- Empower those with a clear Purposehood that is aligned with the Purposehood of your business. Those are the creators who live their own Purposehood at work and feel they are on a mission there.

- Help those coworkers who are misdirected (toward being a consumer or a martyr) in finding the Purposehood of their lives first and then help them align it with the Purposehood of the business or organization.

- Find the destroyers and remove them from the organization.

Once you do so, then you will have an unstoppable business that will evolve and expand exponentially, positively impacting the lives of everyone touched and the future of your organization, humanity, nature, and existence.[83]

You ask, "What is the primary role of a parent or a guardian?"

Every child is born to serve a role that nature, the universe, and existence need of them. In order to grow into their unique roles, they are equipped with many types of intelligences, as explained by Harvard University professor Howard Gardner. The key role of a parent, a guardian, or a teacher is to discover the type of genius intelligence the child possesses and to make sure it is unobstructed and unleashed. Then with role modeling, clear Purposehood, and collaboration, a child will grow to become the creator they are meant to become. Discovering and unleashing your unique genius, or that of a child, a family member, an employee, or friend, is the most impactful action you (or anyone) can do for any organization, humanity, and nature.

My friend, you are a creator among creators. Semideums are not meant to be collectively led like sheep or ordered to perform tasks like dogs. They are meant to be unleashed, like creators, to do the best they can do and become the best they can be. Lead by example and remove the barriers in the way of those you influence. Nourish their potentiality and show them a common vision so you all may create together a better outcome for all.

———

I BREATHE IN LEADERSHIP.
I BREATHE OUT INSPIRATION.

Mysteries of Reality

What is reality?

On one side of this question, you have many scientists who believe that reality is the physical existence and nothing else; the mysteries of our consciousness are merely neurons firing in our brains through causality and chance.

On the opposite side, there are religious dogmas that propagate the concept of a God who created everything in this existence and who keeps a watchful eye on his subjects as he controls causality. Yet, his area of influence has been shrinking as scientists discover how nature actually works, prompting religious believers to reinterpret their scriptures and teachings.

Between these two schools, there are many other interpretations of reality and consciousness, such as holographic construct, pure math, one to many and many to one conscious agents,[84] oneness of existence, duality, dream state, stream of consciousness, or countless understandings of God. Could it be that none of those are right? Or could it be that all of them are right?

At the core of the mystery of reality there are three questions: What is the fabric of existence? Was there a conscious agent that created it? Is there free will?

With the following propositions, I will introduce some clues to possible views that might help you reflect on the nature of reality. Some Purposehooders might find it easier to never bother with such questions and focus instead on choosing empowering beliefs and practices that help them grow with ease. Others might find that their existence is not complete without a theory on reality, or at least the pursuit of such theory.

You need to choose, and I hope the following propositions will help guide your choices.

Proposition 21: Three-Dimensional Views

"Observable existence is projected in three views: a mechanical view, a universal view, and a quantum view." – PoET Proposition 21

Our pursuit of understanding reality has moved over the ages from the realm of imagination to science. Scientists, philosophers, clergy, and mystics have very differing views on reality. The only way we can discover its true nature is by proposing a theory, creating scientific experiments to prove it or disprove it, iterating on the same concept until it's proven correct, or coming up with a new theory and starting the process all over again. This is a methodology that must be used for every claim in order to progress to the next stage of awareness. It's a methodology nature used in developing humanity as an expo-agent, and the dinosaurs were a failed experiment.

It's hard to argue reality with a clergy who only sees it through their own dogmas, or with a mystic who only sees it through their own experience. Reality is best argued with philosophers and scientists. The best modern philosophers are scientists in their process, and the best scientists are philosophers in their visions. Philosophy is interdisciplinary and can be used to create theories of subjects beyond current science.

In other words, we need to look through as many windows as

possible to view what is out there. Science digs deeper into a subject, revealing to a philosopher a new layer of knowledge that expands their awareness of the whole. Some scientists, on the other hand, realize through their specific discoveries a larger truth that leads them into philosophy.

Several prominent computer scientists, including the inventors of the first programmable computer, Konrad Zuse and Edward Fredkin of MIT, believe that biology reduces to chemistry, which reduces to physics, which reduces to the computation of information. They believe that, in principle, there is "a program for a universal computer that computes the evolution of the universe."[85] And just as computers are able to transfer codes with ones and zeros to a 3-D game, so is the information in the universe as it is transferred, through a universal computing process, into the reality we have.

The concept of a computational universe theory, which needed a proof of the conservation of information, was contradicted by Stephen Hawking's black hole theory, since information disappears into a black hole. However, Hawking was proven wrong by Professors Leonard Susskind and Nobel laureate Gerard Hoof when they introduced the holographic principle to prove that there's no loss of information inside a black hole, and that the most basic law of physics, which implies that information is conserved, still stands.

What kind of a program would it take to run a vast simulation like the universe? Professor Jurgen Schmidhuber argues that, like a complicated fractal image, it basically could be only a line or two of code. Another way to imagine this program is to imagine a code that uses machine learning—a self-learning process similar to how the human brain works. The artificial intelligence (AI) code learns from experience and evolves and expands its knowledge exponentially in a process that aims to select the optimal outcome from all possible outcomes in order to solve a challenge.

"Go" is a 3,000-year-old abstract strategy board game that has more possible moves than there are particles in the universe. In March 2016, Google's AI—AlphaGo—beat one of the best Go players in the world, Lee Se-dol, using its sophisticated methodology. A year later, it won three games in a match against the world's champion, Ke Jie, who is considered to be one of the greatest Go players in history. Ke Jie stated afterward, "Last year, it was still quite human-like when it played, but this year, it became like a god of Go."[86] In 2019, Lee Se-dol decided to retire because, as he put it, AI "cannot be defeated."

Could the universe, life, and we ourselves be a product of an existential intelligence (EI) program that has been running a universe intelligence (UI) for the past 13.8 billion years? Or is the UI merely a user interface into existence? Are you a human intelligence (HI) subroutine within the EI?

Coding, which utilizes a language that is easily accessible to everyone, is nothing short of the power of creation itself as talented coders can take a creative idea and turn it into a reality in a very short time. It's as easy as—or even easier—than learning a new language. And just like a book communicates abstract thoughts or feelings into words using the construct of letters, grammar, and syntax, programs communicate creative visions into a composite of sounds, pictures, and data using a language with two numbers— one and zero.

Isn't it fascinating that the advancements of today, which are exponentially growing into the future, are due to two digits (1 and 0)? What seemed like a world moving toward complication, chaos, or entropy before computers is actually being brought into order with the power of two states: the state of oneness and the state of nothingness.

At the core of everything, however, there is one state, one phenomenon that has two sides, like a coin with two faces or a word with two letters. Could this reality be a result of a two-letter code that triggered the exponential evolution and expansion of this universe? Is the two-letter code, BE? Is the EI program in a constant state of BEing? To be or not to be indeed is the question.

As scientists reverse-engineer creation, programming allows us to code new creations. But at the core of all our creations, there are always nature's laws that we don't seem to be able to bend. Our digital creations are growing so exponentially that soon they will be indistinguishable from what we perceive as real. But reality itself is becoming questionable as we uncover the mysteries of existence. Reality is certainly never what we think it is, and it reveals its true nature to us in stages—like a book revealing itself with every turn of a page, and we are like children learning to read it. The more letters we learn, the more vocabulary and grammar rules we comprehend, and the clearer the book becomes. Reality is the ultimate book of existence, and we are still in the first chapter.

We have already discovered three faces to what seems real, and we can't imagine what will be revealed next. The universe was a clock for the level of knowledge developed by Newton. Then, with Einstein, it became a fabric of spacetime governed by the speed of light. Quantum mechanics changed that view to the magical properties of subatomic particles, communicating faster than the speed of light with entanglement, passing through barriers with tunneling, or behaving based on belief or measurement with the observer effect. As computers give us a different view on creation, some scientists, like those I mentioned among others, are further contemplating the idea that the essence of reality is basically information processed through an existential computer. Others are arguing that the universe is merely a mathematical abstract construct.[87] And some recently started scientifically exploring the mystic dimension of consciousness as a base for reality.

You ask, "Why is it important to identify reality?"

My friend, a creator needs a construct to create with and within. If you are creating a novel, you need the construct of language; if you are writing a song, you need the language of music. To create reality, you need to understand what that is, and to most seekers nowadays, reality is what each sees through the window of their beliefs. But just like a window from your living room shows a framed, comforting view of what is out there, opening other windows in the solid walls of limiting beliefs will expand your view of the reality outside your framed view.

Expanded awareness allows us to view events through more windows. The various views don't change events, but they surely change our perception of them. It's like filming a documentary where people seem to be acting as they wish, but in the background, there are producers, directors, editors, and camera operators who are deciding what will go into the film. Still, the entire crew is merely following the script of the documentary as envisioned by the creator.

Is reality the events being filmed, the selected scenes, or the script? Does it even matter to you if you never watch it? Does reality have to be only one aspect? Is the reality of that email you just sent the meaning you conveyed, the words you typed, the program you used, the device that housed the program, the particles the device is made of, or the code that creates the program?

Reality seems to be multilayered, and the more awareness you have of its various layers, the more accurate your conclusions are, and the more tools you have to create the future.

You ask, "What views should I consider for a better understanding of reality and events?"

My friend, there are three spatial coordinates (x, y, z) needed to determine the position of an element in spacetime in addition to time. The least we can do in this spacetime construct is to use those as guidance to consider the three views of reality I previously shared with you.

In the *mechanical view* of reality, we consider the short-term of a dual reality driven by causes and effects, actions and reactions, positives and negatives, and so on. In this view, we consider internal beliefs and habits developed within ourselves to unconsciously respond to events, intentionally or unintentionally. We also consider desired immediate and short-term effects such as survival in a case of imminent danger or accomplishing a task, or an objective like building a house. In this view, we desire to be positively reactive, consciously and unconsciously.

In the *universal view* of reality, we consider the long-term outcome of events where the line between past and future is blurry, and the present seems like an arbitrary reference point in that timeline. In this view, we desire to be positively reflective with detachment from what happened and could happen. We consider a longer timeframe into the past that was and the future that could be.

In the *quantum view* of reality, we look into the most possible details of what happened and the various outcomes the event inspired if we are looking through the past to present timeframe. If we are looking into the present to future, we imagine all the possibilities an event could potentially create. We want a detailed view of the impact of a past event on aspects beyond the obvious, and we want to intentionally create a positive future by considering an improvement we can introduce.

Looking through the prism of each of these three views is like you being asked the simple question, "Where are you from?" In the mechanical aspect, you consider the obvious and you name a country or a city where you are living or where you were born. Yet, when you reflect on the question, you notice that your life has taken you to various places, so the better answer through a universal view might be "Earth." Still, as you think further, you realize that where you are from is not just a place, but also people, food, smells, events, thoughts, and emotions that shaped your belonging. You also realize, in this quantum view, that you are made of particles that came from exploding stars from all over the cosmos, and you answer with confidence: "The universe." All of these answers are correct individually, but more complete collectively.

Consider another example of an event like an emotional breakup or a divorce. In the mechanical view, you would look at the positives in this negative situation, such as the end of a painful relationship and a chance for each to move on with their life. Then, you try to add positive actions to improve a bad situation. You would look at the details of how to split assets, manage custody, and plan the next phase of your life.

In a universal view, you would expand the timeframe and space to consider major factors that led to the good and bad times in the relationship, and you imagine how, many years from now, everything and everyone will be all right. Your reflection will help you extract lessons to improve future responses to other events while feeling at ease that ultimately things will be better for all.

In the quantum view, you would consider the future impact this breakup would have on each person involved, extended families, common friends, your work, and the pet you both love, and for each, you try to do something to increase the probability of a positive outcome while decreasing the negative one.

Any one view, even if correct, wouldn't give you a complete understanding, but having at least these three views will expand your awareness. In one, you are in the event looking around, in the second, you are above the event looking down, and in the third, you are breaking the event into many smaller events and considering its widespread influence.

Here's another example: World War I was directly instigated in 1914 by one event, the assassination of Archduke Franz Ferdinand. This assassination was committed by a 19-year-old man. One action of one man ignited a war that lasted for four years and claimed 20 million lives. Reading the historical accounts of how this event unfolded gives you a mechanical view of the devastation it caused, and how the winning allied powers reshaped the world map at the time and hoped for this monstrous war to be, as President Woodrow Wilson said, "a war to end all wars," to "make the world safe for democracy."

However, when you look at the event with the universal view, you will always discover that the actual impact on the future wasn't the same as the one felt by the participants at the time. World War I ended with a humiliated, unstable Germany having to pay heavy reparations, which led to the rise of the Nazi Party and World War II in 1939. This conflict was even more devastating, with over 50 million people killed.

As you widen the view, you realize that most of the advancements and many of the troubles we currently have in this world are a result of World War I. The conflict in the Middle East today is a result of the redrawn map of the region, but also the advancement in transportation and communications that reshaped the world is the result of World War I. This is definitely a different view from those who were suffering during the war itself.

A quantum view would consider the smaller details of the event and view their impact. Each individual life of those who lived under the Ottoman Empire changed forever, and so did the lives of their descendants. Many migrants from the Middle East moved to the Americas, their descendants contributed to the development of new countries, and with that, changed their futures. This is a different view than the other two views.

In the first case, you mainly see the impact of opposing forces in actions, along with counter-actions—positives, and negatives. In this situation you focus, as you should, on having a positive impact on current events as much as possible. However, once you expand a universal view wide enough with a longer timeframe, you will realize that the outcome is always net positive as life moves toward a better state of being. And if you consider the quantum view with the impact on every person involved, you would realize that any little action is still vibrating through existence and influencing events near and far.

My friend, in all views of reality it's comforting to know that *everything that exists has the existential purpose to evolve and expand exponentially toward a better state of being.*

———

I BREATHE IN VIEWS.
I BREATHE OUT REALITY.

Proposition 22: The Balance of Opposites

"Positives and negatives are the nature of creation. When you see the negative aspects of something positive and the positive aspects of something negative, then you will have a balanced view. A balanced view will help you make better decisions in the present, heal the wounds of the past, and accept future outcomes with ease." – PoET Proposition 22

From iSH, the mystery beyond, came a magnificent existence that is full of opposites, contradictions, and forces that interact to attract and repel. Even the conceptual design of this universe is contradictory; on one hand, it's extremely complex, and yet on the other, extremely simple. When we look more closely, we see that simple things are made of complex parts, and complex things are made of simple parts.

In the simplicity of a flower, there are many complex parts and interactions down to every one of its atoms, yet at its core, is a field of energy made of vibrations and simple equations. Scientists believe that at the core of all complex interactions in the universe are four fundamental forces: gravitational, electromagnetic, strong nuclear, and weak nuclear. With the recent awareness that the expansion of the universe is accelerating, some scientists are speculating that there is a fifth force, *quintessence*, which is a form of an unknown energy called *dark energy*. Others have proposed *protophobic force* (meaning proton-ignoring) as a fundamental force to explain additional observations that do not fit existing theories. Are there other fundamental forces that shape our existence waiting to be discovered?

These forces of an existence made of opposites seem to have been around since the Big Bang wove them into the fabric of the universe. And just like a road is made of straightaways, ups, and downs, the smallest constituent unit of matter, the atom, is made of neutral, positive, and negative subatomic particles. Each element plays a crucial role. Without it, there would not be matter in the universe, and you would not exist.

Everywhere we look we see positive and negative charges dancing together to keep the universe moving. Positives and negatives, actions and reactions are intertwined in the nature of creation as they emerge at the same time—just like the meaning of "what it is" is not clear without also understanding "what it is not."

My friend, at the essence of every event in your life there are positives and negatives generated at the same time. It's important, for your own balanced view and for a life of ease, to see the negatives in every positive event and the positives in every negative event. Looking for the positives in a negative event that occurred in your life is not an act of optimism or positivity, but an act of realism and awareness. That's because *not* seeing the inherited positiveness in such events is not objective, and it's due to limiting beliefs or misdirected unconsciousness. When you are able to look at past events in the rearview mirror while you are moving forward toward your positive destination, you will easily realize that this point of time, as well as the road leading to your destination, is not possible without that negative event.

It's important to clear your past events from toxic negativity by realizing the positiveness in those negative events, so your roots may find empowering nourishment in the soil of your past. What is more important and effective is finding the innate positiveness in negative events as they occur. If you do that, you will not only eliminate toxicity, but also increase probabilities of positive outcomes. Armed with a balanced view and a positive attitude, you can consider corrective actions to the negativities to increase the chances of a better outcome.

How many of our failing relationships are built on positive first impressions made by our misdirected subconscious mind, without pausing to consider the opposite view? Aren't many of our regrets the result of a one-sided consideration? We regret a negative outcome of what we totally believed to be a positive opportunity, and even more so, we regret missing out on a positive outcome because we only saw negatives. But when we pause to consider the positives and negatives and make a balanced decision, regrets of the outcome become lessons to improve our evaluation process for the future.

You ask, "Is it possible to be in total harmony with the movement of the universe instead of zigzagging with a positive tension?"

A human is not a tree or a bird born to sync perfectly with the vibration of life and the universe. Humans are made of opposite forces and will always live in contradictions, zigzagging between positivity and negativity, mindfulness and mindlessness, altruism and selfishness, gratitude and rejection, ease and suffering, abundance and scarcity. However, as a creator of your intentions, you can always tip the scale one way or the other for a net positive or a net negative.

These opposing forces are there to be celebrated as the forces of growth, as long as you are aware of their impact and ready to shift from one to the other before you are totally consumed by one of them. You can't be mindful without relegating mundane actions to mindlessness, nor altruist without taking care of yourself, nor grateful without rejecting injustices inflected on others, nor live with ease without suffering from a misdirection in order to repent and correct, nor live with abundance without knowing how scarcity feels. If you have never experienced the opposite, how would you know that what you are experiencing is even positive?

You ask, "If positive and negative forces balance each other, how could there be a movement toward a better state of being?"

Newton's first law of motion states that every object will remain at rest or in uniform motion in a straight line, unless compelled to change its state by the action of an external force. There seem to be two forces creating that accelerated movement in existence toward exponential evolution and expansion: a pulling force and a conversion force. One is linear, the other exponential. One pulls and the other pushes this existence to a better state of being.

My friend, if you have entered the address of your destination into your GPS, then you won't be lost in detours. On the contrary, every detour will expand your awareness of yourself and your environment, inwardly and outwardly.

There is always a salvation from a life of rejection, suffering, and scarcity, as long as vacuum is not your final chosen destination. It all starts with finding your Purposehood Guiding Star and entering that address into the GPS of your life.

Regardless of your direction, humanity, life, and the universe will always move forward. Nevertheless, you need to choose for yourself which role you want to play, the forces with which you want to interact, and the consequences with which you are ready to live.

I BREATHE IN BALANCE.
I BREATHE OUT POSITIVITY.

Proposition 23: Purposehood Pulling Force

"Everything in existence is being pulled toward a better existential state of being." – PoET Proposition 23

In 1928, physicist Paul Dirac developed an equation that reconciled Einstein's theory of relativity and quantum mechanics and won him a Nobel Prize. It was a breakthrough except for one dilemma: the equation predicted the existence of something that was never imagined before, an *antimatter*. It's like having positive and negative solutions to the square root of 4, which could be either +2 or -2, or a mirror image to every particle in the universe. The equation predicted the existence of exact replicas of matter with an opposite charge in which an electron, which has a negative charge in matter, would be positively charged in an anti-electron (a positron), and a positively charged proton in matter would be negatively charged in an antiproton. Also, in a deeper view, the quarks within a proton would have the reverse charges in the antiquarks, and in a higher view, an atom would have an anti-atom. Antimatter was proven true in 1932 when physicist Carl Anderson was able to photograph a positron in a cloud chamber.

Since matter and antimatter are of opposite charges, the moment they interact, they annihilate one another. This presented an existential mystery since at the Big Bang, energy produced an equal amount of matter and antimatter, so why do we even exist at all? All matter and antimatter should have been annihilated, or there should have been an equal number of stars and planets in an anti-universe that would have been formed from the antimatter. But that's not the case, as we are made of matter and we do see matter in the whole observable universe with little antimatter detected. There must have somehow been a tiny imbalance in favor of matter that left enough to form the universe, life, and us. Scientists have even calculated the imbalance needed to create everything we see in the universe today. For every one billion antiprotons, there must have been a billion plus one protons.

We are all a product of this tiny positive imbalance toward matter in this mystery of creation. There are currently several other imaginative hypotheses and major experiments being conducted around the world to solve the puzzle of how this extra matter survived the annihilation, or was additionally created, and I am sure humanity will find an answer soon. And once we know the how, I'm sure we would continue searching for an answer to why matter has been favored in this observable universe.

You ask, "Why do you think there is matter instead of nothing?"

My friend, to answer "why" questions it helps to believe there is a purpose to existence. I am perplexed by some intelligent people and scientists who can clearly see the purpose of a bee or a tree in its drive to survive and reproduce, contributing selfish-altruistically to the ecosystem within the species itself and the larger surrounding environment, and based on that purpose, scientists are able to establish accurate understandings and predictions of the animal or plant behavior. Yet, when it comes to humans and the universe, they seem unable to find a purpose for their existence.

But with PoET, any person can clearly understand everything in existence has an existential purpose, to evolve and expand exponentially, and that they are pulled by this existential force toward a better state of being.

Imagine this pulling force as the gravitational pull of a Purposehood Guiding Star toward exponential evolution and expansion. It's the same invisible force that pulls a bee or a colony of ants toward the desire to evolve and expand through the basic urges of survival and reproduction, and a desire to exponentially expand if not impeded by environmental constraints.

This same Purposehood pulling force is what is pulling individuals, humanity, and the universe itself, to evolve and expand exponentially. We can apply the laws of physics from studying one natural phenomenon to the study of others. Therefore, we also can presume that things in existence that don't seem to us to have a clear existential purpose would nonetheless have the same Purposehood of an exponentially evolving and expanding universe, and the existential desire that we see in nature to do the same.

You ask, "Is there a Purposehood dialectic in existence?"

My friend, just as with Newton's third law, which states that for every action, there is an equal and opposite reaction, we can assume that any positive or negative occurrence will always produce an equal and opposite occurrence. However, just as the transformation of energy at the Big Bang produced an equal and opposite matter-antimatter, somehow iSH, existence, or whatever universal law there is, favored the emergence of matter in that collision. This shows that higher positive occurrences are always the result of the collision of initial opposing occurrences.

There is an existential force that pulls the universe toward the Purposehood of an exponential evolution and expansion. This subtle but powerful force pulls everything toward a more evolved and expanded higher positive state, which we can term *a better state of being*. Regardless of the positive or negative charge of any occurrence, an opposite charged occurrence emerges immediately, and the collision of the two occurrences always results in a higher positive state due to Purposehood's pulling force. As soon as that

PURPOSEHOOD PULLING FORCE

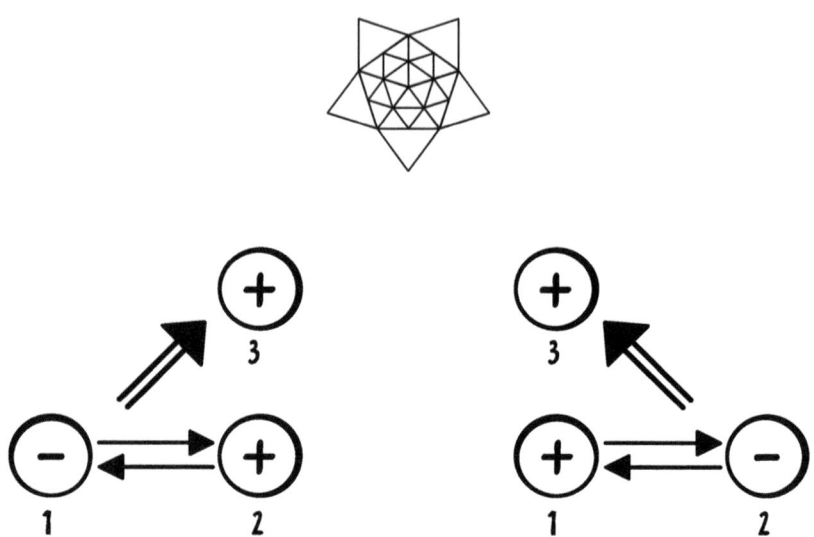

happens, an opposite negative occurrence will emerge, and the process continues forward toward the universal Purposehood.

Philosophers since Heraclitus have discussed this natural phenomenon as opposites emerge, leading to a higher state. Through the Purposehood dialectic, we now can understand why this happens and we can define that state more precisely. It happens because of a universal Purposehood that pulls the universe and everything in it toward the *final destination*. The higher state resulting from this process will have the three characteristics of *exponentiality, evolution,* and *expansion*. This is why we always see progress accelerating linearly or disruptively with time.

> You ask, "Wouldn't all occurrences then be linked together which will cause only negative occurrences to emerge to counter the newly formed positive ones?"

My friend, they are connected and not connected at the same time. In one view of existence, everything is connected and the universe is woven from one thread or exists in one block. But even the mysterious creation of matter and antimatter from nothing is a result of energy transformation. A human's ability to transform mere thoughts into a form of reality, combined with the directional choice, allows negative occurrences to emerge even without a direct cause or a previous occurrence. Yet still, that negative occurrence would necessitate an anti-occurrence, and the process continues toward a better state of being.

You ask, "How do we define the positive or negative charges in occurrences in our lives?"

A positive occurrence is whatever moves you to evolve and expand exponentially in the direction of your Purposehood. A negative occurrence is whatever causes you to devolve and contract or slow down your progress toward your Purposehood. You can apply this definition even beyond yourself to all occurrences in family, business, society, politics, communities, and nature.

For example, the future of societies is moving in the direction of more integration, connectivity, and the removal of obstacles that limit humans from developing their potentialities. This future is in the direction of Purposehood, as it would lead humanity toward exponential evolution and expansion. A negative occurrence in politics would be the election of an official whose views are anchored in the past and who is elected by a wave of citizens who are not at ease with the forward direction of a society.

Yet, a Purposehooder would be at ease with such a situation, knowing that this negative occurrence would necessitate the emergence of a positive one, which would ultimately lead to a positive outcome regardless of how long or how much struggle it would take. A Purposehooder would not dwell on the negativity of the occurrence, but rather focus their energy on adding probability to the best possible positive outcome without being attached to that specific outcome.

This forward movement toward a better state of being negates the idea that history repeats itself, as even what seems like a recurrence is merely a rotation in a higher space in a spiral move forward. This is just like the rotation of the Earth around the sun, which seems to reoccur in the same orbit, but actually is moving in a spiral movement in coordination with the sun's forward path through space. Social reoccurrences like nationalism might have the same labels, but they are never exactly the same. They, in turn, create new occurrences of multiculturalism as societies move toward one humanity on one Earth, and ultimately to one consciousness in one universe.

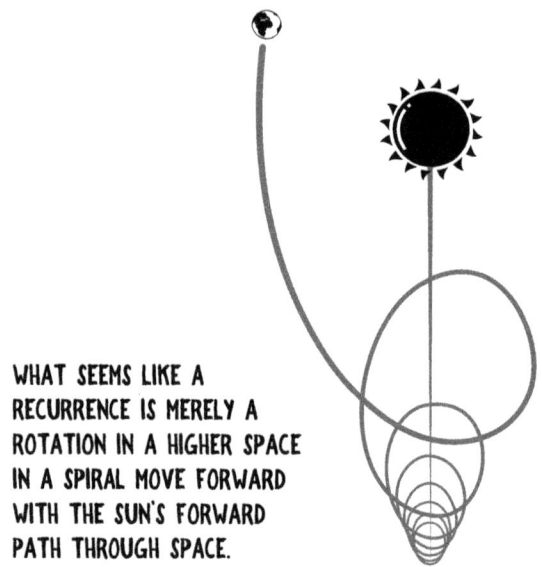

WHAT SEEMS LIKE A RECURRENCE IS MERELY A ROTATION IN A HIGHER SPACE IN A SPIRAL MOVE FORWARD WITH THE SUN'S FORWARD PATH THROUGH SPACE.

You ask, "Will an individual's state of being always be better?"

My friend, the universe's movement toward its Purposehood seems orderly yet unpredictable in a mechanical view, uniform in a quantum view, and intentional in a universal view. The intentionality of the persistent movement of the universe toward its Purposehood also seems to drive all of its elements to fulfill the roles they are meant to play. Every action contributes to the universe's orderly chaos, uniformity, and intentionality at the same time.

The Purposehood pulling force of existence is clearly driving the universe to exponentially evolve and expand in its journey toward its Purposehood, even if we might not notice its direct impact on us (just as an ant might not notice the impact of the gravitational pull of the sun on it). But since the universe is being pulled toward its Purposehood, you can rest assured that everything within it is being pulled by the same force regardless of whether you can detect it. Those who realize this force and harmonize their Purposehood, thoughts, words, and actions with it will grow to a better state of being with ease and gratitude. Those who are not in harmony with that existential pull force will contract with suffering and rejection.

Imagine our universe as a spaceship that is being pulled by the gravitational force of its Purposehood Guiding Star. It holds some neutral passengers who are split between those acting either as a balancing weight, like the ones needed on flights, and those who are weighing the flight down. Among the rest of the passengers, half are trying to slow the ship down, and the other half are trying to accelerate it. Still, half of those who want to slow it down are doing so with malicious intentions to render it stranded in space, while the other half are doing so out of concern for everyone's well-being, as they believe a slower journey is safer.

On the side of acceleration, half of those passengers are doing so with the negative intention to crash the ship with everyone onboard, and the other half want to make the trip faster so everyone could enjoy the destination sooner.

The Purposehood dialectic predicts that on one level the forces of safety would eventually result in a safer journey, and the forces of acceleration would eventually result in a faster journey.

While the spaceship never alters course as it's being drawn by the pulling force of its Purposehood Guiding Star, the opposing forces within continue to exponentially evolve and expand it.

Those passengers with negative intentions will have a journey of scarcity, suffering, and rejection, filled with stress, anxiety, and regrets. Those who believe that the spaceship will ultimately reach its destination soundly, and are willing to contribute their thoughts, words, and actions to increase the probability of achieving that mission regardless of the role they play, will journey with gratitude, ease, and abundance as they are drawn by the Purposehood Guiding Star's pulling force.

By being in harmony with the universe and nature, a Purposehooder has no regrets in a past that is the foundation of a better state of being, no stress in a present that increases the probability of a better state of being, and no anxiety knowing that all forces of existence are interacting to create a better future for all. A Purposehooder is grateful when their expectations are realized and patient when they are not.

There will always be opposing occurrences in your life with positive and negative forces. Even though they might seem equally powerful, and sometimes it feels like what you perceive as negative is overwhelming, everything will be all right as long as you are in harmony with the universal Purposehood. Its pulling force will always ensure that the winning internal force is the one that leads to a better state for all your Five Extensions of Being. When you recognize this pulling force, you will realize that even chance is purposeful.

———

I BREATHE IN PURPOSEHOOD.
I BREATHE OUT EASE.

Proposition 24: Neutral Conversion Force

"Humanity's unleashed potentiality is an exponential driving force toward a better state of being." – PoET Proposition 24

Existence is amazing. It seems to hide all its mysteries in plain sight. It's as if the creating force wants us to discover all its secrets and to use this knowledge to create tools to accomplish its mission. All the science we have today are discoveries of processes of nature. All technologies and advancements we have developed are tools to expedite the evolution and expansion of life. Even the surviving ancient philosophical and mystical thoughts have found parallels in the physical nature, and new metaphysical concepts are being generated from new discoveries. Quantum mechanics seemed to inspire some mystics and philosophers to become scientists and some scientists to become philosophers and mystics.

One of the intriguing discoveries in the early twentieth century was a neutral subatomic particle in the nuclei of atoms called a neutron. Neutrons are made of three quarks: one with a $+\frac{2}{3}$ charge and two with $-\frac{1}{3}$ charges resulting in a neutral zero charge. Even though the neutrons don't affect the chemical property of an atom, they are crucial for its stability. Neutrons bond with positive proton in the nucleus, forming together nearly the total mass of an atom, since the negative electrons and other nuclear binding forces are almost negligible. The contribution to the mass of the atom by neutron is important in motion, since Newton's second law states that a force acting on an object is equal to the mass of an object times its acceleration.

On the journey toward Purposehood, it is important to have alliances and bond with neutral masses. As more people discover their Purposehood in the search for meaning, happiness, success, and fulfillment, this positive mass of Purposehooders will contribute to the forces that exponentially drive all humanity toward its Purposehood.

But until every human is a Purposehooder, you need to gain the support of the neutral masses to ensure they are attracted to bond with the positive side. How many positively charged activists, scientists, explorers, artists, teachers, or parents wouldn't have been able to pursue their mission and make a difference in the world if it wasn't for the support of their family and friends who supported them even without fully believing in their causes? And, how many positive forces in society have failed because they couldn't bring the neutral masses to join their cause?

A neutral mass can add to negative forces or become an extra weight dragging progress down; but when neutral masses are on the side of positivity, then they can be a powerful force toward exponential progress.

A neutron can be converted to a positive proton by ejecting a negative electron and an electron antineutrino. This is another force that moves everything to a higher state of existence and a better state of being. It's the force of conversion that moves neutrals from zero to plus one.

There is another intriguing hypothesis about the reason we have matter in the universe instead of nothing. This one posits that as matter and antimatter canceled each other after the Big Bang, enough neutrinos and antineutrinos were left over to coalesce into stars, planets and, ultimately, life. Physicists are developing experiments to examine this hypothesis.

And just like that, when you help a person to discover their Purposehood, not only will they become a positive force changing the properties of their life, but they also become an added positive force to your own journey, making it easier for both of you to succeed in your missions. This expanded positive force could be your family, your business, or your communities as they maximize the force of the organization by unleashing the positive forces of potentiality in each member.

Your responsibility as a Purposehooder is to ensure that neutral people are at least attracted to your desired positive outcome until they naturally decay into positivity, just like a neutron decays into a proton in a neutron beta decay. You attract those people by being a leader and a role model. Preaching without role modeling is not effective in turning neutrality into positivity. iSH and existence have given us a positive pulling force to counter negativity, but we are tasked with and capable of adding another force by guiding neutrals to the path of clarity.

With the Purposehood pulling force and the neutral conversion force, you will have two positive forces pulling and pushing you *toward* your Purposehood against every negative force taking you *away* from your Purposehood. This 2:1 ratio is what ensures that you, humanity, life, and the universe are moving toward a better state of being.

Just like the flux of existence transitions from one state to another, oscillating between opposite states like the day and night transition into each other, you will never be left hanging long in a state of suffering. Live with ease knowing that as long as you are in harmony with existence, you will always move forward to a better state than the one before, and that the existence of abundance will always have plenty to satisfy your desires.

Haven't you found yourself, at times, lonely only to soon find belonging? Weren't you, at times, lost only to soon find guidance? And weren't you, at times, in need only to soon find satisfaction?

My friend, be the belonging for the lonely, be the guidance to the lost, be the provider for a person in need, and spread gratefulness to everyone and everything in your extensions of being. This is how your life will be at ease and suffering will cease, so you may be known as a positive force of good in this existence. Remember that with every negative there are two positives, one existential and one as a result of your positive deeds. So, rest, reflect, and positively recharge your existential desire to create a better world for all.

You ask, "How will these last three propositions help me with my life?"

When you realize that positives and negatives are the nature of a balanced existence, you will see every past negative event with a balanced view as you discover the positive side of it. And when you realize that existence is determined to pull you gently toward your Purposehood if you direct yourself toward it, then you can live with ease knowing the journey will be filled with happiness, success, and fulfillment. And finally, when you realize that you hold the power of adding another force to propel your forward movement, then you will become a role model leader, attracting and converting people in your extensions of being toward a common Purposehood journey.

Once you understand these last three propositions, you will also reflect on the past without regrets, look toward the future without anxiety, and live in the present without stress. You will know that for every negative there are two positives, and your intentional actions will create a better future for yourself, family, work, community, and nature. They will be your alliances in a life of gratitude, ease, and abundance.

———

I BREATHE IN OTHERS.
I BREATHE OUT BELONGING.

Proposition 25: Oneness

"There are many layers to reality, and the essence of reality is oneness of existence." – PoET Proposition 25

Nature is wondrous. What we see is never the full story. With the invention of the microscope, we observed a whole layer of nature that was hiding in plain sight. The better our microscopes became, the more we were able to look into the nature of existence and discover yet more layers, down to atoms. At some point, we couldn't see any further with our current technology, but we could theorize and later prove the presence of elementary particles. With the invention of telescopes, we observed other layers of existence above us that we couldn't imagine by just looking with our naked eyes. We first realized that our Earth is not the center of the universe but merely one of several planets orbiting the sun. Soon, we realized that this solar system is just a tiny part of a galaxy filled with hundreds of billions of stars. Then, we learned that our galaxy is only a smaller one among trillions of galaxies in the observable universe containing more stars than all the grains of sand on Earth. From there, we have been theorizing about a multiverse system with yet other countless universes.

This vast existence and layers of reality waiting to be discovered seem to have similarities, as if existence doesn't like to invent new laws if not absolutely needed, nor create unique rules for every system within the universe, opting instead for repeating designs and processes. We see the same patterns and laws from the atomic level to the universal scale, which is extremely helpful for humanity to unlock the mysteries of existence. It might be that all the mysteries of existence are contained within us if we look inward with expanded awareness.

In nature and the universe are the secrets to understanding the mysteries of our individual physical, mental, emotional, spiritual, and existential presence. It seems like existence, or iSH, is efficient, utilizing the least energy for the optimal outcome. Some scientists infer flaws in the purpose of a designing force or the nonexistence of purpose in nature because of imperfections of evolution.[88] But nature, or any higher system, is not aiming for perfection at any cost, it is aiming for *optimization* at the least cost, just like any good engineer.

Humanity's awareness of the layers of reality in the physical dimension of existence has been evolving and expanding exponentially. We have been peeling the layers of physical reality away from the pure imagination of the ancients in their religious beliefs. As we incorporated scientific methodologies of observation and experimentation, we discovered layers of matter, biology, chemistry, and physics in its mechanical, universal, and quantum forms. With the recent information revolution, we have developed a deeper understanding of the information structure of existence.

Certain mystics still see existence as one flow of energy. Some scientists see, at the core of reality, an ocean of quantum waves or vibrating strings that compose the universal symphony, while others see abstract math and numbers.

An ancient Sufi master claimed that the whole existence is simply a dot, a singularity point, where *pi* hides in the ratio of the circumference and diameter, and within its infinite non-repeating pattern there lies every possible number combination, mapping everything in our universe. Another believed iSH is the dot at the center of the circle of existence, which is created with a radius of 1. This oneness of existence is always circulating around the dot between (+1) and (-1), positive and negative, yet it couldn't have been realized without the permanence of that dot in an everlasting dance between the center and the circumference: the zero and one.

However, as the circumference of our awareness circle expands with each scientifically uncovered layer, so does the area of the unknown we touch. For some, it is exciting to have so much more to discover, but for others, it is frustrating to be further away from a full understanding of existence. But even if we discover all the layers of the physical existence, could there still be other dimensions to existence? Could consciousness be another dimension? Or maybe reality, in all its layers, is based on an existential purpose intended by iSH, just like the reality of your action is a result of your intention. Doesn't everything you create start with a purpose for your creation?

You ask, "Aren't these layers manifestations of one reality, or is each structure an independent reality?"

My friend, is a computer hardware or software? And is the software the user interface, the various programs running in the background, or the code? And is the code the syntax or the binary 1 and 0? And is the hardware the various parts or the atoms they are made of? And is the atom a particle or a wave?

Reality doesn't have to fit into our understanding. On the contrary, our understanding needs to evolve and expand to comprehend the many faces of reality.

Every time humanity arrogantly concludes that we have discovered the true face of reality, existence hints to yet another layer to keep us evolving and expanding. Without a mystery to be solved, will there be a purpose to humanity's existence? But even with many faces, the dice is one and so is reality, and regardless of the dimension you examine, there is one persistent property to existence—oneness.

There is oneness in the origination of existence and oneness in connectedness in all its layers. Could it be that there was one code, one formula, one will, one consciousness, one Purposehood, one beginning, one singularity point that started the whole of existence? Could it be that all there is today is entangled in a dimension of reality? And when it comes to connectedness, existence seems to be linked through causality, spacetime, or vibration.

Just like a drop of water is one with the glacier, one with the river, one with the ocean, one with the cloud, one with the Earth, and one with the creature that drinks it, you are also an example of oneness and connectedness. There is only one of you in this whole vast universe, and you are one with the universe. Your body is made of particles generated from colliding galaxies, galactic winds, and exploding stars, and you won't survive if you don't constantly renew your cells with this cosmic dust that continuously connects you with all of existence.

You are also one with life as, daily, you exchange particles of your body with the rest of nature. What you eat, drink, and breathe become you, and what was part of you becomes part of other creatures and nature in one process of constant exchange that applies to the whole universe. Through this state of flux, you remain connected with Earth and all its creatures as you replace all your body parts several times during your lifetime (except for some brain cells). Wouldn't it be fascinating to read the life story of an electron as it travels through billions of years with countless short stories, each with their own beginning and end, without realizing that they are all merely chapters in one book?

You are also one with humanity, not only through DNA, but also through constant exchanges of ideas, words, and actions. On one hand, you are in a state of flux, always changing; on the other hand, the particles you are made of would probably last as long as the universe itself. Just like everything existing before you and around you make you, you are part of what makes them and everything that will be in the future. In the flux state, you are never really whole, and you have, at every second, the choice to decide who you are at that moment and who you want to become. You are one with existence, and by simply changing yourself, you can change existence itself.

Existence is a symphony and you are a composer. Your notes will not only compose the sonata of your life, but also all there is and all that will be. You are as important to this symphony as everyone else, and everyone else is as important as you are. You have the power, as long as you're still breathing, to add the most beautiful notes ever composed to this cosmic symphony. The notes left by those who passed before you are being played right now—vibrating throughout existence. Nothing is lost, negative notes are being countered, and the music always gets better.

In this one existence, you are an intentional creator, and by being the change you want to see in the world, you will undoubtedly impact your family, your coworkers, your communities, and the nature you are one with. Realizing the oneness of existence will expand your Five Extensions of Being, where humanity becomes your family, all creatures become your coworkers in the business of improving life for all, nature becomes your community, and the whole Earth becomes your fifth extension. For some, family is all creatures, coworkers are all the forces of nature, communities are our galaxy, and nature is the universe. And for a few among us, there is only iSH and everything else is merely iSH's reflection.

So my friend, shed all the labels of yesterday and choose today who to become tomorrow, as you are not the same person that was. Hold on to a Purposehood that pulls you through life's challenges and be the universe you want to create.

———

I BREATHE IN MANY.
I BREATHE OUT ONENESS.

Proposition 26:
Timeless-Cloud

"While everything is possible, an efficient existence creates only what is optimal for its Purposehood." – PoET Proposition 26

Multiverse is not a new concept of quantum mechanics. It is a product of humankind's limitless creativity, combined with the essential desires to explore beyond the obvious and to belong to a higher existence—one that created works of literature, philosophy, religious beliefs, music, and art with imaginary creatures, parallel worlds, other dimensions, and gods. Every limit imposed is countered by an urge of exploration beyond the artificial wall of limitations.

Scientists resisted those temptations until the discovery of quantum magical properties, which made it possible for some of them to venture beyond the limits of experimental science. The quantum equations used by scientists and engineers to build the technology of today and tomorrow predict (in some interpretations) other dimensions—perhaps 11—and the possibility of the existence of parallel universes. This is where, for example, every choice not made in this universe would continue in its own timeline.

All the information of a system is there in its wave function until it collapses with observation in what's called *superposition* in quantum mechanics. However, information is always preserved. Some argue that if existence is information with infinite storage and processing capabilities, then there is no reason why all simulations could not be running at the same time. If everything is possible, then everything must be there.

As I reflect on this interesting hypothesis, a fly is caught in a spider web outside my window. The possibility of the existence of another universe where the fly was not caught might be a meaningful possibility to my existence (or not), but for sure, it is meaningful to the fly. However, is it meaningful to existence and worthy of creating another universe for that? Maybe, maybe not. Are the choices I have in front of me worthy of creating parallel universes with all possibilities? Maybe, maybe not. Is it useful to create a new universe for every thought that is produced by every human in this existence?

In his short story, *The Library of Babel*, Jorge Luis Borges imagined an infinite library made of every possible combination of the alphabet that would inevitably contain within it every possible book ever made or that would come to be made. Such a collection is actually possible if there were enough storage and processing power to run the program. For example, imagine a simple program that uses letters of the alphabet to create a file with every word, sentence, paragraph, chapter, and compilation of chapters possible to infinity. In this file, you would find hidden within the infinite gibberish not only every book, but also every word uttered by humans, every thought, all the knowledge there is and will be, and every life story told or untold. Such a file would require a storage larger than our whole universe.

If such a file were to exist, maybe in an existence beyond our universe there in the realm of iSH, would it make sense to actually create every possibility in that file? My friend, if you were to have such a file, would you print it all in a *Book of Endless Possibilities,* or only what made sense in a *Book of Existence*? Or, if you were to make movies about the life stories of every human, wouldn't you only use the legible stories and not the gibberish?

My sense tells me that existential laws play on every level of existence, and one of the most important of these is conservation of energy or the resource efficiency usage. This is where a system does not consume energy except to serve its existential purpose.

It would be counter-efficient to run all simulations, regardless of how much processing power or storage there is. My sense is that while the equation is capable of generating all possibilities, the only ones activated are those that serve the existential purpose in the most efficient way. Is it efficient for iSH to run another simulation of existence where that unfortunate fly is not caught in the spiderweb? Maybe or maybe not, or maybe the fly's final contribution to this universe is not unfortunate at all.

You ask, "Is everything that happened and will happen already predetermined in a book of existence?"

My friend, I can imagine a storage device, there in the beyond; let's call it a *timeless-cloud*, where all possibilities are generated by an equation of existence. In the timeless-cloud, all that happened and will happen is already there among all the possibilities from the emergence of the universe until its end. If you were there when it was first generated and before the BEing program had started, it would've looked like a graph of possibilities branching out from one another, all looking the same. You would see the past highlighted with a bright marker, and as choices are made, it would highlight the possibilities ahead. And if you were to look at the timeless-cloud at the end of the universe, you would see all that happened highlighted.

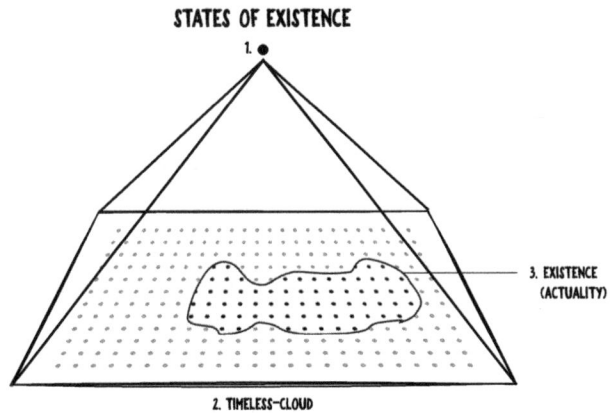

STATES OF EXISTENCE

THE IMAGE ILLUSTRATES ONE WAY TO VISUALIZE THE SYSTEM OF EXISTENCE (1) A DOT
GENERATING ALL POSSIBILITIES, (2) THE TIMELESS-CLOUD WITH ALL POSSIBILITIES STORED,
AND (3) EXISTENCE WITH ACTUALITIES.

The existence of all possibilities in the timeless-cloud and the highlighted events by the executed BEing program, from beginning to end, doesn't negate your ability to choose while you are in this universe. For a timeless observer, like iSH and maybe your consciousness in that realm, the universe would look like highlighted choices among all possibilities in the timeless-cloud. However, for you in this existence, time is progressing forward, events are unfolding, and your choices are highlighting possibilities.

With every thought, word, and action, you highlight new possibilities for other humans to see. Your highlight would make the possibility more likely to be noticed by others, who would then contribute to achieving it. Have you ever noticed how a thought you kept in your head comes to life somehow through someone else? How many words spoken by others do we have in our minds?

OPTIMAL EXISTENCE OUT OF ALL POSSIBILITIES

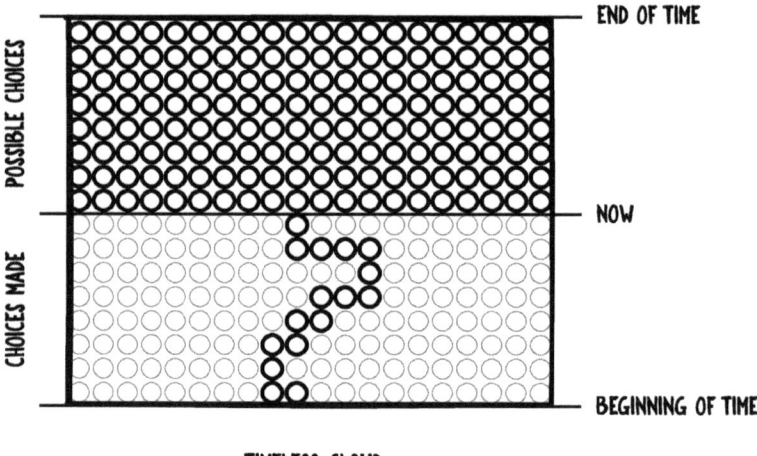

In this existence, you were born as an answer to humanity's pressing need in order to play a role—one that only you can perform with what you were gifted. You grew in your lifetime to become a creator of a future you make probable with every choice. Later, when you're there in the beyond, you would not only see all that led to you and see yourself making those choices, you would also see the ripples of your choices all through existence until the end of time. There, you would realize that your lifetime didn't end with death, but with the universe itself. The awakened would want to be proud as they review their legacy in the beyond.

You ask, "Is there an afterlife?"

My friend, if you ask a dead body if there's an afterlife, the particles will surely answer yes as they continue living in other beings. If you ask your thoughts and emotions the same questions, they would answer yes, as they continue living through your other extensions. In this existence, we see conservation of energy and information, and we also see that with every end there is a new beginning, so it can't be inconceivable to imagine the same rules apply beyond this universe. Still, there is no portal between these existences, yet, so we can't be sure of what truly happens.

For me, the afterlife is a matter of a belief. A belief is unlike faith, which is based on blind acceptance. It is based on weighing probabilities and making a choice between empowerment or limitation. I choose to believe in a continuation of existence because there is a scientific possibility of another emergence in a universe with different laws and dimensions, and because believing in an afterlife empowers long-term planning and consideration of the consequences of our words and actions. But I also choose to believe in a wonderful afterlife, where those who generated positive notes in harmony with existence would pass with ease, and where the others would also pass after their negative notes had been attuned to fit the new existence. This is my belief, and to each their own.

You ask, "How do I use my time to ensure a positive state of being in all states of time?"

My friend, time, in a mechanical view, could be viewed as a small clock that represents the present time and the immediate future—which is best for planning. In this case, you can plan to generate a positive return on time (ROT) on your actions, like making sure the time you spend with your family and at work generate positive returns.

In a quantum view, time is merely an emergent phenomenon for internal observers within the universe; however, time is absent for external observers of the universe from the beyond. In other words, time existentially *is and is not there*. In this case, you can simply measure the return on time (ROT) by keeping positive intentions and thoughts regardless of circumstances and challenges.

In the universal view, you can view time as one unit measured by a lifetime. This is most relevant to your feeling of fulfillment as you generate a positive return on lifetime (ROLT), such as when making sure that your impact and legacy is net positive while you consciously counter your negative actions with positive ones

Every author will perish, but their words are saved in a timeless-cloud.

So only scribe what in the beyond will make you proud.

———

I DOWNLOAD HAPPINESS.
I UPLOAD INTENTIONS.

Proposition 27:
iSH of Curiosity

"iSH is the mystery beyond existence that is asking to be solved. iSH's holy book is the universe and iSH's temple is nature." – PoET Proposition 27

iSH, THE MYSTERY BEYOND

I BREATHE IN ONENESS.
I BREATHE OUT ISH.

A Pause for Reflection

PROPOSITIONS	STRONGLY DISAGREE				STRONGLY AGREE
Proposition 1: Seed of Potentiality	1	2	3	4	5
Proposition 2: Five Extensions of Being	1	2	3	4	5
Proposition 3: Selfish-Altruism	1	2	3	4	5
Proposition 4: Semideum	1	2	3	4	5
Proposition 5: Limitless Creativity	1	2	3	4	5
Proposition 6: The Pyramid of Desires	1	2	3	4	5
Proposition 7: Directional Choice	1	2	3	4	5
Proposition 8: Life of Purposehood	1	2	3	4	5
Proposition 9: Life of Gratitude	1	2	3	4	5
Proposition 10: Happiness	1	2	3	4	5
Proposition 11: Success	1	2	3	4	5
Proposition 12: Fulfillment	1	2	3	4	5
Proposition 13: Life of Ease	1	2	3	4	5
Proposition 14: Life of Abundance	1	2	3	4	5
Proposition 15: The Modes of Time	1	2	3	4	5
Proposition 16: The Future	1	2	3	4	5
Proposition 17: The Past	1	2	3	4	5
Proposition 18: The Present	1	2	3	4	5
Proposition 19: Principled-Flexibility	1	2	3	4	5
Proposition 20: Leadership	1	2	3	4	5
Proposition 21: Three-Dimensional Views	1	2	3	4	5
Proposition 22: The Balance of Opposites	1	2	3	4	5
Proposition 23: Purposehood Pulling Force	1	2	3	4	5
Proposition 24: Neutral Conversion Force	1	2	3	4	5
Proposition 25: Oneness	1	2	3	4	5
Proposition 26: Timeless-Cloud	1	2	3	4	5
Proposition 27: iSH of Curiosity	1	2	3	4	5

PART III

Unleashing Potentiality:
Practices

PURPOSEHOOD PRACTICES

Purposehood Guiding Star: Purposehood Statement

In the dense jungle of life, a jungle full of distractions where everyone is running away from fears and after infinite desires, direction is elusive. The short-term goals you set for yourself seem to give you a temporary focus, but once you achieve them, you discover that they also were diversions from the path you are meant to take on the journey of your lifetime.

GUIDING STAR PRACTICES

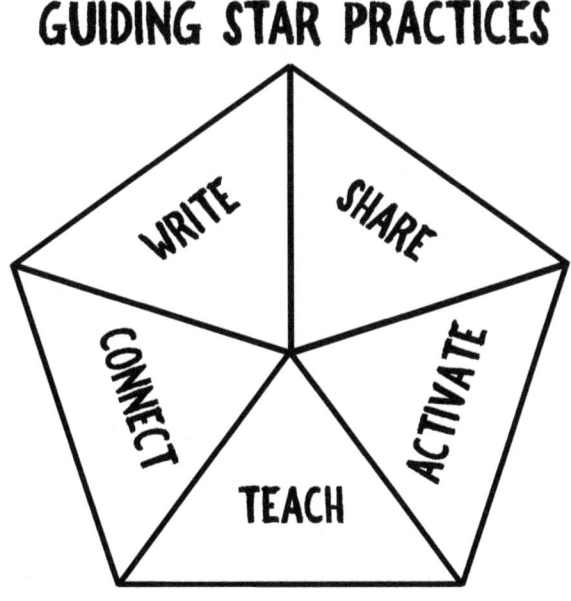

You need to pause and look up at the expansive sky of possibilities through your Pyramid of Values. You need to choose a direction guided by your existential purpose, not fears and basic desires. What you need is clarity of an overarching goal; a guiding star for the ultimate journey through existence; a *shining star*, way up in the sky and away from the jungle's distractions, with a bright enough light to illuminate the path to your Garden of Eden; a *Purposehood Guiding Star.*

The human ingenuity that created the GPS to help you identify your position on Earth also created religions, philosophies, the science of psychology, and self-help industries to aid you in identifying your position in life. Those GPSs of life became useful tools to understand where you were and how to make sense of your immediate surroundings. But without an address to your final destination, all they can do is describe your state of loss accurately, warn you of immediate pitfalls on your directionless road, and expand your situational awareness. They cannot provide you with direction.

Many people confuse awareness with direction as they follow dogmas, step-processes, and practices that comfort them with situational awareness to the point where they forget they are still lost. Situation awareness is positive when you have a direction, but negative when you don't, as it could lead to a false sense of enlightenment.

If the address you enter into your phone GPS is in the opposite direction of where you need to be, then even the most advanced receiver won't get you to where you need to go. You must have the correct address first. Likewise, in the GPS of life. Once you determine the correct address of your Purposehood Guiding Star, you will never be lost in life again. After your destination is set, you will always find the path—regardless of how many U-turns, delays, or obstacles you meet on the way.

Purposehood is a practical philosophy that can guide you to design and construct your GPS of life, one that is made especially for you, one that provides you with a framework to develop your own empowering beliefs based on values and not impulses, one that lets you select practices that can keep your system charged to receive the signals emanating from your Purposehood Guiding Star: the signals of happiness, success, and fulfillment.

Science tells us that each person is made of particles from the stars, but perhaps we're also linked with an existential anchor to a guiding star, as Plato once suggested in *Timaeus*. Plato believed that each person's soul is made from the leftover material of a star, and when a person dies after living a just life, their soul would reunite with that star.

Maybe that's why when you're exhausted by this mundane world and from peering down and around in the jungle of life, you seek relief by turning your gaze to the sky, wandering your tired eyes among the countless shining dots. Perhaps the life of stress, anxiety, and regret is the result of directionless pursuits, stretching and twisting this invisible cord tying you to your own Purposehood Guiding Star. And maybe once you start moving toward that star, then the constant negative tension you experienced will become a positive force pulling you forward.

You are a forward-living creature who may have lost the path by remaining stuck in the present like a plucked vegetable, or in the past like a rusty relic. There is only one rope you need in your life; the one pulling you into the future in the direction of your Purposehood Guiding Star. When you move forward toward it, you move in life with ease, and when you move away from it, you create negative tension. This tension is a blessing if it prompts you to correct your heading, but if you don't, it becomes excruciating, filling your life with suffering.

Any other anchor is a limitation on your potentiality, causing negative tension in your life. Every other anchor must be a detachable one; use it to change your direction and go forward, but once you do, you must let go.

That is true with every attachment you have in life. If you're at work with an anchor attached to your family, you aren't totally at work. And if you're with your family with an anchor attached to work, then you're not totally with your family. Even an attachment to a thought within yourself is great for a while, but then you must let go and find a better one before it becomes an obsession—and that's also true with emotions. How many people do you know who were destroyed by a misdirected anchor of love or trust?

If you think your spouse, parents, children, siblings, friends and communities, your possessions and wealth, businesses, houses and places are your anchors, what will you do when they inevitably disappear? When stability is dependent on the impermanent, then it is not worth much in the long term. Stability in the constantly changing seas of life comes from the pursuit of your existential purpose in the direction of your Purposehood Guiding Star.

You ask, "How do I find the address of my Purposehood Guiding Star in a sky full of possibilities?"

My friend, looking up at a sky full of stars is like staring at a huge white wall where your eyes can't focus on any one point. But if you take a purple marker and put a dot on that wall, where would your eyes focus next time you look at it?

●

On the purple dot!

Now that you have a point to focus on, you can reflect and see if it feels right or if it should be moved a little bit to the left or right, up or down, or even to the opposite side. With this reference point, your eyes will never again get lost staring aimlessly at this white wall. This is exactly what happens when you write your Purposehood Statement.

It is the draft address to your Purposehood Guiding Star.

Here are five simple practices to ensure you will always have a clear view to your Purposehood Guiding Star:

- Write your Purposehood Statement.
- Share it.
- Activate it.
- Teach it.
- Connect with those who share similar Purposehoods.

Write It

You may follow these abbreviated instructions to craft your Purposehood Statement or use the worksheets provided on **Purposehood.org**. You also can download the Purposehood app for your mobile device.

The following is a simple process that anyone of any age can use, and I hope you will find it easy enough to share with people in your extensions of being. Before beginning your Purposehood Statement, you will need some supplies and to participate in a guided imagery activity.

Supplies:

- Your imagination.
- Able to sit in a quiet place (preferably in nature, but anywhere will work).
- A pencil with an eraser, an electronic device that allows easy editing, or the Purposehood app.
- This worksheet.

Guided Imagery Activity:

- Imagine you're sitting in a nice, comfortable place surrounded by nature, or actually sit in a pleasant natural environment outdoors.
- Imagine it's a warm night and the sky is clear and filled with countless stars.
- Take three deep breaths, breathing in for four seconds and breathing out for eight seconds, and try to relax.
- Imagine the world around you is totally quiet and still, and you are starting to feel relaxed in your body and mind.
- Imagine there is a lamp. As you stare peacefully at its warm, gentle flame, a genie jumps out of the lamp!

**You are now ready to begin writing your
Purposehood Statement.**

Follow these steps to write your Purposehood Statement:

PURPOSEHOOD STATEMENT DRAFT 1:

1. The genie looks at you and says, "Today is your lucky day. I'm going to grant you one wish, and only one wish. But it must include the following:

   a. It must start with 'I want to …'

   b. It must be very clear and specific, and

   c. It must be **selfish**."

2. The genie asks again, "What is it that you want for yourself?" Go ahead and write your wish (your **selfish** desire) below, thinking only about the self extension of being.

SELFISH WISH: *I want to …* _____

_____

_____

Let's look at some examples:

When I worked through this process in my workshop, a successful developer, let's call him Peter, wrote: "I want to be the richest real estate developer in my city."

Another person, let's call her Julia, wrote, "I want my family to be healthy and happy."

While Peter's statement is selfish and meets the genie's guidelines, Julia's wouldn't be accepted by the genie because it is not totally selfish. Her statement clearly relates to another extension of being, not the self. Whatever you want must be exclusively selfish in nature, as going against your selfish genetic coding is a losing battle in the long run. She rewrote hers to "I want to be healthy and happy."

This was her selfish motive behind her first attempt, but like many people, she felt more comfortable expressing it indirectly in a selfless way. It's imperative to be at ease with your selfish nature in order to guide it toward your ultimate goal.

As for Peter, he was content with being the richest real estate developer in his city, but he could have also desired to be the richest in his state, country, or the world. It's a wish and you are asking the most capable genie—life, the universe, or iSH—for it, so you might as well aim very high if you so desire.

3. After you write your wish (**selfish** desire), the genie reads it and says: "I think I can immediately begin the process of granting you this selfish wish, but before I do so, tell me what is it that you want to do for the world? Your answer must include the following:
   a. It must start with 'I want to . . .'
   b. It must be very clear and specific, and
   c. It must be **altruistic**."

4. Go ahead and write your altruistic wish below, thinking only about your selfless desire to make the world a better place.

SELFISH / ALTRUISTIC WISH: *I want to …* _____

_____

_____

This desire could be related to solving problems humans have created for nature and its creatures, or ones that help unleash human potentiality, such as gender equality or easier access to necessities for all or those in an underprivileged region or community.

For example, Peter wrote, "I want to build dignified shelters for the homeless in my community." Try to make your statement as wide as possible, going to the furthest of your extensions or even beyond. It must be an issue or a challenge you personally care about, and you must be determined and willing to be a part of the solution.

When you select a wider extension of your being, it would most likely benefit all the other extensions within it. For example, helping your community such as Peter wanted to do would benefit his business, his family, and of course his self. Julia, whose mother had recently passed away after a long battle with cancer, wrote, "I want to help cancer patients feel at ease as they battle their illness."

5. Now that you have your selfish and altruistic desires clearly stated, you're ready to produce the first draft of your Purposehood Statement.

   You create a Purposehood Statement through a causality link between the self and the world, connecting your selfish and altruistic desires with the most profound awareness: the *why*. Causality leads to creation.

   Many times, you seek what might be bad for you and avoid what might be good, but when you forge a clear partnership with existence through your Purposehood Statement, then life will give you happiness, success, and fulfillment, and show you with growing clarity how to get there.

6. Write both your wishes together but write the word, "because" **between** the two wishes.

SELFISH WISH: *I want to ...* _____

_____

_____

   because

SELFISH/ALTRUISTIC WISH: *I want to ...* _____

_____

_____

   Clarity is transformational, and this statement will be a transformational purple dot on the white planes of your future, a shift between ambiguity and clarity, and between an unintentional life and one that is intentional.

7. Read both linked parts out loud together as one long statement. Reflect a little on this moment of clarity.

   • How do you feel about it?

- Does it explain the trajectory of your life so far? Does it resonate with your existence?

- If not, would you like to change some words or select other desires?

- **Go ahead and make any changes you feel would bring more clarity to your Purposehood**.

Peter's Purposehood Statement read, "I want to be the richest real estate developer in my city, because I want to build dignified shelters for the homeless in my community."

When Peter read it to the group, they couldn't help but applaud with admiration. Peter shared with the group the profound clarity he felt. In his case, it wasn't that he was totally oblivious about these desires before, but he wasn't that clear. It was like looking at the sky with the correct prescription glasses. The clarity of the beautiful sky is awe-inducing, and I hope you are feeling the same.

Julia's Purposehood Statement read, "I want to be healthy and happy, because I want to help cancer patients feel at ease as they battle their illness." Julia felt that this clarity will drive her to pursue health and happiness as she dedicates time and effort to help ease the suffering of others.

Once you complete this section of your Purposehood Statement, you can make minor adjustments by switching your selfish and altruistic desires to see if that adds clarity or not.

This process is like when an optometrist narrows down the selection of the correctional lenses so that you can choose which one is more comfortable.

PURPOSEHOOD STATEMENT DRAFT 2:

8. Now flip the order of the two wishes. Then link them again with "because."

SELFISH / ALTRUISTIC WISH: *I want to …* _____

_____

_____

because

SELFISH WISH: *I want to …* _____

_____

_____

- Which one sounds better to you?
- Which one touches your inner voice more?
- There's no right answer; it is all about you and your feelings.

9. Select your favorite draft Purposehood Statement.

PURPOSEHOOD STATEMENT DRAFT 3:

10. Write down the one you selected from the previous two. As you recopy it, reflect on every word and feel free to change any of them or recraft your wishes to become clearer.

*I want to …*_____

_____

because

*I want to…*_____

_____

PURPOSEHOOD STATEMENT DRAFT 4:

11. Try one last variation of your chosen statement: Replace both of the "I want to…" phrases in that statement with "I will…"

I will… _____

_____

_____

I will… _____

_____

12. This time, instead of linking your wishes with causality, you will link them with *intentionality*, which is the power of creators. Write the word, "therefore" between the two wishes instead of "because."

13. Reflect on this intentionality statement (Draft 4) and the causality one (Draft 3) you selected before.

   • Which one sounds better to you?

   • If you feel like changing words or desires, please feel free to do so.

Your existential purpose is yours to decide, not for anyone else to dictate. This is why iSH, the universe, and nature, evolved you to be a human. Remember, *there is no right or wrong answer.* Choose what speaks to you in the clearest voice. You are just finely adjusting the prescription of your clarity glasses as an optometrist would do.

PURPOSEHOOD STATEMENT DRAFT 5:

14. Write below your final statement linking your selfish and altruistic wishes with causality or intentionality:

I _____

_____

Choose one: *because* or *therefore*

_____

I _____

_____

Draft 5 is the address of your Purposehood Guiding Star. Congratulations!

Peter finally chose, "I will build dignified shelters for the homeless in my community; therefore, I will be the richest real estate developer in my city." He felt that by paying it forward through helping his community, stakeholders in his business would be aligned toward making the company even more successful.

Peter also reworked the Purposehood Statement of his business to sync with these desires.

Julia chose, "I want to help cancer patients feel at ease as they battle their illness, because I want to be healthy and happy." She felt her engagement with patients will help her have the drive to live the healthy and happy life she's been lacking.

Remember, this is just the first draft of your Purposehood Statement—the first location of the purple dot on the limitless white wall of possibilities, or your best guess at the address of your Purposehood Guiding Star. It's the best guess at the moment and, as you grow your awareness with the five daily practices that follow in this book, you'll find that you'll adjust your statement accordingly until it becomes your bright, shining star showing you the way.

In the Purposehood app you can enter the same information and you will have several more versions of your Purposehood Statement to choose from. There is no right or wrong selection. There are very subtle differences among them, so select the one that feels the most comfortable at this time and feel free to go back to your statement on the platform to adjust and try different versions.

You ask, "What is YOUR Purposehood Statement?"

My friend, I've adjusted mine many times since my first draft, and I continue to do so as every day I learn something new about myself.

I recently noticed that my adjustments have become minor tweaks. My current Purposehood Statement is: "I will inspire people to live their Purposehood, because I want to live mine." The previous one said: "I want to inspire people to be happy, successful, and fulfilled every day of their lives, because I want to be happy, successful, and fulfilled every day of my life."

In Life Design courses, workshops, and retreats, a Purposehooder often works with a coach or a mentor to help them dive deeper and expand wider to cover all extensions of being. You can examine your statement with PoET in mind and ask yourself:

• Will this statement help me evolve?

- What kind of a person will I become if I follow this direction?
- Will this statement help me expand?
- Will it help me be exponential with my impact and legacy as I influence others?

You also can examine the statement with your extensions of being as you reflect on the impact of this direction on all. How will it exponentially evolve and expand your family, your work, your communities, and your relationship with nature?

If you don't yet have a coach or Purposehooder friends to assist you, you can do this yourself by reflecting often on your Purposehood Statement and questioning the motives behind every word in it. You ultimately want to get to the fundamental desires that are driving your selfish and altruistic wants. With a clear statement, you can slowly transform your backward-pulling desires into forward-pushing values.

Share It

Once you're clear on your Purposehood and you commit to your practices, you will notice the whole world is conspiring to get you what you desire. *But first you need to share your statement with the world.* If the world and other people don't know what you need and what you are willing to give back, how will they even know to help you on your journey?

The next step is to share your Purposehood Statement with all your extensions of being so they might be inspired, and at the same time, help you move toward your Purposehood. Who can you send this statement to right now? Go ahead and do it. Share it right away with at least one person. Post it on your social media channels and on Purposehood.org.

Sharing the selfish-altruistic intentions expressed in your statement will activate the mysterious powers of existence to make your wishes come true. You will be pleasantly surprised with the offers of assistance, the thoughts and prayers of support, and the energy you will have on your path toward this clear guiding star.

Your Purposehood Statement is what you're willing to contribute to the world for what you want to get out of life. And if you're clear enough, then the universe—and all its known and unknown forces—will either help you get there or show you a better way. This is the power of selfish-altruism, which links what you want with what you're willing to give back for a win-win relationship with existence. When you're in harmony with your existential purpose and that of the universe and life, you will not only get what you want, you will also have a life of gratitude while growing with ease.

Activate It

Now think about one simple action you can do immediately to activate your Purposehood Statement. It could be as simple as sending a text message, an email, posting a note, or making a phone call. It could also be an intention to do something that will move you toward your Purposehood, or stop doing something that is moving you away from it. Write down this simple action!

This is a great practice for the days when you feel down or unmotivated. Just think about one simple action that will move you closer to your Purposehood Guiding Star and *do it right away*. That small step forward will add resilience, motivation, and a positive mindset to your day.

Teach It

A great way to reflect on the process is by helping others write their Purposehood Statements. Their reflections, thoughts, and questions will inspire you to reflect on yours. Since you are connected to all the people in your extensions of being, any person without a clear Purposehood is a drag on your movement forward. When you ensure everyone shares the same clarity, then everyone will become a source of strength to all the others. Also, when you teach someone else, you empower them to teach others, which creates a positive viral expansion that will be linked to you till the end of time. Consider making a list of people in your extensions of being whom you will offer the precious gift of existential clarity.

But you don't have to stop there. Some of my most fulfilling experiences come from helping complete strangers write their Purposehood Statements. Witnessing the moment of transformation as people link their wishes with causality brings joy beyond measure.

Who do you intend to help in the next 48 hours? Write down at least three names.

_____, _____, _____

Connect With It

Your statement and the statements of others serve as an easy way to seek, find, and connect with others who share a similar Purposehood Guiding Star. The ancient grouping by tribes, ethnicities, nationalities, religions, or even common interest has served humanity well in its past, but today these are limitations on our growth. The road to the future will be paved by people who connect together with a shared Purposehood.

The easiest way to find your community of Purposehooders is to connect with people who share the same altruistic part of your statement. As you work together to make the world a better place for all, you will also help each other achieve the selfish parts of the statements.

Technology is making it easier to connect people around shared Purposehood regardless of their localities, nationalities, expertise, and affiliations. As the AI algorithms improve on the Purposehood technology platform, it will become an even better place to build and belong while achieving your goals and making a difference. By creating meaningful connections around the corner and across the globe, you will unlock the power of the individual and collective to enhance the economies and societies of the world.

You ask, "How will I know when I find the right Purposehood Guiding Star?"

My friend, your Purposehood Guiding Star is in the opposite direction of the path where you feel stressed, anxious, and full of regret. It is located where happiness, success, and fulfillment meet. Use these signals as coordinates to your guiding star. If you're receiving these signals, then you're on the right road; if not, then adjust and keep fine-tuning until you do. Your inner voice will tell you when you're on the right path. Trust it.

Another way to test it is to ask: "If I had six months to live, would I still spend my time pursuing this Purposehood?" Be true to yourself. If the answer is yes, then you're probably on the right track.

You ask, "Do all Purposehood Statements take you in the right direction?"

My friend, if a person chooses a black hole as their guiding star, then their statement will lead them toward an existential vacuum and destruction. That's why it's crucial to have the right system of beliefs. Without the right GPS of life, such a person would have a statement like, "I want to rule the world because I want to empower my Aryan race to save the world from other inferior races." A person who believes in the oneness of existence, the potentiality of every human, and the freedom of each to choose their direction would never write such a statement.

Your Purposehood Lifebook

A Purposehood Lifebook is a journal of missions, goals, and actions to implement in your daily life. Your Purposehood Statement will be the title of your Lifebook. It's the overarching selfish-altruistic purpose of your existence.

Inside your Lifebook, there are five sections with five subsections under each one of those. Within every subsection, there are many chapters.

The section titles are extension statements for each of your Five Extensions of Being. Answer questions such as: "What do I want from my family?" and, "What do I want to do for my family?"

The subsections are the five sectors of each extension where you answer, for example, within the family section, "What do I want from my parents and what do I want to do for my parents?"

The chapters within the subsections are your goals and the paragraphs in those chapters are your milestones to reach those goals. All these are wonderful milestones and landmarks you are adding to your existential journey on your GPS of life.

Once you have written the titles, then you can dive into exploring these goals with the Five Streams of Potentiality in order to develop the how, who, and what.

This exercise in the Purposehood Method sounds like an involved process, and, like anything worthwhile, it is. However, the process is simple and straightforward, and anyone can do it regardless of age or background. The clearer and more specific you are, the easier it will be to navigate through life and grow to your potential.

Since this is an editable Lifebook and is not written in stone, feel free to erase and revise any of the milestones, goals, extension statements, or even your Purposehood Statement. You are in total control. The more aligned your goals are with your Purposehood Guiding Star, the more likely you will receive happiness, success, and fulfillment pursuing them, regardless of the outcome. With this simple process, you can start designing a life worth living, and with the five daily practices, you can become sensitive to the universal signals telling you whether to stay on course or adjust your heading.

You will find more details, and you can download Purposehood Lifebook materials, on **Purposehood.org**.

Making Decisions Easily

You ask, "How does my Purposehood Statement help me make the right decisions in my life?"

My friend, you are a creature of choice. With infinite desires come a tremendous number of decisions you need to make daily. The result of those decisions is who you are today, and if you want to change your life, you need a process to make better decisions. Thankfully, the majority of your daily decisions are trivial and are made by your unconscious mind through habits, social and environmental cues, and prior experiences. You don't need a logical decision-making process to react to a horn sound while you cross the road.

However, significant life choices such as a college major, your career, relationships, investments, and any major commitments require a thoughtful decision-making process. Decisions are too often made based on mindless urges and misguided values, and often rely on emotions, not logic, so in order to make better ones you need to first ensure that your inner processor is aligned with your Purposehood. You can do this primarily through the five daily practices and the Five Streams of Potentiality, which I will discuss later.

While people think they are making logical choices and weighing the right information, researchers have found that even "thoughtful" decision-making is much less logical than we think. A Purposehooder with the right orientation, starting from their existential desire and moving toward their Purposehood Guiding Star, will have a binary decision-making process that simplifies their life and makes every decision they make a source of happiness, success, and fulfillment.

The Purposehood Binary Decision Process

Use the binary process for your straightforward decisions by simply asking this one question while looking at your Purposehood Statement: "Will this decision [insert the decision] move me toward my Purposehood or away from it?"

If the answer is toward your Purposehood, then proceed. If not, then don't choose that option.

It basically comes down to this: "Will eating this cake, seeing this movie, watching this video, listening to this music, going to this concert, meeting this person, buying this product or service, and so

BINARY DECISION PROCESS

on, move me toward or away from my Purposehood?" You get the idea. The right decision is always the decision that moves you closer toward your Purposehood.

The Purposehood Decision Matrix

For more complex decisions that require further reflections, you can use a 2 x 2 matrix to make the right decision. I use this process for deciding what business ventures I take on, which relationships to build and maintain, what meetings and events I decide to attend, what trips I take, and basically any decision that involves a considerable investment of my lifetime.

The x-axis represents the movement away from your Purposehood (negative) or toward it (positive); the y-axis represents your negative or positive return on lifetime (ROLT).

DECISION MATRIX

When you think of a decision and you consider whether to proceed or not, place your choice A in one of these four quadrants based on positive or negative ROLT, and away or toward your Purposehood.

- If both outlooks are negative, then whether to proceed with a choice should be a natural no;

- When they are both positive, then it's an easy yes.

255

- If choice A has a positive ROLT but takes you away from your Purposehood then ask, "How can I make choice A more aligned with my Purposehood?" If you can, then do so and move it to an easy yes. If you can't, then ask, "Can I replace choice A with another option B, which has both positives?" If yes, then disregard A and choose B; but if you don't have a better option, then go ahead and select choice A anyway.

- If choice A has a negative ROLT but takes you toward your Purposehood, ask, "How can I increase the ROLT on choice A?" If you can, it becomes an easy yes. If not, then ask, "Can I replace choice A with another option B, which has both positives?" If yes, disregard A and choose B; but if you don't have a better option, then go ahead and select choice A anyway.

If I am invited to an event, I consider the content, people, and time needed to travel and attend in the context of my Purposehood Statement.

If the event has relevant content, the right connections, and efficient lifetime investment, then it is an easy yes. If not, then it's an easy no.

However, sometimes I get offered a large contribution to my favorite charity in exchange for giving a short talk about business strategy, leadership, or employee engagement, topics I enjoy but don't necessarily move me toward my Purposehood. In this case I ask myself, "Can I make the engagement more aligned with my Purposehood?", I then ask the organizers if I can adjust the topic of my talk to fit with my Purposehood or add an extra workshop session for those interested in discovering their Purposehood. If the answer is yes, then the event moves to both positives, and it's a go. If no, then I ask myself, "Can I replace this event with another engagement that would have both positives?" If yes, I skip this event and do the other one. If no, I say yes and go the event.

At other times I am asked to deliver a Purposehood workshop on another continent, a major investment of lifetime, which is hard to justify even though the event, no doubt, takes me toward my

Purposehood. In this case, I ask, "Can I increase the ROLT?" On a long trip like this I try to see if I can do more workshops with different audiences, such as college students or young entrepreneurs. I also check whether anyone from my extensions of being lives close by, or if there is a local nature reserve I can visit. If the answer is yes, I've got two positives, and it's a go. If the answer is no, I ask myself if I can replace it with an engagement with two positives. If yes, I do the second option, and if the answer is no, I say yes anyway.

I say yes in both cases when no other obvious alternative is present, because life always has amazing surprises that emerge from no expectations to help you move toward your Purposehood.

With the Purposehood binary process and decision matrix, any person, family, business, and organization can maximize the return on their lifetime, declutter, and stay on the path of their Purposehood. These are simple tools to ensure happiness, success, and fulfillment every step of the way. I have seen firsthand the impact of this process on people who have struggled with major decisions for a long time, only to make them all after they write their Purposehood Statements and learn this process. You can easily do the same.

Five Daily Practices
(20 Minutes)

FIVE DAILY PRACTICES

AFFIRM

BALANCE

PAUSE

FOCUS

EXPAND

Life is wasted when you live mindlessly driven by fears and desires, but is beautiful when you live mindfully with conscious intentions. Intentional living expands your awareness in three-dimensional views of the future, past, and present—and of the quantum, mechanical, and universal impacts of every day of your lifetime.

The following five practices are simple but amazingly powerful, and collectively take 20 minutes per day to bring mindfulness and intention to your life. Will you invest 20 minutes per day for an intentional life of happiness, success, and fulfillment?

The five daily practices are:

1. Affirm
2. Balance
3. Focus
4. Expand
5. Pause

———

Daily Practice 1: Affirm (0.75 Minute)

The first thing in the morning, and as you move from the dream state into awakening, simply declare your Purposehood Statement to yourself and to existence. You are restating your intentional choice of direction in life and shining the light on your path as you open your eyes. This daily affirmation will help you start the GPS of your day with the correct address to your ultimate destination, and will ensure that you're moving in the direction of your Purposehood.

ADVANCED PRACTICE

Place your Purposehood Statement on your social media profiles, on your screen saver, or even frame it and hang it on the wall. The more you remind yourself of your heading, the more likely you are to arrive there with minimal distractions.

Share your Purposehood Statement with your family, friends, and coworkers, and use it as a way to introduce yourself to new people. This sharing will expose your ultimate selfish-altruistic goal to the forces of the universe. You'll be amazed at how many people want to help you get there. People want to help others do what's beneficial for the world they live in, and if your selfish desire is linked to that same goal, then they will want to help you achieve that too.

In some mysterious ways, I found that even nature, with all its creatures, has given me cues in the most unexpected ways on the road to my Purposehood. If no one knows what you desire for yourself and for the world, how could they even try to help you?

When I meet someone new, I often ask, "What's the purpose of your life?" It always sparks an interesting conversation that eventually leads to them asking me about mine—which I state from memory without hesitation. Often, those people then volunteer stories, connections, and recommendations that I wouldn't have received if I hadn't stated my Purposehood Statement. Moreover, by learning about their purpose in life, I have the privilege of knowing them better and in a more meaningful way. It also gives me the opportunity to offer them advice, a connection, support, or at least a word of encouragement that might help them live their Purposehood.

Sharing your Purposehood Statement is pivotal for receiving happiness, success, fulfillment, and growing with ease. Without this daily practice, your other practices will be directionless.

This simple affirmation evokes a potentiality-empowering *belief* that you can make a positive difference in the world and achieve your personal highest goal; creates a *mindful* intention—an inner awareness of your unique role in existence and outer awareness of the world and its needs; generates a *giving* intention to yourself and to the world; arouses an implicit commitment to *wellness* as you prepare your body and mind for the journey ahead; and reminds you of the value of *belonging* to a better world you help create.

———

Daily Practice 2: Balance (1 Minute)

In the evening before you go to sleep, reflect on your day and determine if it was spent mainly in selfish pursuits or altruistic ones.

Then, if your day was mostly selfish, answer this one simple question: "For all the blessings I have in my life, what selfless act do I intend to do tomorrow?"

If your day was mostly altruistic, then answer this question: "For all the blessings I have in my life, what selfish act do I intend to do tomorrow?"

Then pick one simple act that you can easily do and set the intention of doing it. This could be something you already do anyway but without a clear intention, such as watering the plants, walking your dog, or taking your children to school. By simply adjusting your intention beforehand, you can make the same action selfish or altruistic.

On the next day, make sure you get it done. Accomplishing little daily goals on the path to your Purposehood is a major motivation to keep pursuing it, giving you a sense of accomplishment and completion.

ADVANCED PRACTICE

Before you go to sleep, take a few minutes to reflect on your day and write down in your journal a few selfish and altruistic actions from the day and finish by marking the day as mostly selfish or altruistic. This process will help you conclude your day with total awareness. You're looking for a general feeling, not a scientific measurement, so pick whatever answer first comes to your mind. If you've spent the day volunteering in an orphanage, then clearly, you've been largely altruistic, and if you've spent it on the beach sunbathing, then you might want to consider that you've been selfish. But most days are mixed with selfish and altruistic activities, so in which do you think you invested more time?

People who are excessive givers or work in jobs that require altruism—like mothers, nurses, firefighters, teachers, and so on—might want to make sure they intentionally spend some of their life-time's currency on selfish activities and vise-versa.

Because all your extensions are linked through selfish-altruism, it is very easy to confuse selfish and altruistic acts. This is why it is extremely important to be aware of your subconscious intentions and switch them to conscious intentions.

For example, if you walk the dog because you like the exercise and enjoy your pet's company, then the activity should be considered selfish, but if you walk the dog because it enjoys the walk, then the same activity would be altruistic. If you work at your job with the intention of unleashing the potentiality of your coworkers and helping them live their Purposehood, then your work hours are mainly altruistic. However, if your intention at work is to achieve selfish goals such as earning money to buy your dream car, or to be admired by others (neither is wrong), count that time as selfish. If you intend both, then which one do you think was the dominant driver in the back of your mind? Be honest with yourself when you pick the daily selfish or altruistic question to answer. This moment of reflection is priceless.

As for what act to select for the next day, most of the time you can simply just pick one you do anyway, and just adjust your intention to fit your need. This simple reframing will modify your perception of the same exact act. If a mother who spent her day in a spa intends to do an altruistic act the next day, she could simply take a task she does anyway—such as driving her kids to school—but shift her intention from getting the kids to school on time, a chore, to being there for the children while on the road. In this case, before driving the kids to school she would state her intention as, "I intend to make my children feel loved, supported, and cared for while I drive them to school." You can make a similar intention for taking care of your pet or garden, for example, if you water the plants for the plants and not for your love of greenery.

Another thing you can do to enhance the balance practice is to pause for a few seconds after you say, "For all the blessings I have in my life…". At that point, recall at least one of them and feel grateful for it. Feel free to write them in your journal.

If you recall a person who has blessed your life, why not send them a message with a few appreciative or loving words? If you recall a creature of nature, like the squirrel you saw on your nature walk, try sending it a grateful thought, wish, or prayer. If you don't believe this grateful thought of yours will help the squirrel, at least know it will for sure help you better connect with nature. If you've enjoyed a nice meal, send a grateful thought to the people and creatures who made it possible—from the farm to the table.

Try to recall a different blessing each day. You might even want to add each one to a reference list of all the blessings you have in your life. This practice might be particularly beneficial on a day when you're feeling down and you need that extra shot of positivity.

One last great use of this practice is as an icebreaker. For example, as you sit at the dinner table with your family or friends, suggest that everyone shares their selfish or altruistic act of the day and how they felt after accomplishing it.

This balance practice is a simple way to increase awareness of your habits and actions, and of the people and creatures you interact with in your daily life. It also creates intentional success with sustained growth as you oscillate between your chosen selfish and altruistic actions and accomplish them. Additionally, it will help you live a balanced life and increase awareness of how you invest your currency of lifetime.

This practice also evokes a potentiality-empowering *belief* of your selfish-altruism and your ability to forward-balance your desires toward your Purposehood; *mindfulness* as you intend with awareness a positive action and reflect with gratitude on the blessings in your life and the chain of people, creatures, and events that brought this blessing to you; *giving* as you choose an action for tomorrow that rewards your selfish side for being altruistic today or your altruistic side for gratefully accepting your selfish day; *wellness* as you rest your mind with the gift of reflection, awareness, intention, accomplishment, and gratitude before you sleep; and *belonging* as you choose an action for the next day that drives stronger connection and closer bonding with your extensions of being.

———

Daily Practice 3: Focus (9 Minutes)

Take three minutes to focus, rest, and recharge three times a day. The objective is to bring your attention to only one thing and let everything else fade away. Be still, be silent, be bored, gaze without thoughts and judgments at an element of nature around you such as a flower, a plant, a tree, or an object such as a piece of art, a piece of furniture, a photo, or even an empty wall. Or maybe focus (preferably with slightly open eyes, but okay with closed ones) on a sound, a scent, the feeling of the wind on your face, or even a taste in your mouth, but intentionally focus on that one thing for the full three minutes, letting go of everything else.

ADVANCED PRACTICE

It's a good idea to start the practice by declaring an intention such as, "I intend to focus on this yellow flower" or "I intend to focus on the sound of raindrops." And for those who find it hard to focus on one sensory input for three minutes, you might want to close your eyes and focus on your breath as you build your ability to focus while gazing.

The objective of this practice is to take charge of the type and amount of information being collected by your mind so you may slowly learn to focus on receiving the universal signals of happiness, success, and fulfillment. You want to learn to intentionally tune in to what benefits you instead of the countless distractions around and within you.

This is also a blissful practice, and the more you become comfortable with it, the more you'll experience the joy it brings. The more you experience the joy, the more you would want to expand it. You can expand this practice by resting longer and more often. You can add to your focus practice meditations, prayers, mindful nature walks, and making your daily activities mindful ones by simply focusing on the activity itself and nothing else. When you eat, just eat.

At the end of the practice, why not add a loving-kindness thought to the object of your gaze like, "May you grow with ease."

You also can add a creativity practice to your focus by spending a few extra minutes to become aware of all the details of the object of your focus and experience it through all your senses. Then you can think about three other novice functions for the object beside its obvious ones. For example, after gazing for three minutes at your empty lunch plate, take time to notice the variations of colors, the material, the shape, and the curvature with all your senses. Then think about three other uses for this plate beside serving your food. Maybe it could be part of a sculpture or a painting you create in your mind, or it could be the tablet of your eating commandments, or maybe it could be a Frisbee used to play with your dog.

The simple focus practice of three minutes, three times a day (3x3), evokes a potentiality-empowering *belief* in your ability to focus away from distractions and to assert control over your sensory input, *mindfulness* of your inner processing and expanded awareness of one input at a time, *giving* as you gift your creativity focus and your mind rest, *wellness* with a physical and mental rest as you nourish your restless body and mind with focus and stillness, and a deeper sense of *belonging* and connection with the object in your focus.

——

Daily Practice 4: Expand (5 Minutes)

Sit comfortably with your back straight so your head and neck are in line with your spine. Think about one thing you wish for yourself today. You might want to wish for happiness, success, fulfillment, healing, clarity, courage, ease, abundance, and so on. Close your eyes, and for a few seconds imagine a bubble filled with that wish as you breathe. With every breath the bubble expands until it surrounds your body and you are totally immersed in that wish. In the remainder of the first minute, repeat in your mind invocations such as, if you wished for healing, "May I be healthy. May my body be free of pain. May I be healed."

In the second minute, and with your breath, the bubble expands to include your family. With you and your family members immersed in your wish bubble, you change your invocation to include them, such as, "May we be healthy. May our bodies be free of pain. May we all be healed."

In the third minute, and with your breath, the bubble expands to include people you work with. As you repeat your invocations, you imagine them included in the "we."

In the fourth minute, and with your breath, the bubble expands to include your friends, neighbors, and people in your communities. As you repeat your invocations, you imagine them included in the "we."

In the fifth minute, and with your breath, the bubble expands to include your pets, your mother tree, the nature around you, and the creatures in it. As you repeat your invocations, you imagine them included in the "we."

Finish this Purposehood Bubble Meditation with a big smile of fulfillment and gratitude.

ADVANCED PRACTICE

This expand practice is at the core of every religion in the world. It's a practical interpretation of the Golden Rule as you wish for others what you wish for yourself.

There is no limit to how much your bubble can expand. Make your bubble large enough as it expands to sometimes include your distant family members and departed ones, and even your customers, suppliers, shareholders, and coworkers. Occasionally include in your communities the people who live in your city or the places you visited, or maybe people in places you are about to visit. Your community bubble is extremely flexible and can include all humanity if you wish so. Can Earth or the universe be included sometimes in the "we" of nature?

If you are practicing in a public place like a park or outside your office building, try to include all people and creatures in that area in one of your minutes. They are all sharing that space and time with you and deserve to be in your wish.

Sometimes, make an effort to include people you don't agree with or even might have angered you. You might want to include a family member you try to avoid, a coworker you're not on good terms with, a competitor, a neighbor who annoys you, a friend who abused your trust, maybe even a tax collector or a cat that scratched you. Wishing them what you wish for yourself is a healing experience to many mental and emotional wounds.

The expand practice evokes a potentiality-empowering *belief* in the impact of including all your other extensions with their qualities and resources in your self-extension, *mindfulness* of your current state of need and what is needed to fulfill it, *giving* as you expand your wish for yourself to include all your extensions, *wellness* as you give your mind a healthy dose of calmness with active visualization and your emotions a powerful charge of compassion, and *belonging* with a daily conscious link to all your extensions of being.

———

Daily Practice 5: Pause (4.25 Minutes)

This is one of the most powerful practices that anyone could use to control basic desires and impulses. It creates a tiny space between a stimulus and your impulsive reaction. These seconds of awareness will allow you to ultimately take charge of your responses.

Pause, breathe, and smile five times a day:

1. Pause for 10 seconds bringing your attention to one thing, or nothing, in order to create a tiny space between what is going on around you and your reactions (*10 seconds total*).

2. Breathe in for 4 seconds and breathe out for 8 seconds. Repeat three times, shifting your attention from the object of your pause to your breath (*36 seconds total*).

3. Smile for 5 seconds with a sense of gratitude for taking charge of your time and your responses (*5 seconds total*).

This amounts to *10 seconds, plus 36 seconds, plus 5 seconds*, totaling *51 seconds*—a simple practice that anyone of any age can do. Do this five times a day for a total investment of 4.25 minutes!

We run through most of our lives autonomously, driven by the programs of our adaptive unconscious mind. Neuroscientists estimate that our actions, thoughts, and emotions are activated by our unconscious mind 95 percent of the time. Only 5 percent of our decisions are made consciously. Living an intentional life isn't about operating consciously, but about awareness of how your subconscious is operating and having the desire, ability, and process to reprogram it if you so choose.

You want to live a fully intentional life, but not a fully conscious life. Living a fully conscious life is an impediment to growth, just like living fully in the now. If you have to consciously turn on all the programs needed to run the operating system of your computer, you won't have time to be creative or do the work you need to do. It's better to have your operating system running "unconsciously" in the background so you can focus on future-driven creativity to create tasks.

Shift from being a mindless operator of your unconscious programs to a programmer of your unconscious algorithms.

Unconscious programs are mainly written by genetic codes of your ancestors, beliefs passed on to you (especially in the first seven years of your life), and memories and interpretations of your experiences. Use your consciousness not to operate but to *program*. Use the present to create awareness of how your unconscious programs operate and keep the intentions to reprogram them for your future living.

With awareness, you can notice what is positively and negatively influencing your thoughts, words, and actions. Then, with the Five Streams of Potentiality, you can consciously rewrite the code, eliminate negative unconscious viruses and replace them with positive codes to run your unconscious positively.

ADVANCED PRACTICE

The *pause, breathe, smile* practice mixes various ancient practices with the latest neuroscience discoveries to create more awareness of your behavior in the smallest amount of time and allow you to intentionally reprogram your subconscious with a positive decision-making process.

Pause

Can you pause by focusing on nothing? This is your ultimate goal, but until you can fully do it, try focusing on just one thing. When you pause for 10 seconds, bring your attention to one thing around or within you. This could be the person next to you, a tree outside your window, a scent of a flower in the room, a clicking sound of a fan above you, the sunlight's warmth you feel on your face, a thought sitting stubbornly in your head, the beating of your heart, or an emotion rising within you. Just pick one point to bring your attention to and continue pausing for 10 seconds. You don't have to think or feel anything, just observe and notice without expectations or judgments.

When you pause, you create a space between the event input and your unconscious reaction. This tiny space is all you need to expand your awareness of how you're interpreting the information generated by the observed event and the thought, emotion, and action you're about to create. Pausing is not like hitting the pause on your video, because you can't freeze what is happening around you. It is an internal pause as you focus your input receiver on one thing. Let go of all other inputs or totally turn off your receiver so a spacetime is created. Observe how you're interpreting the input you received from the current event or from your past experiences so you may decide later if your interpretation program is generating limiting or empowering beliefs.

Breathe

Breathe deeply in for four seconds and breathe vigorously out for eight seconds. Repeat that three times, shifting your attention from the object of your observation during the pause to your breath. This process will take you a total of 36 seconds. You can close your eyes or keep them open. The best is to focus your mind silently on your breath, but if it is restless, you can simply count—breathing in: 1-2-3-4, and breathing out: 1-2-3-4-5-6-7-8. You also can use silent mantras as you breathe in and out, such as the ones shared in various chapters. You also can try using a giving mantra, directing it to the instigator of your pause, as you repeat the following in your mind:

Breathing in: *May you be happy*

Breathing out: *May you grow with ease.*

If you are very agitated you can add seven-second hold between breathing in and out. So, you breathe in for four seconds, you hold your breath for seven seconds, and you breathe out for eight seconds (4-7-8), and you repeat that three times.

Breathing in and out is a great selfish-altruistic practice as you take in oxygen from plants and return carbon dioxide to them. You also download information from the universe and upload your intentions to the timeless-cloud. Isn't it interesting that we start life by downloading our first breath and we leave life by uploading our last breath, and in between, we're in a constant download and upload mode?

Smile

Smiling is another great happiness practice. It is self-rewarding, causing your brain to release hormones such as endorphins and serotonin, and reduces stress hormones like cortisol.

When you smile for five seconds, try to squint . . . and why not show some teeth too? This is how other people's brains read your smile as being an authentic one. Smiling is also contagious and spreads the joy around. You can smile with gratitude to the people and nature around you, to congratulate yourself for taking charge of your life, and with a determination to make the right decisions for your future.

When you observe, with a pause, the active subroutine at that moment and reflect, with your breath, on the positives and negatives of the situation, then you can smile with gratefulness for the positivity and with determination to correct the negativity. Smile because life is always beautiful in all its negatives and positives.

The pause practice is about taking charge of your life by turning mindless reactions to mindful responses. You can use it to change negative habits through awareness by simply pausing, breathing, and smiling as an urge arises, such as the urge to drink sugary products, eat processed food, or smoke. And after pausing, breathing, and smiling, you can reflect on this urge and acknowledge it by naming it. Then you simply continue with your behavior.

This simple exercise of awareness will give rise to positive internal forces that can change your negative habits, or at least prepare your unconscious for a positive intervention. By making a habit of consciously running the pause practice subroutine at least five times a day, your human intelligence self-learning program will reprogram your unconscious to get rid of the limiting beliefs and habits plaguing your life.

Another way to use this transformative practice is to introduce it to all your extensions of being. When everyone in your family, at work, or in your community has the privilege of requesting a pause, where everyone present honors that request by joining in, three great things happen: The person is given a chance to respond mindfully to a situation to the benefit of all; they are given the opportunity to expose their vulnerability, which will help them in their growth; and as everyone shares in the practice, it creates a common bond and sense of meaningful belonging among the group. When a person is given the privilege by those around them to request a pause, it is important to understand that it is about their own need to interrupt their internal processing, not about interrupting someone else's.

When you're in an argument with your spouse, for example, and you request a pause, you're simply exposing your vulnerability at that moment and your need to reprocess, and you are asking your spouse to honor you by joining you in the pause practice. It's not about interrupting them because you don't like what they're saying. If you're arguing and one of you requests a pause, then pause, breathe, smile together for 51 seconds and continue where you left off. It's that simple. The same approach would apply in a business environment with coworkers.

You can also connect this wonderful practice with nature by taking time to pause, breathe, and smile every time the rain starts, when you hear thunder, as the sun rises and sets, or even when you hear the annoying buzzing of a fly. You also can connect it to common annoyances like a phone ringing or message alert where you pause, breathe, and smile before you answer.

My friend, I have witnessed this simple practice helping families and teams to resolve conflicts and strongly bond together. It's a practice for all ages and all situations and definitely worth the investment of 51 seconds.

This pause practice evokes a potentiality-empowering *belief* that you can control your impulses and reprogram your unconscious mind to respond positively; *mindfulness* with a pause of intention, breath of awareness, and smile of gratitude; *giving* as you give yourself control over stimuli and impulses; *wellness* as you rewire your brain for calmness to reduce stress, anxiety, and regrets while strengthening self-control and the will to deprive harmful urges from their power over your life; and *belonging* as you practice with others composed responses for a better family, work environment, and improved relationship with friends and nature.

On Your Way to Purposehood

With the clarity of your existential purpose as stated in your Purposehood Statement and these five daily practices, you're already on your way to a life of happiness, success, and fulfillment. Now you can tap into the Five Streams of Potentiality to remain charged for your journey toward your Purposehood.

———

I BREATHE IN IMPULSES.
I BREATHE OUT A SMILE.

Five Streams
of Potentiality

FIVE STREAMS OF POTENTIALITY

BELIEF · MINDFULNESS · BELONGING · GIVING · WELLNESS

With constant suffering in the jungle of life, it's understandable that people are desperate for quick fixes in their search for relief. Trends come and go promising healing, ease of suffering, a life of joy, unleashed potential, happiness, success, fulfillment, and a cure to every ailment in family, business, and society. All you need to do is solve this one problem, buy this one book, subscribe to a program, follow a few step process, eat a certain diet, do this one lifestyle change, practice yoga, exercise, meditate, or buy into whatever is the latest product or service designed for desperate people. Yet, the suffering from stress, anxiety, and regrets continues to rise with no solution in sight.

The solution comes from realizing the following:

To begin with, people are not just 4 or 16 types, as some psychologists would like us to believe, but 7.76 billion types and growing. Every human has a unique personality, life experience, challenges, and gifts.

Second, solving our human challenges starts with personal transformation; a transformation that unleashes the potentiality of the individual in the direction of their Purposehood.

Finally, it's true that people in positions of influence should help unleash the potentiality of those they impact. However, ultimately, this transformation is a personal responsibility of every adult. You have the power to transform yourself by choosing your Purposehood and unleashing your own potentiality.

This transformation can't happen without addressing five areas in your life: belief, mindfulness, giving, wellness, and belonging. These are the Five Streams of Potentiality.

The First Stream: Belief

"Beliefs are the ultimate expression of free will. Regardless of how you acquired them, you always have the choice to replace limiting beliefs with empowering ones." — First Stream of Potentiality

You ask, "What is belief?"

My friend, belief is the most formidable force in forming reality and creating the future. As theoretical and experimental physicists try to solve the mysteries of quantum mechanics, they propose many theories to explain the "observer effect," where the mere observation of a phenomenon inevitably changes that phenomenon.[89] In other words, the position or manifestation of a wave-particle is determined by an outside observer. One of these interpretations is *QBism*, which proposes that the belief of the observer is what drives that manifestation. In this view, the observers of all possible realities, you, me, and others, are participating through our beliefs in creating the reality we live in.

I've seen the power of belief in shaping reality in people who convert from one religion to another, and with the new belief, their lives and the lives of their extensions also change. It's not hard to observe how changing the beliefs of a society impacts the future of everyone, as we've seen from the rise and fall of ideologies like communism.

Beliefs also impact our minds and bodies. In what's called the *placebo effect*, researchers found that sham treatments with fake medicine created physiological responses, activated neurotransmitters, and altered chemical productions in the brain such as increasing dopamine, which affects emotions, pleasure, and reward.[90] For Parkinson's patients and others who suffered from depression, stress, and anxiety, placebos changed electric and metabolic activities in various areas in the brain. Further research revealed that the more believable the treatment, such as when it is administered by professional-looking practitioners in clinical settings, the more effective they were, even if the patients were told the truth about the administered treatments. Believing, consciously or unconsciously, that the treatment would help was enough to activate the body's natural ability to deal with some of the symptoms.

In the same study, doctors administering placebo treatments were asked to spend 20 minutes with patients in healing rituals such as conversing compassionately, telling them about the healing effect of the placebo treatment, touching their hands or shoulders, and spending a short period in mindful silence. Those patients reported more relief than others who were rushed through the procedure. The researchers concluded that the rituals strengthened the beliefs of the patients.

I wonder if the same rituals might also have impacted the doctors' beliefs, which in turn, contributed to the healing. Maybe an empowering belief in your healing power and the ability of our bodies to heal themselves combined with compassion would rub off on others. Isn't that what often happens in support groups, or when a parent believes in the talent of their child, or when a manager believes in the ability of an employee?

You might not believe that beliefs create reality, but what is clear is that beliefs are at the core of who you are and who you could become.

My friend, you are today the product of your beliefs. The greatness in you is a result of your empowering beliefs, and your weaknesses are a result of your limiting beliefs. Do you even know what they are?

Beliefs are often like programs that run in the background without being noticed on your smartphone or computer. When your mind is running the malware of limiting beliefs, your magnificent being becomes corrupted and dysfunctional, and soon you start suffering from stress, anxiety, and regrets.

Many of your limiting beliefs are unconsciously captured in the first seven years of your life from your guardians. More are later caught from trusted and notable people, since your doubting guards are lowered and your blind acceptance is heightened. These pieces of malware rapidly evolve and expand, producing more self-limiting beliefs of what you can't do or why you can't achieve what you want. They also become judgments and labels you place on others, limiting your ability to genuinely love, connect, and collaborate. Limiting beliefs are like cancer cells: if left untreated, they will multiply and take over your life, destroying any positivity and leading you toward suffering, rejection, and vacuum. Even one simple limiting belief is capable of causing suffering, and we have many.

If you believe that cleaning your house and cooking meals is a waste of your time, then anticipating those chores makes you anxious, doing them makes you stressed, and reflecting back on them fills you with regret of time wasted. However, if you believe them to be physical exercises that keep you moving, or mindful practices that increase your awareness and connect you with your environment, then anticipating those chores makes you happy, doing them makes you successful, and finishing them makes you fulfilled. The chores are exactly the same, require the same effort, and take the same time, but the outcome is totally different: one of stress, anxiety, and regrets, and another of happiness, success, and fulfillment. And it's all because of a simple belief.

You ask, "Could a belief be limiting to someone and empowering to another?"

Yes, my friend. Belief is based on weighing evidence and consequences and then choosing to adopt those views and values based on your best judgment at the time. If other evidence appears with more convincing views, then you simply adjust your beliefs to fit your new convictions, unlike faith.

Faith is a blind, absolute belief. Any absolute belief is limiting for a person looking to grow. However, even blind faith can be empowering to those who are in constant suffering, and lack the will and motivation to change their current state. A person who is cognitively impaired because of their addictions and in urgent need for specialized care can be empowered to change their life by having faith in a dogma. The same dogma, though, is limiting for someone who is looking to unleash their potentiality toward their existential purpose, as any dogma negates all others and reduces all viewing windows on life to one.

Sometimes, the damage in the jungle of life is so severe that a person might need a drug or a dogma, even with the risk of harmful side effects, just so the pain could stop long enough to seek other, more beneficial, treatments.

You ask, "Will changing my core beliefs change my life for the better?"

Empowering beliefs will absolutely change your life if the ones you hold now are limiting you from having the life you deserve. Transformation only happens when you change the beliefs within. My friend, belief is a choice, and when you expose, examine, and express your belief, you can choose to replace a limiting belief with an empowering one.

Awareness of your beliefs is important for changing your present situation, and to design your future life. If you are not satisfied with your life, then you need to discover the limiting beliefs that are holding you back. And if your life is wonderful, then why not identify the empowering beliefs that led to such life and share them with your extensions? Your empowering beliefs can inspire others, and seeing your positive impact on them firsthand will surely add more fulfillment to yours.

However, changing core beliefs by accepting a ready-made dogma is never the answer, as you will become a hostage again to another set of limiting beliefs, even if they are better than the ones before.

The Three Brooks to Belief

There are three brooks that feed into the belief stream: exposing, examining, and expressing.

EXPOSING YOUR BELIEFS

Some beliefs are easy to expose, especially those you share with others as in social values and articles of faith. The vast majority of your beliefs, though, are hidden in plain sight—within your habits, decisions, and judgments. Most people go through life unaware of their guiding beliefs; yet, without awareness of what is guiding you, it's almost impossible to transform your life and reach your full potential. It's important to expose the empowering beliefs behind all the wonderful things in your life in order to make sure they remain your pillars of strength and to share them with others in your extensions. Maybe you can even improve those beliefs to become more empowering.

Exposing your empowering beliefs is important for your growth, but what is crucial for any transformation is to expose the limiting ones that are negatively driving your life toward vacuum, rejection, and suffering or holding you back from reaching your full potential.

To expose your beliefs properly, identify them by answering questions such as, "Why was I able to achieve this goal?" to identify an empowering belief, and, "Why wasn't I able to achieve this goal?" to identify a limiting one. Additionally, when you listen to others expressing their beliefs, ask yourself if you hold similar or different beliefs. You might not be able to expose all your beliefs in one setting or one workshop, so keep an active list and add to it as you identify new ones. You also could seek the assistance of a Purposehood coach or people in your extensions who know you well to help you identify beliefs you might have missed.

A great way to expose your core beliefs is to write down a sentence or a paragraph about your own beliefs next to each concept

I introduce in this book. There are 114 core beliefs in this book that you can reflect on to uncover some of your own. These are meant to ignite your own reflections and help you create your own empowering beliefs, not to introduce yet another dogma. Start your sentence with: "I believe...".

Next, categorize them by the source of those beliefs like a parent, a friend, a religion, a book, a school, and so on. If a belief is self-created, then try to recall the event that led you to form it. This categorization will help you reflect on the belief, people, and events that influenced your life.

Then classify each belief as empowering or limiting. This is an important step in the process as you need to have clarity of your Purposehood in order to correctly classify them. I consider the beliefs that unleash my potentiality toward my existential purpose as empowering and the others as limiting.

EXAMINING YOUR BELIEFS

Once you have exposed a belief, examine it through the process of doubting, learning, and debating. Beliefs rely on what's called *motivated reasoning* to reinforce their validity. The brain is always looking for evidence, regardless of how dubious, to make you comfortable with a belief, so ask yourself several times, "Is this belief true? Is it really true? Is it really, *really* true?" Also ask, "How would I be or feel—or how would the situation be—if this belief wasn't true?" In this process, you are looking for reasons to create a doubt, a little crack, or an opening to allow your curiosity to seep in.

One who doesn't doubt wouldn't look, one who wouldn't look wouldn't see, and one who wouldn't see will always be lost in the jungle of life. You don't need to be afraid of doubt, as it is the first station on the train of certainty.

When a doubt is created, the next step is to expand your knowledge about the subject, considering various views. The learning will either reinforce your belief or alter it. Once you have raised confidence in your belief or the adjusted one, then you can debate it with others.

Debating is the best learning opportunity, as it gives you access to someone else's research, thinking process, and views. They either can show you what's wrong with your beliefs so you may abandon or adjust them, convince you with evidence of a better one, or reinforce your own. In all cases, you will win a debate if your intention is to learn from the other person or from your own reflections. With this intention, you will never lose a debate, since when you lose, you still win!

A wise person once said that when he started a debate with someone, he would pray for the truth to be revealed by either of them. He also started the debate with the thought: "I'm right, but I could be wrong, and the other party is wrong, but they could be right," which created a principled-flexibility instead of absolutism.

EXPRESSING YOUR BELIEFS

Once you have exposed and examined a belief, express it to yourself and your extensions. A belief is more effective when you write it, look at it often, and say it to yourself like an affirmation. And, once you share it with others, it becomes a commitment and a subtle call for them to help you reaffirm it.

If you are someone who believes in iSH or the unknown forces of the universe, you might want to share your belief in a prayer, a wish for others, a thought, or a meditation, calling on those forces to reinforce your belief or show you a better way.

Finally, insert this belief into your subconscious by creating habits from consciously repeated actions related to it. For example, the belief that you don't have time to eat during the day might be the driver of your habit of eating a heavy dinner late in the evening. When you examine this belief, you learn that you can always make time to eat a proper meal if it's ready in your office. You also learn about negative health effects of eating heavy meals late. So, you develop a new belief: "I am the master of my time and I can take a break to eat a healthy lunch so I may eat an early, light dinner," which you repeat often as an affirmation. You share and debate this belief with your spouse and reach a mutual understanding of what a light dinner is like and when to stop eating. Then, every evening you stop eating by 7 p.m. and you link the time with brushing your teeth, a habit you already have. Then you prepare your healthy lunch for the next day. After 40 days or so of this new habit, you will intuitively change a negative belief and habit into a positive one.

Removing limiting beliefs through the above process is a monumental step toward developing empowering ones.

You ask, "How do I develop empowering beliefs?"

My friend, I offer the Purposehood practical philosophy as a framework to develop empowering beliefs that will unleash your potentiality in the direction of your Purposehood. Regardless of the beliefs you hold now, once you declare to the GPS of your life the address of your new destination—your Purposehood Statement—and choose your role as a co-creator of your future and the future of your extensions, humanity, and life, you can build the empowering beliefs of a creator instead of a consumer, martyr, or destroyer. To be the creator you are meant to become, what beliefs should you have? Start by creating core beliefs like the 114 expressed in this book.

In a Purposehood "Life Design: The Purposehood Method" course and retreat, participants combine theoretical knowledge with exercises related to every topic covered in this book. The course is broken into three main units:

1. Directional Choice: Finding your guiding star.

2. Desire: Building your value system.

3. Creativity: Unleashing your creative genius.

From the first day, participants start identifying their limiting beliefs and creating empowering ones by following the outline in this book. In the subsequent days, they add more beliefs to their lists as they become aware of their own strengths and limitations while exploring PoET propositions, the Pyramid of Values, and their Life Graphs. On the last day, they leave with an extensive list of beliefs to empower a life of happiness, success, and fulfillment. You can follow the same process on your own, with your forum mates, with a Purposehood coach, or on the Purposehood.org platform and app.

By following the Pyramid of Values, you can develop empowering beliefs based on the correct order of desires. You can go over each desire and ask yourself, "What does this desire mean to me?" Then write down your beliefs relating to all the 33 desires as those desires create both empowering and limiting beliefs and, in the process, drive your life.

Since you are guided by your existential desire, the beliefs you will develop will be empowering ones. For happiness, I stated, "I believe happiness is a byproduct of living my Purposehood," and for excessiveness, "I believe excessiveness is only justified in knowledge gained or learnings shared." Those beliefs, and others related to my Pyramid of Values, are the guardrails for my journey in life.

Beliefs are choices, and you can simply choose whatever you want to believe, so why wouldn't you want to believe in what empowers your journey toward your Purposehood and unleashes your potentiality?

You ask, "Can you share with me some of your core beliefs?"

My friend, my first empowering belief is *"Everything in existence has an existential purpose."* This belief provides direction, instigates creativity, and encourages me to connect to other people and creatures. When you believe everything has a Purposehood, then your curiosity is awakened to discover it in everything and everyone you encounter. You will be at ease with life and you will treat all people, animals, and nature with reverence. Most importantly, you will become future-oriented, focusing on the road ahead for yourself and all your extensions of being.

I also believe:

- I have an existential purpose that only I can fulfill, which will positively impact the whole of existence.
- The universe has invested 13.8 billion years of evolution and expansion through colliding stars and countless complexities to create a life on this precious planet, which, against incredible odds, produced me, a human, a semideum, an expo-agent, a co-creator of the future, a genius of limitless creativity and infinite desires.

- I am made of five extensions, which include my family, coworkers, communities, and nature in addition to the self, and all are linked through selfish-altruism so I may grow through their growth and they may grow through mine.

- I have the choice to flip the Pyramid of Desires and convert my desires into positive values, focusing on my Purposehood.

- By doing so I will live in abundance with ease and gratitude receiving happiness, success, and fulfillment.

- Happiness is as natural as the air I breathe on the path of my Purposehood, success is to keep evolving and expanding regardless of the setbacks and obstacles, and fulfillment is investing my lifetime in what gives me positive returns.

- I am the co-author of the future, and my past events are interpretations that can be rewritten to provide me with learnings, experience, and fuel to recharge my present actions toward the future I will co-create with others.

- I am a principled-flexitarian full of curiosity, openness, and confidence, and I am always happy to be shown a better way.

- I am a leader among leaders and my primary responsibility is to unleash the potentiality of those I encounter.

- Reality reveals itself in many ways and through many dimensions, and I am open to looking at events wide, deep, and from high above in order to have a more holistic view.

- In every person and every event of the past, present, or future, there are negatives and positives, and through awareness of both, I can have a balanced view of life.

- Everything that exists is one in substance and structure, and an existential force is pulling the universe and life toward a better state of being, where humanity will be the exponential driving force toward that state by evolving and expanding life throughout the universe.

- I may pass to another dimensional existence where I can proudly look down timelessly, with iSH, on a universe I helped to create.

- iSH is the mystery beyond, the creating force of this existence, a mysterious friend, a soulmate of sort, a pillar of strength, an instigator of wonder and creativity.

- iSH is whatever I need iSH to be in order to live my Purposehood.

- By having a Purposehood Statement I have an address to the GPS of my life, so I will always find the way, regardless of how many times I am misdirected and how many diversions are in my path.

- By committing 20 minutes a day to my five daily practices, I can immediately improve my life with directional clarity, balancing my selfish-altruistic nature, improving my focus, expanding myself, and having control over my impulses.

- I can unleash my potentiality with empowering beliefs I choose, mindfulness that expands my awareness, giving that fuels my altruistic nature, balanced wellness, and belonging that connects me with others who want to help me grow with ease.

- I, you, and everyone else are entitled to become Purpose-hooders and to receive happiness, success, and fulfillment, regardless of the circumstances of our birth.

You ask, "How is belief supported by other streams?"

The practices in the other streams will help you remove limiting beliefs and build empowering ones as the Five Streams of Potentiality reinforce each other in a holistic approach. Use *mindfulness* to expose and monitor your beliefs, *giving* to reinforce your altruistic beliefs and to ensure you provide the self with selfish needs, *wellness* to connect your beliefs with your physical body, and *belonging* to examine and share your beliefs and receive the support needed to live them.

You ask, "What is the essential practice for a Purposehooder to access this stream?"

My friend, create an affirmation by adding the following phrase to your Purposehood Statement:

I have an existential purpose and my Purposehood is: I ...

As you replace limiting beliefs with empowering ones, nothing will be able to stop you from reaching your potentiality. What you need next is to nourish the mental, emotional, spiritual, and existential components of the self, and the best nourishment is the second stream of potentiality: mindfulness.

The Second Stream: Mindfulness

"Mindfulness is the process to unleash your potentiality from within. You can always choose to live a mindful life through intentions, awareness, and gratitude." — *Second Stream of Potentiality.*

You ask, "What is mindfulness?"

My friend, in Purposehood, mindfulness is the intention of increasing awareness of your extensions of being and the beyond in order to instill a grateful state within yourself. It is the ability to awaken your conscious mind at will. It is the liberty to enter the realm of higher beings, where actions are not driven by mindless impulses but by intentionality. It's the ability to observe, recognize, and intervene if needed in order to create a positive outcome. Having this ability is what makes you, me, and every human an active participant in creating the future.

Contrary to some views, mindfulness is not a passive state. It is an active state that puts the mind in the pilot seat as we navigate through life. And just like a navigation system operates mainly on autopilot, a pilot is present to set the destination, monitor progress, and take charge when needed. A mindless person's thoughts come after their words or actions, while a mindful person's thoughts come before their words and actions.

There are three main desired outcomes for mindfulness:

1. Improving Focus

Thoughts are impermanent. It's not easy for the mind to stay focused on a thought, and when an emotional response is created, the mind tends to think of more reasons to keep you in that state until other distractions occupy your mind. It's as if the mind refuses to observe the first part of Newton's first law of motion but still obeys the second part. The mind refuses to rest, not even in sleep, and stays in constant motion until acted upon by a force. My friend, mindfulness is that force. While mindful practices are incapable of putting the mind at total rest—thankfully, as a totally rested mind is a dead one—they are capable of reducing distractions, enhancing focus, and calming the mind.

Focus is about total engagement with what matters and detachment from what doesn't. It not only provides the ability to bring focus when you need it in order to be more productive, but also to focus on *nothing*, giving your mind the rest it needs to function at a higher state of consciousness. The mind is built to constantly jump between the past and the future. The past contains the roots that nourish you from the ground of your experiences. The future is your leaves, where you generate energy from the light of your guiding star. The present is where the mind struggles to remain, and with mindful practice you can learn to keep your mind in the present, as long as needed, to rest or plan.

2. Strengthening Connections

How connected do you feel to a person who is often checking their phones or not paying attention to what you say? A mindful Purposehooder is totally present at every encounter, gifting their time and attention and profiting from connectedness. They also invest a focused time with compassion and love on themselves, people in their life, animals in their care, and the nature that gives them air to breathe and food to eat.

Mindful practices also strengthen your connections with the

past, present, and future, in addition to your extensions. Mindful people don't surrender to negative memories, they reframe them. They don't react to present events, they pause and respond thoughtfully; they don't face the future with negative backward theories, they form forward-pulling ones.

For those who want to be infinitely curious, transcend beyond their five extensions, or focus on the most abstract of all, mindful practices help them connect with iSH and the beyond.

3. Reprogramming Subconsciousness

We live most of our lives mindlessly, and that is not a bad thing. Since we are fashioned to be future-driven creators, our unconscious drives most of our behavior, allowing us not to think about the mundane tasks of everyday living and decision-making. Imagine how burdensome it would be if you had to consciously make driving decisions on your routine commute to work with all the cars, people, and signs on the road. If this enormous amount of data had not been processed in your unconscious mind, you wouldn't be able to listen to the radio or converse with other passengers. Our unconscious frees us to consciously focus instead on reframing the past and creating our future.

The challenge, however, is that many of our unconscious behaviors are built with the DNA of negative habits and limiting beliefs, and are fueled by misdirected infinite desires. We need a tool that is capable of observing, recognizing, and intervening in order to remove, revise, or replace negative subconscious routines.

You ask, "What is the tool to reprogram our negative subconscious routines?"

My friend, biologists studying viruses that prey on bacteria discovered an amazing process to remove, revise, or replace damaged DNA through a gene editing tool, CRISPR. This tool reprograms the protein RNA, which then can guide an RNA molecule designed to recognize a particular DNA sequence. As their techniques continue to improve exponentially, researchers believe that not only will they be able to cure serious illnesses and edit the DNA of sperm and eggs, but also they will be able to create new species and revive old ones.

Mindfulness is the CRISPR of unconscious routines. With mindfulness, you can recognize the corrupted routines that are holding you back, and then attach mindfulness to your beliefs, giving, wellness, and belonging to repair or replace the negative routines with positive ones.

The success of mindfulness is measured by how mindlessly positive you can be. When you practice mindfulness correctly, ultimately, your decisions, judgments, and responses are unconsciously guided by empowering beliefs and intentionally developed goals, habits, and traits. Some people, when stressed, react by grabbing a carton of ice cream. The goal of mindfulness is not to make them aware of the stress every time or even the negativity of injecting sugar into their bodies, but to ultimately change the subroutine from, "when I am stressed I grab ice cream" to "I walk in nature, go for a run, or donate to a charity."

So, mindfulness is also the state of awareness of these negative habits and limiting beliefs, the gratefulness for such awareness, and the intention to change them with the other streams of potentiality.

You ask, "What is the purpose of mindfulness?"

My friend, mindfulness is about changing the world from within.

As we are, the world will be.

This is a most profound statement, not only about the nature of reality, but also about yourself, family, business, communities, and even nature. If you are living alone in a cave in the mountains, then reality will be what you perceive it to be. But since we all live connected with others, reality is what we collectively perceive it to be.

To realize a reality, which is basically a projected construct of the mind, you need to align the perceptions of every member of the group toward that reality. This is done by having shared goals that align with each individual's Purposehood, then developing shared empowering beliefs, mindfulness habits, giving activities, wellness practices, and belonging through reciprocation. You always start with yourself and then inspire others in your extensions. This is how you thrive and build a strong family, a flourishing business, and rewarding relationships. Our reality, our future, our societies, our businesses, and our families can only change through individual transformation of every member of the organization. And this starts with you.

The Three Brooks to Mindfulness

There are three brooks that feed into the mindfulness stream: intentions, awareness, and gratitude.

INTENTIONS

If imagination is the drawing board of creativity, then intention is the brush. Intention is the tool of creators. It's the magical power bestowed on humanity to build the future. Just like with reflections you can reframe the past, with intentions you can frame the future. If the observer effect impacts the outcome in the present, according to quantum mechanics, then intention is how the observer can impact the outcome in the future.

With intention, you can mindfully turn a thought into a plan of action. Mindful intentions are based on researched information, well-thought-out plans, and a clarity of the intended results, while mindless intentions are generated either from mindless desires or naïve wishes. How often do we see disasters as a result of good intentions that were not based on facts, a proper plan, nor a serious consideration of the possible outcomes?

Intentions have three superpowers: they focus the mind on a desired outcome, they multiply the benefits of the same action, and they can even change the nature of the action without changing the action itself.

You ask, "How do intentions focus my mind, multiply benefits, and change the nature of an action?"

My friend, the human brain is built to generate limitless creativity and to constantly imagine future possibilities. With every possibility, a light bulb is lit in your mind. But, just like how staring at the sun could damage your vision, too many thoughts blur your vision of the future and lead to paralysis. With an intention, you turn off the distractions and shine a flashlight on one or a few possibilities.

Intentions act like an agenda of a meeting that ensures everyone stays on topic and works toward a desired outcome. With an intention, you also set a goal and a direction to your actions.

Studies have found that Americans spend an average of more than 10 hours of their days staring at screens, a rate which is on the rise. There are endless possibilities to view, and more information than ever before to consume. A typical person today receives more than five times the information of a person who lived only 30 years ago.[91]

When you create a clear intention before you start flipping through channels, scrolling through posts, or picking up your phone, you can limit the distractions and the amount of your lifetime spent on such activities. If you simply state to yourself before staring at any screen what you intend to do, how long you want to spend, and what outcome you plan to achieve, such as, "I will spend the next 20 minutes on social media to share my thoughts and connect with my close friend," then you instruct your mind to avoid the urge to open other apps, to read other posts, or spend more time than you can afford. The more precise your intention, the better the outcome will be; just like the more precise your online search phrase is the more relevant the results are.

Intentions are also multipliers, as you can add many of them to the same action for multiple outcomes. The meeting you're having with friends could be about having fun only, but it also can be about much more, with additional intentions such as sharing a useful practice, picking their brains about what they recently learned, debating a new belief, and bonding through shared practices such as pausing, breathing, and smiling together. If you expand your intentions before you leave home, maybe on the drive there you can think about an icebreaker to start with, and a few questions to spark meaningful discussions.

Additionally, intentions have the power to change the nature of an experience without having to change the event itself. Giving a donation to a charity could be with the intention to show off material wealth or display gratitude. The action is the same, but the nature of the experience is totally different. You can simply change the nature of the experience by examining your intentions and making sure you set the right tone to create positive outcomes.

You ask, "How do I create an intention?"

My friend, intentions come in many shapes and forms; they could be positive thoughts like the ones sent to an ailing grand-mother, prayers like the ones asking for forgiveness or blessings, goals like the ones set in a business plan or a personal journal, and statements like the ones in your Purposehood Lifebook, starting with your Purposehood Guiding Star. Just think it, state it, and evaluate it.

An intentional life is built on intentional thoughts that move you closer to your Purposehood, and when you state your intentions, you clarify them to yourself and others. Once you have done that, evaluate the outcome with gratitude. If the outcome is not what you intended, then gratefully accept the expanded awareness and intend to improve the next time. Repeated positive intentions turn into empowering beliefs that instruct the unconscious mind to drive an intentional life.

A mindful life is an intentional life. A Purposehooder pauses before reacting to create a space for a positive intention.

AWARENESS

You ask, "What is awareness?"

Awareness is the basic requirement for consciousness and the ulti-mate goal of mindfulness. While some believe everything in exis-tence is conscious to one degree or another, consciousness is as wide as awareness is. It's tempting to think that a person who lives in a cave is not as aware as the person living on a mountain top, or to think a university professor living in San Francisco is more aware than a villager in India. However, awareness is not only about having a wider view of your surroundings, nor having more knowledge about a specific topic. It is about inner, outer, and beyond awareness and your level of awareness is as high as the lowest of the three.

Haven't you met amazing people with self-awareness but total ignorance of others, or with situational awareness but no self-reflections, or mystics and monks who are connected with something beyond to the detriment of their self and their relationships?

My friend, to achieve inner awareness you need to be aware of your past, yourself, and your Purposehood. The past is where your roots are planted and where the nourishments of your potentiality are provided. You need to ensure that only positive nourishments are feeding your growth, and you can do that by examining your life, as with the Purposehood Life Graph—a process of recognizing, reflecting, and reframing past events. When you realize that the past is a story you narrate, a present you activate, and a future you create, then you are always in control of the past; and it all starts with the intentions to expand your awareness of your past.

To expand your awareness of the self, you need to expand your awareness of your body, your thoughts, your emotions, your spirituality, and your existence. The best way to do this is through science and meditation. With science, you learn available facts, theories, and boundaries that still need to be crossed. With meditation, which has been proven by neuroscience to calm the mind, you let go of all you learned so you may hear the whispers of existence.

If yours is a restless mind, start with a mantra, such as a relevant word or sound, or repeating silently, "I breathe in for myself," as you breathe in, and "I breathe out for the world," as you breathe out. Focusing on the breath is another step of meditation. There is nothing more important than a breath; yet most people are not even aware of the 23,000 breaths they take daily from their limited account of lifetime reserve of approximately 700 million. Even the richest multibillionaire is not a breath billionaire. Aren't you amused that the poorest and the richest among us own, more or less, the same number of breaths? Focusing your attention on the breath is the most effective tool to bring focus and open awareness. Ultimately, exponential awareness comes with stillness and silence.

The other part of inner awareness is knowing that you are moving in the direction of your Purposehood, and you can achieve that by triangulating your position with happiness, success, and fulfillment. You should be receiving those signals if you're on the right path, but if not, then pause, breathe, smile, and adjust.

For outer awareness, be aware of your present by observing without judgment, as judgments change the nature of experience, distorting its actuality. Also, by intentionally connecting with your other extensions with compassion, you expand your awareness of all the outer elements that make you who you are. Lastly, by exploring the history of humanity, geology, biology, and cosmology, you become aware of how the present came to be and how to extrapolate a possible future.

One of the best practices for outer awareness is slowing down for a short while. How much would you notice if you were looking through a window of a speeding train? Not much. By intentionally taking a snail walk in nature, or even on a familiar route, you will start noticing sights, sounds, smells, and sensations you haven't experienced before.

Slow eating is another way to expand your awareness of what you eat and how your body is reacting to it. Another exercise is to fast weekly for a day; abstaining not only from food and basic desires, but also from electronics and other distractions. I call it a "Nonday," a sabbath of sorts. Taking this short break will free your mind from the bondage of addictions and impulses so it may instead focus on connecting with your extensions, and maybe even the beyond if you decide to add silence to some of your fasting days.

As for awareness of the beyond, the least you can do is be aware that there is so much you are not aware of. Exploring the borders of your unawareness is a type of awareness of the beyond. Yet, for some, awareness of the beyond comes through imagining a future, connecting with their iSH, and contemplating the next phase of their existence.

Regardless if the iSH you choose, be it God, a grand mystery, or nothingness, or if the afterlife you select is paradise, reincarnation, or oblivion, be aware of the options, your choices, and the impact of those choices on everything you do. Mystics swear that connecting with the beyond opens an exponential door of awareness. Alas, a statement that cannot be verified except through personal experience. How many diggers strike gold? It is for you to decide if it's worth the investment in lifetime, but maybe it's worth exploring and experimenting.

Total awareness, if even possible, simply puts you in one state with iSH. But even with a fraction of this awareness, you can reach a state of gratitude.

A mindful life is an aware life. A Purposehooder re-centers awareness on their breath when they feel pulled by impulses.

GRATITUDE

If intention increases mindfulness of the future and awareness increases mindfulness of the present, then gratitude increases mindfulness of the past. The first one cures anxiety, the second cures stress, while gratitude cures regrets of what was done or could've been done. Gratitude is not just saying thank you or naming what you are grateful for, but a state of intention and awareness of your past, present, future, and all your extensions of being. It's unlocking joy by being grateful for what you have instead of suffering from the burning desire of what you don't. It's being grateful for all the causes and effects that led to your existence; for being here and now to breathe this air, drink this water, eat this food, and be with those you love; and for the gift of the seed of potentiality that empowered you to create the future.

Gratitude has three aspects. It is linked, temporal, and dual.

The Link of Gratitude

Gratitude is not about what you're grateful for, but *who you are grateful to*. My friend, whatever you are grateful for couldn't have happened without yourself, others, and iSH. In a state of gratitude, you are thankful for the whole link.

Many people express a sense of gratitude for having the food they are about to eat, but this food wouldn't have been there without the chain of people who brought it from the field to the table, the farmers who planted and tended to it, the plants that provided the seeds, the animals who pollinated the plants, the sun that provided the energy, the Earth that provided the nourishment, the evolution that changed a burst of energy into the life you're having and the food you're eating, and iSH, the grand mystery beyond it all. When you generate a good thought, wish, or prayer of gratitude as you're about to eat, for example, include all those in the link.

Other people, especially religious ones, give thanks to their iSH without remembering the chain down from there. iSH shouldn't be an escape from being grateful to a long chain of credit we owe to people and to nature for the valuable existence we are gifted, but an encouragement to recognize the link from iSH to us. If your chain of gratitude is broken, then you never truly thanked your iSH.

Gratitude and Time

When you live in a continuous state of gratitude, you are mindful that every moment of your lifetime is a gift and an opportunity for reflection, joy, and impact, and for that you are always grateful. Reflecting on the past, you recognize that whatever happened couldn't have happened any other way, and it created a better state of being, regardless if the wisdom had already revealed itself to you or not. So, you're always thankful when you see the positivity and patient when you don't.

When you are grateful for a pain or a challenge, you're saying "I see the wisdom and I know the end result will be a better state, so I'm thankful." You also can be grateful for a future outcome you desire as a way to add even a tiny probability to your wish among all possible outcomes. Visualizing a positive future outcome and being grateful for it, as if it already happened, adds calmness to your mind and an intention to your actions. That increases the probability of finding an answer to a thought or a prayer, or gaining wisdom. A gratitude for what you'd like to happen evokes the pay-it-forward effect. For example, if you plan to feed the hungry if you were to win a contract, why don't you go ahead and do the grateful act before? You will feel the reward of the giving act regardless.

My friend, be grateful for the life you had, are having, and will have. A life of gratitude is a combination of moments of gratitude. How many points of gratitude have you collected? This is the recipes for happiness, success, and fulfillment.

The Duality of Internal and External Gratitude

Gratitude is felt internally but expressed externally. Intentions and awareness are mainly internal states of mindfulness, but gratitude is both internal in feelings of acceptance of what was and appreciation of what is, and external in authentic appreciation to all who brought the blessings to our lives. We are usually grateful of what we have already received, so internal gratitude is awareness, acceptance, and appreciation of the gifts from others, nature, and iSH, and external gratitude is an intention to reciprocate to people and nature.

When practicing gratitude, list what you are grateful for and remember the entire link for the subject or object to iSH and plan a giving action in reciprocity.

A mindful life is a grateful life. A Purposehooder smiles with gratefulness for all that was, is, and will be.

You can practice this external gratitude to others with words like "thank you" or "well done," and actions like gifts of time and possessions, and thoughts like prayers or loving-kindness meditations.

Meditation

You ask, "There are so many meditation techniques, which one is the most beneficial?"

My friend, for the past 45 years I have experienced and shared a wide variety of meditation techniques developed by various traditions and practiced by millions of people across the world. I've spent time meditating with Sufi masters, Buddhist and Christian monks, Hindu and New Age gurus, silent and loud, guided and unguided, with and without mantras, sitting and moving, open and closed eyes, minutes short and 10 days long, and with and without religious connotations. I have found the diversity as enjoyable as tasting the fruits of various trees. And just like mixing a variety of food is the best nourishment for a healthy body, mixing various meditation techniques is the best nourishment for a healthy mind.

In a study over a nine-month period, 300 volunteers practiced three different meditation techniques both solo and with others. Researchers found through MRI scans that parts of the cortex grew thicker depending on the type of practice.[92] For example, attention-control practices such as focusing on the body or breath increased the thickness in the prefrontal cortex and parietal lobes, while compassion meditations increased the limbic system and the anterior insula, which deal with emotions. Additionally, various techniques generate different reactions by the body, such as compassion meditation reducing cortisol levels by up to 51 percent in comparison to others.[93]

My friend, someone who is as sophisticated and unique as you are would require a personalized plan for their own needs. The days of one-solution-fits-all is behind us. Every human needs their own prescription to greatness, and the mindful way of finding the right potion is by learning, experimenting, and observing. I have found that experimenting with the many techniques is just like trying different cuisines—and with mindfulness of your body, mind, emotions, and the feedback of people you interact with about changes in your behavior, you can choose what works best for you.

It's always good to find a stable practice you enjoy and add a variety of others for different needs. Also, just like a nutritionist would develop and monitor the progress of a health plan depending on your needs, an experienced Purposehood coach who is not totally invested in one school can help you design a combination of practices depending on your needs. Some people find it easier to meditate by repeating a word or a mantra.

You ask, "How should I select a mantra?"

My friend, a mantra doesn't have to have a meaning to help you meditate. You can select any word or phrase to repeat. However, when I recommend a mantra, I like to use an old Sufi method in which you select a word from 99 attributes. The chosen word is selected to counter a negative desire the individual aims to control or a positive one they wish to empower. You will be able to do this process on Purposehood.org or with a Purposehood coach.

You ask, "How do you choose your meditations?"

My friend, meditation is about expanding awareness, increasing gratitude, and focusing intentions in order to have a better connection with yourself and other extensions of your being. Through meditations, you can connect with existence, and with that connection, you can upload your giving thoughts and emotions and download wisdom and clarity.

While meditation works from the inside to expand your awareness internally, externally, and existentially, its true measure of effectiveness is the degree of control you reclaim over your impulsive basic desires.

An effective meditation is the one that frees you from the bondage of mindless infinite desires and puts your mind in charge of your desires. For me, meditation always starts with an intention, clearly stating to myself the reason for investing that time to meditate. Am I meditating to send thoughts of love and compassion to others as I capture it for myself, and if so, to whom? Or is it to receive a healing, clarity, relief, or a download of existential wisdom? Or is it to simply connect, observe, and be with my various components of the self, my extensions of being, life, the universe, or iSH?

There are mainly three kinds of intentional meditation: those for giving, receiving, and being.

Giving meditations, such as the expand daily practice, focus the mind on sending yourself and others kind thoughts and prayers such as, "May you be happy, successful, and fulfilled every day of your life; may you grow with ease." The reward of such meditation is felt instantaneously in a feeling of gratitude and satisfaction.

Receiving meditations, such as those for calmness or healing, can employ techniques like repeating a mantra, focusing on the breath, or performing a body check.

Being meditations is the ultimate meditation. With stillness and silence—a prerequisite to connecting to the highest existence—and if you provide the space in your mind, you can download answers to your questions or prayers.

You ask, "How is mindfulness supported by other streams?"

My friend, your other streams' practices will also help you become more mindful. Create empowering *beliefs* about your ability to live a mindful life with intention, awareness, and gratitude. Use *giving* to give your mind the rest, focus, and clarity it needs and give loving-kindness meditations, time, and possessions to others. Use *wellness* to help your mind by having a healthy and balanced body. And use *belonging* to expand your self-awareness, looking through other's eyes, and to strengthen your practices by practicing with others.

You ask, "What is the essential mindfulness practice for a Purposehooder to access this stream?"

As with anything, just do that one thing you are about to do with intention, awareness, and gratitude.

I intend to be mindful of my thoughts, words, and actions.

When you have empowering beliefs that provide direction to your limitless creativity and infinite desires, as well as mindfulness to expand your creativity and awareness of the impulses of mindless desires, then it's time for the third stream of potentiality: giving. It stretches selfishness to include others and provides you with a control over the selfishness of desires so you may regulate them like the flow of water through a tap. With giving, you can ensure that selfishness waters your growth instead of flooding your field of existence, contaminating your seed, and depleting your soil of the nourishments from other streams of potentiality.

The Third Stream: Giving

"Giving time, possessions, and thoughts is how you unleash your own potentiality through helping others unleash theirs." — *Third Stream of Potentiality*

You ask, "What is giving?"

My friend, giving is letting go of something you value. It is the lowest common denominator among all existential purposes. With giving at the core of your goals, you will always find a shared purpose among your family, coworkers, and people in your community. It's the primary practice of selfish-altruism, where you grow the self by helping others to grow.

However, even if giving is an altruistic act, it is in actuality a selfish trait inserted into every living organism to ensure (through nature's genius) life's own evolution and expansion. Through giving, simple and complex organisms develop the urge to reproduce, connect, and collaborate. If it wasn't for the encoded giving, why would a cell or a person share their resources with competing offspring? And with reciprocity, personal connections are built and strengthened when a giver receives equivalent gifts from the recipient of their generosity in return.

Additionally, nature gives evolutionary advantages and better chances of expansion to an altruistic group of shared-purpose individuals over a group of those who are selfish. If you think about any organization, like a family or a business, the chances of sustained growth always favor the organization of individual givers instead of selfish takers.

With giving, selfishness is stretched beyond the self to include assisting others in acquiring the same selfish needs, just like genes see their own survival through the survival of related genes. Creatures expand selfishness to include offspring, collaborators, and their pack. That selfishness of giving is passed on to us so we may evolve our traits and expand our resources through family, reciprocal connections, and group advantages.

While selfishness works superbly for creatures with limited basic desires and creativity, creating controlled growth in nature and a balance between needed selfishness and altruism, we humans have a different situation. We are endowed with infinite desires and limitless creativity that create the possibility of developing unbounded selfishness, which if left unbalanced, could lead to the destruction of our selves, families, businesses, communities, and nature. For example, we share with animals the basic desires to eat, possess, and have power over others, and for most animals, eating is shared with relatives and left for others once full, possessions are limited to immediate needs, and power is confined within a group or an area of influence. But humans, with unbounded selfishness, could eat and possess to depletion of resources and expand their power to the point of abusing everyone else, including those close to them.

This unbounded selfishness is responsible for most of the suffering we see in our personal and family lives and in human-made disasters: polluting land, air, and seas; and trafficking other humans for labor and sex. It is also responsible for destroying forests and animals and condemning our species to miseries and ultimate extinction if we don't learn to control this unbounded selfishness. But most of all, it's the cause of individual suffering.

My friend, if unbounded selfishness is the mother of all suffering, then *intentional giving* is the cure. With intentional giving we transform unbounded selfishness into selfish-altruism, with which we reclaim control over our infinite desires in order to direct them toward a life of Purposehood, gratitude, ease, and abundance.

You ask, "Is it hard to become an intentional giver?"

My friend, iSH, the universe, and life are invested in your success in becoming a co-creator of the future, so they have given you three rewards to make it easy and attractive for you to become an intentional giver.

PHYSICAL REWARD

With fMRI, neuroscientists were able to show that giving stimulates the Mesolithic pathway, the reward center, to activate the same areas of the brain that control happiness. Biologists found that giving releases endorphins and dopamine—addictive hormones that translate into pleasure, happiness, and feelings of peace. Giving has also been linked to what's called a "helper's high" through the release of oxytocin, a hormone that induces feelings of warmth, euphoria, and connection to others.

Other studies found that giving in the form of volunteering, donations, or emotional support helped reduce blood pressure and those who gave recovered faster from heart ailments.[94] Givers over 55 years of age had a 44 percent lower chance of death in the following five years than those who didn't.

PSYCHOLOGICAL REWARD

Researchers have found those who volunteer and help others had higher self-esteem, less stress and depression, and were 68 percent less likely to feel hopeless than nongivers.[95] Also, on average, people who are identical in their circumstances, like income, age, religion, and gender, are 11 percent more likely to feel very happy if they are givers compared to nongivers.

Most importantly, freedom from scarcity and a life of abundance is one of the greatest rewards of giving. Giving frees you from the bondage of scarcity, where you always feel you don't have enough of anything like stuff, time, emotional support, and help. When you give, you break that chain to scarcity. It doesn't matter how little you have; when you share, like when you share your food, for example, you say to yourself, "I have enough." Likewise, when you take 10 minutes to mentor a coworker or simply listen to them, you say to yourself, "I have time."

So giving changes your life of scarcity from "I don't have time," "I don't have patience," "I don't have space in my mind," and "I don't have enough to live a life of abundance," to one where you always have extra to intentionally give, even if it is little.

SOCIAL REWARD

Everybody wants to be around a giver. When you are an intentional giver, you build better connections and stronger bonds with your family members, coworkers, friends, and even your pets. These stronger connections will help you receive emotional support and expand your pool of resources to help you accomplish your goals and live your Purposehood. And, since researchers found that giving is addictive and contagious,[96] those people in your extensions will not only reciprocate, but also spread giving to their extensions, thus exponentially spreading your positive impact and increasing the possibilities of positive interactions.

When you ignite giving in your family or organization, you will spread all kinds of giving there and beyond. A study by James Fowler of the University of California and Nicolas Christakis of Harvard showed that when one person gives, the act inspires observers to give later and toward different people.[97] The researchers found that giving could spread by three degrees—from person to person to potentially influence hundreds of people you've never met.

You have all the incentives built within you to become a giver and exercise control over your infinite desires. All you need now is *intention*. With intentional giving you will turn unbounded selfishness into selfish-altruism, and with it, you can direct your desires toward your Purposehood.

You ask, "How do I practice intentional giving?"

My friend, it all starts with an empowering belief. When you believe your existential purpose is to become a creator so you may co-create the future with others, you will understand that selfish-altruism is the link between the self and your family, coworkers, communities, and nature, and that giving is the tool to build, maintain, and strengthen this link. Giving is the mechanism that drives your exponential evolution and expansion through the connection with your extensions of being.

You can practice intentional giving starting with the self. As you spend a vacation away from your children, for example, have the intention to rest and recover so you can be a more patient parent. And as you learn a new skill so you can ask for a raise, have the intention to also apply that skill to make the company more successful for the benefit of all its stakeholders. Whatever gift you give to yourself, make it intentional, either as a reward for already being altruistic or as a preparation for future giving.

Then, expand your intentional giving to your family members, your coworkers, your communities and friends—as well as to the nature in your care such as your garden, the creatures in it, and your pets.

As you adopt more empowering beliefs and expand your mindfulness, you can expand the circle of giving to your human family and your community of creatures on Earth. You might even see, at some point, that the self includes everything there is.

The Three Brooks to Giving

There are three brooks that feed into the giving stream: time, possessions, and thoughts.

GIVING TIME

Time is the most valuable asset we have; one that diminishes with every breath we take. Yet we are so unaware of its value that we easily waste it on mindless pursuits or useless endeavors. Once we realize the value of time and the preciousness of the lifetime we have left, then we can intentionally offer some of our lifetime as gifts.

You can start down this path by giving yourself the gift of extra lifetime by intentionally reducing all the distractions that are consuming your time. Space and time are woven together in the fabric of the universe; the faster the movement through space, the slower time passes. Likewise, by reducing the amount of clutter you have around you, including the possessions and distractions that occupy the spaces in your life, you can move more efficiently through your own space and reclaim more time for worthy pursuits.

When you think "I'm so busy, I don't have enough time," make sure to give yourself, during this self-inflicted scarcity, the gift of 51 seconds to pause, breathe, and smile. Then, gift 51 seconds of your time to your family, coworkers, and friends so they may have the privilege of calling a pause. When you pause distractions and observe your breath with a smile of gratitude, you expand your perception of time and you shift from scarcity to abundance. And, when you get to spend time with your spouse, kids, coworkers, friends, pets, or nature, why not make the intention to give them your full attention and to interact with empathy, compassion, and understanding? You can listen, share, and be there.

GIVING POSSESSIONS

Our infinite desire of accumulation unbalances the distribution of resources and creates a disparity in economic stature, especially when combined with other basic desires such as power and status. All religions throughout history recognize the importance of giving possessions. Some make giving optional and others make it oblig-atory—as much as 20 percent of a person's income. There is a great wisdom in such practices, as long as they are distributed directly to the needy and not consumed by the institutions themselves.

Some enlightened people gave even more as they realized that ownership is a misconception, since all possessions are made of atoms and all the atoms in this universe are owned by iSH or the universe. You don't even possess the atoms you are made of as you are constantly exchanging your atoms with others during your life-time, and when you die, you surrender them all back to the universe. The best a person can do is to lease a possession for a lifetime before it's passed on to others.

But giving from your possessions is not only about helping others, it's mostly about freeing yourself from the bondage of enslavement to the infinite desire of possessiveness. Every item you have is a weight chained to your existence, consuming your energy and your most valuable currency: your lifetime. When you give from what is weighing you down, add to your gift a "thank you" and a smile of gratitude to the recipient for freeing you from this weight. Then, once free, don't buy what you'd like to have, but like what you have.

If you were to move to the most beautiful island in the world, where you would live happily surrounded by your loved ones and other Purposehooders, but you were only allowed to bring 100 items, what would they be? Make a list and detach from everything else.

The easiest form of giving is to donate all the extra stuff you have, things you haven't used for a while. This is the first step in taming your unbounded selfishness and freeing yourself from the mindset of scarcity and the anxiety of hoarding stuff "just in case." Giving away the clothes you haven't worn in many years or don't fit you anymore is not altruism, but at an act of freedom. The least you can do is to give away an older item when you obtain a newer one.

The second step of giving is to give from what you value and are attached to. Why don't you buy someone a meal when you are at your favorite restaurant, or when you buy a shirt, also purchase an extra and give one away? This is how you start building your selfish-altruism.

The third step and the highest of giving is to give from what you need. True altruism is when you break your last loaf of bread to share with others.

GIVING THOUGHTS

The least any person could give is a simple thought, word, or action. This could be a warm greeting of "hello," a "thank you" with a smile of gratitude, a word of encouragement to a child, a message of support to a struggling coworker, a hug of compassion to a friend, even a thought, a wish, or a prayer for someone in pain. A positive word is like the seed of a fruit tree that will grow deep and high to produce nourishment for a lifetime.

This type of giving could also be as simple as picking up trash from nature on your hike, stepping out of your car to remove a fallen branch off the road, planting a tree, or any simple acts of kindness to nature and its creatures.

Again, these acts of giving are altruistic as they help others, and at the same time, are selfish in that they make you a giver, with all the health and social benefits attached to this wonderful attribute.

True giving is how you express true love and a sure recipe to receive happiness, success, and fulfillment.

You ask, "How is love linked to giving?"

My friend, love is a very misunderstood word and an ill-defined emotion, which is further confused by linking it to basic desires such as sexual attraction or possessiveness, as in loving an object like a piece of art; eating a desired food, such as people who express their love for animals by eating them; physical activities such as loving sailing; power, such as the love expressed to voters by politicians; and the love of other desires. Yet, there couldn't be confusion once we define love as the willingness to give the things we value without any expectation of reciprocity, whether they are possessions or thoughts. The gift must be pure, because tainted objects obtained through negative actions are not worthy of true giving, such as community work ordered by the court as a punishment for misdeeds, possessions obtained by trickery or theft, or thoughts and prayers to people we wronged without attempting to reverse the harm we caused.

The gift must be something of value, because getting rid of what we don't value is an act of tidying up, not giving. If a person doesn't value their lifetime, wasting it on worthless pursuits, then gifting their time is not worthy of love. If you truly love someone, you would need to become your own most valuable asset before you gift yourself to them.

Additionally, if a person offers their prayers, thoughts, compassion, or empathy without offering an available hand they could stretch to help others, it would be an act of hypocrisy, not love. When a gift is not only pure and valuable, but also needed and cherished by the giver, this gift reaches the highest level of giving, and if combined with no expectations, then it becomes pure love.

You ask, "What kind of giver should I be?"

My friend, a Purposehooder is a selfish-altruist who understands that giving is essential for their own exponential evolution and expansion. While they focus most of their giving on their direct extensions of being, they also give, sometimes anonymously, to people and causes beyond their extensions, since giving to strangers is the best expander of our altruistic self and the best controller of our infinite selfish tendencies. Some people are givers by nature, and most are unconscious givers. However, a Purposehooder is an intentional giver with a determination to better their lives and others.

Most people spend a considerable amount of time daily on altruistic activities such as taking kids to school, cooking for family and friends, helping with homework, mentoring a coworker, being there for a neighbor in need, walking and feeding their pet, or watering and protecting their plants. By inserting an altruistic intention before any of these activities, such as, "I intend to help my child or friend with a homework so they may have better future," the same directionless activity becomes an intentional giving one. A Purposehooder often helps their family members, people at work, friends and neighbors, and their pets and plants without any expectation of reciprocation.

A Purposehooder also dedicates part of their earnings to be spent on giving activities—either directly to help those in their extensions, or to causes that help others. Again, most people spend considerable amount of money on gifts, especially to their families, friends, and relatives, and by adding giving intentions, they can expand their altruistic side. One of the most liberating forces toward potentiality is liberating yourself from stinginess.

A Purposehooder intentionally gives small thoughts, words, and actions of kindness to themselves, people, and nature all through the day.

By attaching a giving intention to your normal acts, you will strengthen your giver side and slowly you will see your selfish-altruism exerting more control over your desires. The more control you have, the less the pull of the basic selfish desires on your life—ones that create tension, which, if not addressed, will lead to stress, anxiety, and regrets.

You ask, "How is giving supported by other streams?"

You can use the other streams to spark your giving side. Use *belief* to state, "I'm an intentional giver." Use *mindfulness* to give without expectations and with gratitude when you become aware of another's needs. Use *wellness* to dedicate your healthy body to acts of kindness. Use *belonging* to give time and attention to those in your extensions.

Your five daily practices are also full of giving as you answer the balance question, give yourself the gift of focus three minutes three times a day, use a bubble meditation to expand your wishes to all your extensions, and give yourself and others the privilege and gift of 51 seconds of pause, breathe, and smile.

You ask, "What is the essential giving practice for a Purposehooder?"

My friend, the essential giving practice is to wake up in the morning and have the intention to be a giver.

I intend to be an intentional giver to my Five Extensions of Being and beyond.

With empowering beliefs running your life, mindfulness practices to monitor progress, enhanced awareness for creeping limiting beliefs, and giving to control your selfishness to empower your selfish-altruism, you are now ready to correctly build the proper vehicle of your inner self that will take you toward your Purposehood. With wellness, the fourth stream of potentiality, you will attend to the most essential part of the self, your body.

The Fourth Stream: Wellness

"Wellness is the fertilizer of the ground where the roots of your potentiality spread. It's a combination of nourishment, movement, and rest that take you toward your Purposehood." — Fourth Stream of Potentiality

FOURTH STREAM

You ask, "What is wellness?"

My friend, wellness is optimizing your body for the journey toward your Purposehood. It is living a holistic, individualized, and balanced lifestyle in order to maximize your fitness and best prepare you for the role you choose to play in this existence. No wonder wellness is elusive in a culture of quick fixes, endless visitations to doctors and healers, and waves of short-lived trends in physical exercises, diets, meditations, supplements, and medications.

Wellness must be holistic, as you are a multidimensional being of extreme complexity, created physically from a burst of energy and vibrations that manifested in particles that fused together in the bellies of exploding stars over billions of years to create the Earth that birthed you.

Like magic, you appeared as a single-celled microorganism and evolved for the past four billion years to become a body made of unique cells and trillions of creatures that work hard and nonstop, collaborating together to keep you alive so you may evolve the even more complex functions of thoughts, emotions, limitless creativity, and infinite desires. With all this, you are destined to become a co-creator of the future, a contemplator of the past, and an observer of the present. And just like those creatures within you work together to maintain your body, you were placed in the body of humanity to ensure its forward march toward its mission to spread life across the landscape of the universe. Your wellness is crucial, not only for your own survival, but also for humanity, life, and the universe. You are a part of the body of humanity and life, and when one part aches, the pain is echoed everywhere.

Such layers of complexity are impossible to maintain, repair, and improve with one remedy. Counting on a single remedy to ease your suffering or heal your pain is like taking a medication that masks the symptoms without curing the cause, and at the same time can introduce side effects that damage your other systems.

For true wellness, you need a clarity of your existential purpose and all Five Streams of Potentiality working together to make sure the beautiful complexity that is you grows with ease. You need beliefs, mindfulness, and giving to maintain your software and free yourself from the viruses of stress, anxiety, and regrets that are at the root of most illnesses. You need physical wellness to maintain your hardware and build the appropriate vehicle for the journey you are on; and you need belonging to maintain your connections with companions who are traveling with you toward your Purpose-hood. Any system without all five streams feeding into it will not provide the healing, recovery, and growth you need.

Wellness must also be individualized, as no two humans are exactly alike. Each star athlete has their own unique wellness program that takes into consideration their future, past, and present. It all starts with the goal they want to achieve and the sport they want to play. This program is built for their individual goals and needs, genetics, metabolism, weight, abilities, and traits. A wellness program for a wrestler is very different than one for a sprinter. Even within the same sport, each person needs a different program. A defender in

American football needs a different wellness program than a receiver, and a boxer who wants to compete in a higher weight class would need very different program than the one competing in a lighter class. This determines the type of food they eat, the quantity of food they consume, the frequency they eat, the amount of rest they get, the type of rest they get, and of course, the exercising schedule and type.

Once the future goal is set, a wellness program considers the athlete's past health condition, genetic composition, their parents' health history, the way they were raised, and the environment in which they were raised. Finally, the program considers their current lifestyle, beliefs, relationships, and practices.

You are as unique and as important to your extensions of being, humanity, life, the universe, and iSH as that star athlete. Your potential role in the existence is not less than any other creator. Your wellness program needs to be customized for your uniqueness, your Purposehood, and the ultimate goal you want to achieve, as well as the role you play in the game of life. And once you know your Purposehood and your field of play, you need to customize a holistic program that will give you the maximum capability to reach your goals.

As humanity evolves and expands exponentially with its science, technology, and consciousness, we will soon have individualized wellness programs to unleash human potential. Nurturing humans to their potentiality will be the most important job in the universe. There's no escape from this destiny. Life demands it. The universe demands it. iSH demands it.

We will get to the point in the not-so-distant future where every human is treated like a universal gift, a unique being, a semideum of the ancient Greek, someone who will influence and improve the lives of all and even evolve and expand life itself. Everything will be customized for that goal, from biological enhancements before birth, to education, social systems, and technologies. This will include, of course, wellness programs. But until then, you will need to take charge of customizing your wellness program by becoming aware of the latest science, by tuning in to your body's reactions to the disciplines you introduce, and by enlisting the assistance of experts and coaches if needed.

The Three Brooks to Wellness

There are three brooks that feed into the wellness stream: nourishment, movement, and rest.

NOURISHMENT

A body is not just a combination of body parts, nor only a collection of cells. Your body is everything that makes you experience this existence. This definition evolves the notion of a body to include any new technology or biology that expands your experience of existence. This includes an artificial limb or heart, a hearing aid, surgical lenses, stem cells, and pacemakers, to name a few. In the future, it will include integrated genetically engineered cells, artificial intelligence, and robotics.

Our bodies are made of matter, which is made of vibrating energy, which is made of information. Our nourishment is not only physical, but also includes *all input* that comes into our bodies. Through your five senses you are always capturing information that either nourish or hinder your growth. The songs you listen to, the movies you watch, the news you read, the relationships you keep, and the events you experience are all adding positive or negative input into your body.

Your thoughts and emotions are self-generated input that affect your well-being positively or negatively. In the same way, all we consume becomes us, literally. The carrot, nut, piece of meat, or drink you are about to consume will shortly become your bone marrow, blood, hormones, organs, or a cell. Physically, it has the power to alter your DNA,[98] but you might want to also consider the circumstances and the history of this food or drink that will become you. Its experiences, the way it was grown, and the way it was treated and handled on its journey to become you, positively or negatively, will also be part of you.

My friend, your body is your holy temple of existence. It is holier than any house of worship and more worthy of being honored, revered, and cleansed by only allowing positive nourishment into it.

There are three essential physical nourishments for the body, without which you can't exist. These are food, water, and air. All of these connect each one of us permanently to nature. Truly, Earth is our existential mother delivering through our existential umbilical cords the nourishments we need to survive and grow. Could it be that the source of stress in our lives is the ungratefulness we've shown to our existential mother through pursuing mindless desires? Could it be that our negative emotions of sustained stress, anxiety, and regrets are being imprinted on nature with every mindless step pounding the ground with arrogance, and every breath we take with entitlement, breathing out ungratefulness?

In an experiment with dogs, researchers collected odor samples from people who watched a horror movie, and from those who watched one that was happy.[99] Then these samples were placed in a room with the dog's owner in one corner and a stranger in the opposite corner. The researchers also placed in the middle a random odor (and sometimes no odor at all). When each dog was released into the room, the researchers monitored its heart rate and stress level in addition to behaviors such as approaching, interacting, and gazing at the stranger. The dogs who walked into the room with the samples of happy odor interacted more with the stranger and showed much lower stressful behaviors.

If an odor of a person after simply watching a horror movie is that impactful on a dog, what impact are we having on nature and its creatures, with all the stress and negativity we have in our modern lives? Researchers found that the average dog's lifespan is getting shorter, mainly due to stress, fear, and anxiety. These are diseases that we're inflicting on nature, and then we wonder why with all these advancements we are not feeling well. Could it be that this negative imprint is being recycled back to us through what we eat, drink, and breathe? Could it be that we are forcing nature to fight us back with viruses and pandemics? Could it be the road to healing ourselves, families, humanity, and nature starts by breaking this cycle from within?

When it comes to food, we are omnivores—capable of eating both plants and meat. Meat was essential to our evolution, as it allowed our earlier relatives to access more calories with less energy expenditure. That, in turn, helped develop our modern brains.

Today, meat is still important for people who move constantly like Bedouins, who live on barren lands in the deserts, or in extreme climates such as Siberia or Alaska. However, with modern availability of plant-based food and the knowledge we have of the health risks of eating meat, the damage to the environment, and the cruelty these animals must endure, we have fewer excuses for eating it. I am confident that a day will come soon when most humans will not want to kill an animal for food. We already have plant-based meat imitations and cultured meat cultivated through cellular agriculture to satisfy some people's carnivorous cravings.

Yet, evolving humans are meant to live with principled-flexibility, as absolutism is the enemy of progress. With a flexitarian diet, a person could be a vegan, for example, without closing the door on the possibility of eating meat if their survival depended on it or if they so desired every now and then. Some have suggested that since we have four canine teeth out of a total of 32, then our caloric intake ratio from animal products to plant should not exceed 13 percent.

In all cases, Purposehooders strive to eat mindfully, with intention, awareness, and gratitude. They mute the negative internal and external dialogues and focus on seeing, smelling, feeling, hearing, tasting, and swallowing small bites that are chewed well. They pause, breathe, and smile when they feel the urges of an uncontrolled desire to overeat or to consume what is not good for their bodies. They aim to like what they should eat or drink instead of eating and drinking what they like. They share their meals with others and don't waste what is left as they give some of their food to the needy or as compost back to nature.

When it comes to drinks, about 60 percent of an adult body is water, and it is the source of life itself.[100] If food is our connection to Earth, water is our connection to the cosmos. Scientists believe water came to Earth from asteroids, and within it, there's possibly the energy of the stars and the memories of evolution.[101]

There actually is no need for a human or any creature to drink anything besides water, except a baby does need its mother's milk for a short period of time. Our urge to drink anything else is driven purely by reasons other than survival, such as a desire for social status when drinking expensive drinks or for social contact when pressured to drink with others. If our drinking desires become mindless and uncontrolled, then we risk destroying ourselves with addictions to unhealthy forms such as alcohol or sugary beverages.

Every human should have free access to clean water without having to purchase it in harmful plastic bottles. Water is a living code of life that reacts to conditions that constrain or expand your potentiality. Those conditions will be part of who you become as you drink them into your cells. Humanity's potentiality will not be totally unleashed until it is unleashed for every human. Every person has the ability to alter the course of humanity toward a better future. We have to solve many challenges before then, such as access to education, connectivity, and freedom from all kinds of labels and restraints, but there is no excuse for not providing—right now—access to free and clean water for everyone.

And then there is air. We can survive without eating for three weeks, and without drinking for three days, but all it takes is three minutes without air before we die. Yet, the air we breathe today is polluted with hard-to-detect fine particles, increasing the risk of stroke, heart disease, lung cancer, and chronic and acute respiratory diseases. This is causing an estimated seven million deaths annually, with tremendous cost and pressure on health systems, economies, and living conditions of people around the world.[102]

According to the World Health Organization, more than 90 percent of the world's children breathe toxic air every day.[103] How could a child's potentiality be unleashed if we poison them with pollutants that negatively impact their neurodevelopment and cognitive ability before they are even born and during their most impressionable years?

While you might be able to purify the water you and your family drink and organically grow the food you eat, the air you breathe is a global problem that one person can't solve alone. On the negative side, we seem to be condemned to breathe this polluted air until a global solution is found, but on the positive side, solving this serious and existential challenge is forcing all humanity to work together to solve this problem we created for our own survival and the survival of nature.

Mother Nature has been patiently correcting many of our misdeeds throughout our evolution, but now it's time we take responsibility for our actions and work together as one to solve the existential challenges of climate change and biodiversity. This is humanity's training mission to prepare it for the next milestone in the journey toward its Purposehood. It's time to unleash the potentiality of every human and learn to collaborate in solving existential challenges so we may use the learning to rehabilitate distant planets to welcome life.

You, my friend, can do something positive immediately, first by becoming aware of your breath, then reconnecting mindfully with nature, and finally, by inspiring people in your extensions to do the same. This change from within will eliminate negative habits in the ways you consume, manage your waste, travel, and consume energy, and eventually will empower you to develop positive habits and work with other like-minded people to influence our societies, businesses, and political leaders to do the right things.

Sometimes when you pause, breathe, and smile, you can bring your attention to an element of nature, and as you breathe you can use a mantra such as:

———

I BREATHE IN HEALING.
I BREATHE OUT GRATITUDE.

To reconnect with nature, consider getting adopted by a tree. Find that tree and make it representative of Mother Nature. Feel free to show her all the love, emotions, reverence, and respect you'd show to your human mother. Tell her your aspirations and concerns and reveal to her the pressures you've been bottling inside of you. Remember, this mother tree will always listen and only do what's good for you. And maybe, just maybe, one day as you sit silently and still next to her, she will speak to you without a voice.

The ancients wisely advised never to fill your stomach, but if you must, then fill one-third with food, one-third with drink, and leave one-third empty so you may breathe with ease. With the right compositions and proportions, we can energize our bodies to keep moving.

MOVEMENT

Long before the advancements of science, the ancients also realized that everything flows, changing all the time and never standing still. The nature of this existence is movement. The vibrating waves of our existence are in constant movement, the particles manifesting as solids are in constant movement, even the spacetime fabric of this universe is in constant movement. Evolution and expansion happen from this constant movement. You are made from the same moving parts of this universe.

Everything in you is moving, and all your nourishments are meant to energize your moving body parts. They are made of and for movement. Even as they lay still, they are always processing something—a chemical reaction, an electrical charge, a thought, or an emotion. When our parts cease to move, we're dead. But even then, we keep moving as we disintegrate and transform. You are made from movement and for movement in order to become an expo-agent of life.

When you are still, you create a pause in you, disrupting your urge for constant movement. This pause is necessary to recharge your body and mind, allowing you to reflect on your past, dream of your future, and observe your present.

With a pause, you slow down the flow of input so you may recognize distractions for what they are and refocus your attention to the one thing that matters. But a pause is only an interruption, not a state of being. You need to be still to connect to the source of enlightenment, and you need to keep moving to attain it and expand it.

Standing still in the present is an illusion sold by people who want to escape the pull of their Purposehood. They have the choice to do that, but imagine if everyone bought into this philosophy instead of thinking that the present is just a rest stop on the journey to the future. You probably can imagine life evolving and expanding without any monks, but can you imagine life evolving and expanding *if all of humanity were monks?* We are meant to be on the move, and we are meant to rest to recharge for the journey.

However, moving mindlessly without direction is not positive, either. We need to move through life mindfully and intentionally with empowering beliefs, expanding our awareness, and generating gratitude. Movement that benefits our selves and our extensions of being and connects us with humanity, nature, and all its creatures.

While our ancestors had no choice but to move to hunt for food, plant fields, or perform manual work all day long, our modern world requires very little movement of us. As a matter of fact, soon enough in the near future, with the introduction of autonomous automations and artificial intelligence, all the work required of a human being will be intellectual. Without a clarity of Purposehood and a lifestyle that incorporates the Five Streams of Potentiality, we will have little motivation to move and we will continue to see an increase in stress, anxiety, regrets, and other physical and psychological ailments. We need to wake up every morning with the intention to be physically active regardless of our jobs or physical limitations. Creativity, wellness, and positive desires are generated through movement.

There are three essential areas to consider when you design your own movement program: endurance, flexibility, and strength. They are all necessary for your wellness, so you need to make sure that if you focus on one of these for your physical goal, you still need to maintain minimum levels of the other two. If you like running, for example, add stretching and push-ups to your routines. If you like yoga, add cardio exercises like hiking in nature. And while you're in nature, you can do some exercises that build your muscles like picking up rocks or moving dead logs from the path. The best exercises are the ones that you can incorporate in your work, do with friends and family, and do while volunteering.

With today's technology tools, you can set and track goals such as 10,000 daily steps or my favorite, burning 800 active calories daily. You can make all your phone calls while walking, hold your meetings while moving in nature, volunteer to coach children in sports, or build houses and schools for the poor. You can make an active habit of whatever it is you enjoy doing, fits with your Purposehood, and creates multiple benefits, touching many of your streams of potentiality.

Physical activity is one of your basic desires, but your other stronger desires might mask themselves as fatigue in order to push you to spend hours on vanity or perhaps acceptance on social media. You need to be mindful of your body, know when to push and when to rest, and get the rest you need, as you can't keep moving without a recharge.

REST

Rest is a recharge, a reflection, and a preparation for your forward journey. It's a mindful pause to ensure you are still on the right path. It's a chance to disconnect from forces pulling you in all directions. It's a space you create between your subconscious and actions, between your desires and mindless fulfillments, between thoughts and emotions, between what you think is or was and what actually is or was, between judgment and acceptance, and between infatuation and love.

Your body requires three essential rests: sleep, breaks, and stillness.

Sleep is a forced rest dictated by nature to make sure you don't consume beyond its recovery. It's your chance to reset as you start every day anew, awakened to a new start, and a new opportunity to correct a wrong and initiate a positive deed. It's the preparation for the most important day of your life—the day that you will take all the learning from the past to intentionally create the future. It's a gift to wake up again to watch the miracle of existence unfold in front of your eyes with a magical sunrise, and to know that your lease on life has been extended. It is also a chance for you to recover, recharge, dream, and maybe connect with the timeless-cloud.

So before you sleep, answer your balance question, "For all the blessings I have in my life, what selfless act do I intend to do tomorrow?" Then go to sleep with a mindful reflection and a sense of gratitude and intention.

Most of our days are spent awake, working, doing, socializing, and thinking. In this active state we need breaks from distractions and exhaustion. You can use those short pauses to refocus your mind, play, and explore away from stress. You can, for example, pause, breathe, and smile often, take short walks in nature, simply let your mind daydream, or just jump up and down.

In an ever-moving world, you also need stillness. Stillness slows down time and allows you to observe, reflect, and expand your awareness. Stillness also provide you with one of the best tools for creativity—boredom.

Silent meditations are a great exercise of stillness and also your three-minute focus practice, focusing on one sensation or gazing at one wonder of nature three times a day.

One of the best resting practices is fasting. A day or two a week of fasting and a longer consecutive period once a year is a great way to rest your body from eating habits, your mind from distractions, your emotions from reactions, your relationships from negativity, and your senses from overwhelming inputs.

To fast correctly, you should not only refrain from eating, drinking, and electronics for hours in the days, but also from all the other urges of your basic desires. True fasting allows you to move up in the Pyramid of Values while focusing on your existential and fundamental desires.

You ask, "How is wellness supported by other streams?"

My friend, use all your streams to unlock your true wellness. Start by discovering and clarifying your Purposehood. Make sure that your *beliefs* about your potentiality and role in life are empowering you to have the best body you need. Think about the milestones and goals on your journey toward this existential purpose.

Set *mindful* intentions for your wellness program to maximize your potentiality as you move forward. Be aware of how your body reacts to changes you implement. Challenge the negative desires for conformity and comfort, as often what you like might not be good for you, while what you dislike might be good. Be grateful for knowing your direction and having the will to move ahead and for people, nature, and circumstances that are helping you get there.

Give yourself time, resources, and encouraging thoughts and prayers to accomplish your wellness program. Give your body the nourishment it needs in order to be the best it can be for the journey you choose. If your journey is of creativity, the food you need is different from that required by those who aim to be soldiers fighting against aggressors. Your needed rest would be different. Your exercise would be different. Maybe you need more brain food, more walks in nature, more hours of sleep, and more meditative breaks. A soldier would need something very different.

People with severe challenges, like Stephen Hawking, showed us that wellness is staying in the best shape possible in order to continue moving toward your Purposehood. He lost most motor functions in his body to ALS, yet he still was able to optimize his wellness to become more productive than many others who claim better health. Under this severe circumstance, he fulfilled his existential purpose, which expanded the world's understanding of the cosmos, contributing toward humanity's Purposehood of exponentially evolving and expanding life into the universe.

How many people do we see taking care of their bodies for the wrong reasons and for useless pursuits? They want to be strong to intimidate and beautiful to be noticed. They exercise to look good, and rest for "beauty sleep." They seek fulfillment from the outside only to feel the emptiness inside. This health is not wellness. These people's potentiality is wasted as their quest for staying young, for recognition, for vanity, or power drive them away from their Purposehood.

Once you have clarity, make sure to connect with a sense of *belonging* with people who are walking the same path. People who will encourage you to keep going and support you when you have doubts. Let go of those negative people who want to hold you back. Find others who will push you beyond your comfort zone and challenge your ways. This is the road to true wellness, and only you can take the first step, starting with the right intentions and then helping others.

You ask, "What is the essential wellness practice for a Purposehooder?"

My friend, every practice in an intentional life starts with an intention.

I intend to live well by being mindful of my nourishment, movement, and rest.

Now that you have established your inner strength with empowering *beliefs, mindfulness,* and *giving,* and your body strength with *wellness,* you are ready to connect with others in order to receive all the happiness, success, and fulfillment that comes from *belonging.* Then, with others, you can build the future you want for your extensions of being and for humanity, life, and the universe. The fruits of your first four streams are realized in the fifth stream of belonging.

The Fifth Stream: Belonging

"Belonging is the stream for co-creation, obtained by including supporters, excluding distractors, and expanding with motivators."
— *Fifth Stream of Potentiality*

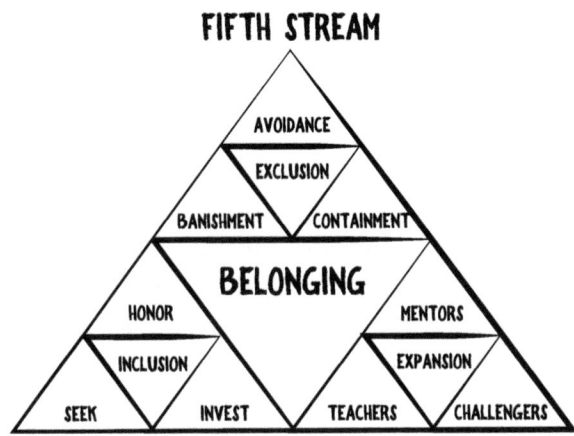

FIFTH STREAM

AVOIDANCE
EXCLUSION
BANISHMENT / CONTAINMENT
BELONGING
HONOR / MENTORS
INCLUSION / EXPANSION
SEEK / INVEST / TEACHERS / CHALLENGERS

You ask, "What is belonging?"

My friend, belonging is a fundamental force of existence. It's how the universe drives evolution and expansion. If it wasn't for belonging, subatomic particles wouldn't have grouped together to form hydrogen and helium, gases wouldn't have grouped to form stars, stars wouldn't have gathered to form galaxies, and galaxies would not have formed groups and clusters. Belonging is the gravitational force that brings things that are both similar and opposite to forge a higher order of being. It drives all the drops of water to form streams, then brings streams into rivers to feed the oceans that host the life we all came from. If it wasn't for the desire to belong, why would single-celled organisms divide and multiply to create a family, a group, and a community?

Why work together with others to create more complex beings and advance life for all? Belonging brought cells together to form plants, and brought trees together to form forests to host life on the surface of the Earth. Belonging is what brought our early ancestors together, and when exponential belonging was triggered in the first Homo sapiens, we developed the desire to connect beyond our gene pools, beyond our tribes, and beyond our work. As our belonging evolves and expands exponentially, we are connecting and belonging beyond our nationalities, our birthplace geography, and beyond our ideologies and religious affiliations.

If the Purposehood pulling force is moving everything in existence toward an ultimate future, belonging is how we get there. We are not meant to be alone. You have no value to humanity, life, and the universe if you live and die alone without any sense of belonging. Belonging and all its benefits of happiness, success, and fulfillment is gifted to you by life, the universe, and iSH for you to create the future with others. Your future and that of your extensions is built by collective vision and collaboration. The future of your family is created through a collaboration of a couple and all their extended families. The future of a business is created by the collaboration of all stakeholders. The future of any group, community, and society is created by the collaboration of all its members. The future of this planet is created through the collaboration of all humanity. The future of humanity and life is created by collaborating in families, businesses, groups, organizations, and communities to unleash the potentiality of every human and make sure no one is left behind— regardless if they are imprisoned behind bars, dogmas, or limiting beliefs. Every human is a stepping-stone toward the future, which is altered by every loss of potentiality.

No potentiality is truly unleashed without the support of others. A lonely person is chained to emptiness from within, wasting their precious lifetime without realizing that they are essential to other lives. You are not meant to be alone, and as a matter of fact, you are never alone, not for a second.

This loneliness plaguing humanity is a false construct of an unaware mind. We all belong to life all the time. How could a person be truly lonely with the movement of life all around them? Even that chair you're sitting on while feeling sorry for your lonely self is alive with movement in every atom that makes it. And if you reflect within, you will find trillions of creatures in your body that ensure your existence and rely on you for theirs. When a person is lonely among trillions of beings within and around them, then loneliness is not the problem, unawareness is.

The moment you are aware of the connection, you will be unable to separate from your extensions, a pet, nature, and even from the well wishes and hopes of people you don't know who pass you by or even live on the other side of the globe. Then you will discover that loneliness is a mere illusion and you always belonged, at least to nature, if to nothing else.

Belonging, my friend, is the ultimate stream of potentiality. It's the stream that exponentially expands the previous four through a network of positive collaborators. All the inner hard work you invested in yourself to become an intentional being with empowering beliefs, awareness, and gratitude, and to become a selfish-altruistic giver with a well-balanced mind and body, will be cultivated in the fruits of your belongingness. With positive beliefs, mindfulness, giving, and wellness, you can form positive belongings to your family, work, communities, and nature.

You ask, "Could belonging be the first stream of potentiality?"

My friend, the force of belonging is so strong that it can easily pull people together for the wrong reasons. A person without the first four streams of potentiality can be effortlessly swept away by the forces of conformity to participate in atrocities like we see in hate groups or by a false sense of superiority or entitlement over other nations, ethnic groups, or religions. When we don't fortify our inner selves, we can become victims to people, propaganda, and ideologies that are well versed in manipulation and use people for their own gains. How many atrocities were committed all through history by political leaders, religious clergymen, and profiteers who fooled masses of followers into committing the most heinous crimes?

Purposehooders will never blindly follow anyone or any ideology and will never belong to groups that limit the potentiality of any human. Before joining a group, Purposehooders fortify themselves with empowering beliefs that remove all the labels of conformity. They nurture a mindfulness that keeps them grateful for the beauty of life and all its creatures, even those with whom they disagree. This mindfulness alerts them to false information and bad intentions.

Purposehooders give to their extensions, but also to others across the globe. They gather strength from wellness that is based on respect of nature and all creatures. Once fortified, they search for people who share their journey toward a common constellation of Purposehood Guiding Stars, people who share similar empowering beliefs and common practices that strengthen bonds and keep open arms to connect with others, people who are invested in helping each other grow for the unique role each is meant to play in existence, people who don't want to dominate or impose, but share and offer. With such people, any challenge will be met with a resolution, and any journey will be filled with happiness, success, and fulfillment.

The Three Brooks to Belonging

There are three brooks that feed into the belonging stream: your lists of *inclusion, exclusion,* and *expansion.* These correspond to three types of people you need to be aware of in your life: those who will always support you (inclusion), those who will always pull you down (exclusion), and those who positively challenge you and expand your awareness (expansion). Keeping these lists will help expand awareness of their impact, allow reflection on their quality, and help devise a plan of action to strengthen belonging.

INCLUSION LIST

These are the people who believe in you when you have doubts, support you when you need help, cheer you up when you are struggling, bring you joy when you are sad, show compassion when you are suffering, provide a shoulder to cry on, and are pillars of strength when you need someone to lean on. They are givers by nature, and you happened to be the lucky receiver and reciprocator to their endless giving. These could be loving parents, spouses, family members, childhood friends, coworkers, and people in various groups you belong to. Everyone has someone like that in their life, as a human can't survive through childhood without at least one giver. You need to identify those people and honor them by at least reciprocating support. Always keep them in your thoughts and prayers and send them messages of gratitude and love often. Invest time in maintaining those relationships, as they are the source of happiness, success, and fulfillment.

If you don't have enough of such people now, then seek them in the right places and you will find them. The time you invest in building those relationships will be some of the most fulfilling time spent, with the highest return on lifetime.

Of course, one of the best supporters you can attract is a spouse. If you invest the time in finding a spouse based on shared Purposehood and empowering beliefs, then you can, through shared practices, build bonds of compassion and mercy that will propel your sails throughout your whole life's journey. There is no better investment in life than having the right spouse.

EXCLUSION LIST

These are people who impact you negatively. It could be the way they express themselves, their beliefs, their way of life, the words they use and gestures they make, the people they keep around them, or it could be simply their presence. Most negativity comes from limiting beliefs, negative interpretations of life experiences, and lack of awareness. People with negative attitudes and behaviors are actually suffering and need help. Just as the negativity of a person living with migraines could be replaced with positivity by simply resolving their health challenge, any negative person could be transformed by finding the source of that negativity in their vision of the future, views of the past, and reactions to the present, and then helping them find a positive alternative.

No human should be excluded from support that can help them unleash their potentiality. However, this exclusion list is about you and how you are impacted by others. It's for you to judge if what you perceive as another person's negativity is pushing you forward or pulling you back. It's for you to judge if you are willing and able to help them change or if you feel that you can't resist or redirect their negative impact on you. It's not about who they are, but how you are impacted by them.

When you list those people, you need to make sure that you are not passing judgment on who they are, but only reflecting on how they make you feel and how you interact with them. They could be wonderful people with good intentions, but only you can judge their influence on you. If you only feel constant negativity, then you need to do something about it.

There are negative people, destroyers, who have ill intentions and are determined to abuse, manipulate, or demean others. They have directed their existence intentionally toward destruction and vacuum. They are the black holes of humanity aiming to dismantle anything good that is sucked into their vacuumed life. You should avoid these people at any cost. One such person could destroy a family, a business, or an organization.

You ask, "What actions can I take for people I have on my exclusion list?"

My friend, there are three actions you can take with your exclusion list: banishment, avoidance, and containment.

For those with whom you experience constant negativity with everything they say or do, or even if their mere presence and the time you spend together is draining, then the simple action is to banish them from your life for your mutual benefit. Life is too short to waste on such encounters and too rich with other people who could help you excel.

It's easy to block unwanted people if they are outside of your extensions or on social media, but it's much harder when those people are part of your surroundings. In that case, try to reduce your encounters as much as possible by avoiding them. There is no need to attend a party where negative people are around. And sometimes, you just need to avoid pain until you have the strength to confront the cause. People with trauma need to recover away from triggers until they have the strength to heal them.

Then there are those you perceive as negative, but whom you can't banish or avoid because they are family members you live with, people you need to work with, or neighbors next door. What you can do is prepare yourself for the encounter to ensure the negativity is neutralized within you. Start with an empowering belief that this encounter will not harm you, if you so choose, as you have control over your responses. Set an intention of what you would like to leave the encounter with, such as "I intend to have a better understanding of this person or what drives them," or "I intend to experience the benefit of my five daily practices by observing the negative emotions within me and the improved control of my responses." Then, try to observe and expand awareness of them, the situation, and yourself, and feel grateful for the insight you gain from such an encounter.

I found magic after preparing myself for a negative encounter with the expand practice targeted at the person or the group. People often react to our attitudes and emotions, hidden in plain sight in our tones and body language. When you mindfully cleanse yourself from negativity with a giving meditation toward that person, they might pick up on your positivity and gratitude instead. You also can try to be a giver by offering your help or at least by being there to listen despite how it makes you feel. There's always an existential reward awaiting an intentional giver.

You ask, "Is it possible for someone not to have an exclusion list?"

A friend shared with me a story about negative people at her work who didn't care about her. They were often loud, even after she told them that loud noises pained her. There were two factors here: loud noises hurt her, and the assumption that her coworkers didn't care. In reality, she controls both of these. She could simply move away from the noises or wear a noise-canceling headset. The assumption that her coworkers didn't care was not a fact. It was her interpretation, which she could easily change. After all, some people might have problems hearing soft noises, yet for them, what is normal is too loud for her.

Many problems in relationships come from having different interpretations, creating assumptions, and building expectations on wrong conclusions. You can only control what is within yourself. This awareness will almost eliminate your exclusion list. We are hurt by others mostly because we let their actions hurt us.

My friend, a person who reaches enlightenment and higher awareness won't be affected negatively by anyone else. *They will have no exclusion list,* as they have total control of what they receive from others, and they even learn more about themselves from those negative encounters. The only criteria you should have for this is whether it is worth investing some of your lifetime in these encounters or not. If the answer is yes because you are trying to help them, then so be it. If it's yes because they bring up negative emotions within you and you need to learn where and how these negative emotions arise, then so be it. But if the answer is no, then simply ignore the negativity and move on.

Most people don't have the level of awareness to deal with internal negativity generated by others and by situations. The easiest way out is avoidance. There will always be negativity, even in the best encounters and even with the most positive people. If you are in a situation where negativity is present, simply leave until the negativity passes, or at least pause, breathe, and smile it out.

Are you on someone's exclusion list? Are you a person whom someone in your extensions is banishing, avoiding, or containing? If you are, try to understand why and see if you can make the needed changes within yourself before you attempt to mend those relationships.

EXPANSION LIST

If the first two lists are essential for your survival, this list is essential for your evolution and expansion. The expansion list includes people who are there to teach, mentor, and challenge you; they are there to expand your window for internal awareness and open new windows to your external awareness; they are there to ensure you apply your beliefs and stick to your practices even if they don't subscribe to them. They remind you to stay authentic while challenging you to explore new beliefs and practices. They are close expansion friends whom you may meet regularly in forums and community gatherings, as well as casual friends and resources whom you intentionally go out of your way to meet for coffee or tea and wonderful conversations and advice.

Such people are gems. They will contribute to your existence. You need to be prepared to benefit from their teachings and to reciprocate by sharing yours with a sense of gratitude for being part of their precious lifetime. You need to be prepared to ignore their faults, as nobody is without some, and to forgive them for any incidental harm they might have caused you.

The best way to benefit from your time with such relationships is to make your meetings totally intentional with clear expectations of outcomes. If a person is your mentor, you don't need to waste time with them on useless gossip or small talk. If they are there to teach you, then be prepared with meaningful questions. If you are meeting to share experiences, then use every minute mindfully, as their lifetime and yours is too precious to waste without objectives. And if the objective is to relax and have fun, then do that and save the serious discussions for another time.

One of the most beneficial experiences I found related to expansion is being in a forum with such people.[104]

You ask, "How do I develop a forum with my expansion list?"

My friend, a forum group is made up of 8 to 10 diverse people with no direct conflict of interest or competition who meet typically once a month for four hours. One of the group members is appointed for a one-year term as a moderator to keep order of the process. In a community, these could be people who don't work together, or those who compete in the same fields or are colleagues in the same department. You start by building trust—emphasizing total confidentiality, with no judgment or direct advice usually conveyed with phrases such as "you should" or "should not." Everyone is there just to listen, connect, and share their own experiences.

1. Start the forum session with everyone stating their name and their Purposehood Statement to remind themselves and everyone else about the journey they are on so they may receive more relevant feedback from the group.

2. Take two minutes for the expand practice where everyone includes the others in their wish bubble.

3. Then the moderator proposes an icebreaker such as: "Name your favorite selfish or altruistic act you have done in the last month." Or one from the second daily practice: "What balance action have you done today and how did it make you feel?"

4. Then everyone takes five minutes to fill out their forum update sheet about the major positive and negative events since the last meeting in personal, family, business, communities, and nature categories.

5. Each person then takes up to three minutes to share their update, which also highlights any major issues they might be facing.

6. Once everyone is done, the members, with the help of the moderator, choose two issues based on two criteria: importance and urgency.

7. The person with the issue selected then presents the details of the issue in 20 minutes, then spends 10 minutes answering clarifying questions and finally, 15 to 20 minutes listening to the group's feedback as they share their experiences with any similar issues they've faced.

8. During the four-hour session, at least once the moderator initiates a three-minute rejuvenation practice such as taking an everyday object and asking everyone to write down 10 ideas on how it can be improved or used, or each person can simply choose to focus on an object, a person, a feeling, or their breath.

9. Everyone has the privilege of calling one pause if they need it, and the whole group joins them for a 51-second pause practice.

10. Finally, take two minutes to end with the expanded practice where everyone includes the others in their bubble of gratitude.

Many people who practice forums in their family, work, and communities report tremendous benefits to all participants, while enhancing their members' and employees' overall satisfaction. You can find more tips and a forum update form on Purposehood.org.

You ask, "Isn't it hard to find people to belong to?"

My friend, when you view people as assets and treasures, you will find that almost every person you meet could be an exceptional member of your expansion list if you are willing to focus on their experiences and stories instead of their judgments and opinions. By asking probing questions, I find when I meet a person who doesn't share my convictions, that I actually agree with 80 percent of what they don't initially say. When I meet a person who shares my convictions, I find that I actually disagree with 20 percent of what they don't initially say. So, the range of disagreement with both people is still about 20 percent.

Then, I ask myself, "Do I want the 80 percent or the 20 percent to govern my view and relationship with this person?" I also found that the 20 percent in either person is the most interesting to discuss.

Maybe if everyone took the time to connect with the other person, they would also find that they agree with them 80 percent of the time. I would dare to say that all humanity shares 80 percent of common norms and values on which we can all connect and collaborate to build a better future. My friend, I hope as the Purposehood movement evolves and expands exponentially, it will become easier to connect with people who share Purposehoods so that we may all forge authentic relationships and mutually beneficial collaboration.

You ask, "Do the five daily practices contain the Five Streams of Potentiality?"

When you communicate your Purposehood Statement and write and verbalize goals, you are stating empowering beliefs. As you pause, you increase your chances of discovering limiting beliefs. The balance, three-minute focus, the expand bubble, and the 51-second pause practices cover mindfulness with intensions, awareness, and gratitude. Giving is present when you plan a selfish or altruistic act in your balance practice, when you give yourself the time to focus and the privilege to pause, and when you expand your compassion to your extensions.

With these practices, you gift your body and mind the nourishment of positive hormones and needed rest for wellness. And finally, as you perform those practices with your family, coworkers, and friends, you will strengthen your belonging.

You ask, "What is the essential belonging practice for a Purposehooder?"

My friend, learning from the examples of the most successful group-based organizations—religions—you would ideally want to meet up once a week in a local community or group, once a month in a forum, and once a year, if possible, in a larger gathering. It's also important to have common rituals to practice together. This includes the five daily practices or those from the Five Streams of Potentiality.

But the one essential belonging practice is the intention to belong.

I intend to belong to those who support my Purposehood and expand my potentiality.

Now that you're ready with your Five Streams of Potentiality, there's nothing that can stop you from receiving happiness, success, and fulfillment, living your Purposehood, and making a positive difference in the world by unleashing the potentiality of others.

Gratitude, ease, and abundance is awaiting you. Become the person you want to be, build the family, businesses, and communities you want to belong to, and in the process, play your unique role in the exponential evolution and expansion of humanity, life, and the universe. Nothing can stand in your way of becoming the creator you were meant to become. It's time to co-create your bright future with others, the bright future of your extensions, and that of humanity.

My friend, time is the most precious of your possessions, and it's time for action.

You, Humanity, and the Future

"True convictions are displayed in actions." – A Purposehood principle

You ask, "Where do I go from here?"

My friend, we are undoubtedly facing tremendous challenges and existential threats. Some are of our own creation, such as climate change and the destruction of biodiversity, others are out of our control—not unlike a collision with an asteroid that wiped out the dinosaurs on our home planet or viruses that killed millions. Today, as we live through the inflection point of exponentiality, we are facing serious and unprecedented challenges in all our extensions of being.

Our selves are suffering from the persistent tension of misdirection in this jungle of life as we mindlessly run away from fears and after desires, twisting the umbilical cord connecting us to nature's nourishments of happiness, success, and fulfillment. As this happens, we experience stress, anxiety, and regrets every day of our lives.

Our family units are falling apart under the constant strain of distractions, addictions, and demands on our time. This tension prevents us from strengthening our bonds and from helping each other overcome challenges and remove obstacles that are hindering our growth toward our potentiality.

Our businesses are consumed with mindless pursuits of short-term profits at the expense of the well-being of employees, communities, and nature, instead of establishing a clear Purposehood that embodies all stakeholders. That Purposehood would treat employees as assets, not as liabilities, and create products and services that ensure a sustainable growth of the business. It would solve pressing problems instead of treating customers as mindless consumers while preying on their fears and infinite negative desires.

Our relationships are transactional. Our communities and societies are suffering from divisions and manipulations by the negative forces of ignorance and malevolence, leading people toward an existence devoid of positive values, reverence for life, and respect for other humans who don't share their views. These same forces are undermining humanity's efforts to solve our collective challenges, including the 17 goals targeted by the United Nations to be achieved by 2030, ranging from eliminating poverty to clean energy and gender equality—a cause that must take priority as it has the most immediate positive impact on half of all humanity.

Women do not yet have equal access to all the resources and opportunities available to men in order to equitably contribute and solve the challenges of our malfunctioning male-led institutions, including politics and religion. Empowering women as leaders might be our best opportunity to achieve the other goals in the targeted time frame. The time of leadership by muscle power has passed; the future needs the intuitive intelligence and compassion of women.

Nature and all its creatures are suffering from our mindless exploitations and growth, which is driving hundreds of species to extinction on daily bases, and could ultimately lead to our own disappearance.

Today, we are still unable to fully collaborate to solve our existential problems due to imaginary divisions based on the limiting labels of nationalities, religious affiliations, ethnicities, competing financial interests, power structures, political views, or even the false construct among all kinds of groups of "us versus them."

Yet, there is no reason to despair, as we are about to emerge on the other side of the inflection point of exponentiality. The progress of technology and growth is becoming exponential, as is our collective consciousness. This growing collective consciousness is awakening individuals to their potentiality, bonding family members closer around shared Purposehood, and initiating businesses that want to make money by making a positive difference in the world. It is creating relationships and forming groups and communities around shared visions, goals, and actions that drive social change, solve global challenges, and force people in power to alter the course of destruction. It is opening people's eyes to the needless suffering of nature and its creatures, and the urgent need to change course now before it's too late.

Awakened people are realizing with this exponential consciousness that we are all one humanity, interconnected to many other lifeforms traveling together on one ship. We increasingly recognize that we all will drown in the sea of extinction if we don't stop and counteract the ill-intentioned and misguided—those who are destroying our ship in the pursuit of instant gratification and immediate gains. Indeed, awakened people are fighting not only for their survival, but for the survival of all life, including those who, consciously or not, are working against them.

You ask, "What does the future hold for us?"

The future of the universe, life, humanity, and your future, my friend, is bright. The mystery of existence has not been fully revealed, the beauty of the universal landscape has not been fully constructed, the wonders of life have not been fully explored, the possibilities of what's ahead have not been fully innovated, and our fundamental desires have not been totally fulfilled. There's still so much influence to absorb and exert, so much belonging to offer and accept, so much value to enjoy and create, and so much love to receive and emanate. So much to imagine and so much to desire, so much to learn and so much to gain, so much to create and so much to anticipate.

My friend, the future is born from the marriage of predictions and unpredictability: predictions of the oracles of creativity and the unpredictability of collective consciousness. The future is created in the tiny space between expectations and surrender: expectations from infinite desires and limitless dreams and the surrender to the pulling force toward an existential purpose.

The only way to see the future from its birth to its end is to be outside spacetime, outside this dimensional universe looking down on a block universe, perhaps one among many, a view only possible from where iSH sits on the throne of infinity.

This doesn't mean that we are not influencers of the future, nor that it's not possible to create the future as we envision it. On the contrary, if we can create a clear vision of the future and we take steps toward increasing its probability, then the possibility of actually bringing that vision into existence is also increased. It's quite possible that our collective actions as humanity toward a common vision of the future is the tipping point of possibilities. Yet, as we explored in the PoET propositions, even though it serves us well to have clear and high expectations, we should rest assured that the future will always be a better state of being, regardless if it meets our expectations or not.

You ask, "What is the future of the universe?"

My friend, the universe, 13.8 billion years old, is a baby that has just been delivered from the womb of existence with a Big Bang. It's full of hope and aspirations as it looks forward to trillions of years of marvelous exponential evolution and expansion before it closes its eyes and surrenders the tremendous wisdom collected during its lifetime to the timeless-cloud. By the time it dies, it will have lived many magnificent trillions upon trillions of years with yet-unimaginable life spreading all over its now barren lands.

Just like we see the coming and going of creatures, structures, and ideas during our short lifetime on Earth, the dying universe will witness countless planets, stars, galaxies, and lifeforms come and go in a constant cycle of birth and death, creation and destruction. And with every cycle, a new evolved and expanded universal conscious-ness emerges from the ashes, with contributions and information of those who came before.

This universe, my friend, is a neighborhood in iSH's many universes. It is still under construction, and soon enough during its lifetime—not yours or mine—it will be filled with vibrant life of amazing creatures, including our distant semideum offspring.

You ask, "Will this existence end?"

Scientists and clergy might not agree on much, but they all agree that this existence will come to an end. Death is the final destination of everything born. How this universe will end is still a guess, but I suspect it will probably collapse into itself, just like a black hole, and re-emerge on the other side with all the information it accumulated during its lifetime with another Big Bang of sorts, but in a different dimensional existence. This is how we might continue to exist, and from iSH's prospective, we might already be there.

You ask, "What is the future of life?"

My friend, life is the expo-agent of the universe and it will fulfill its function to evolve and expand exponentially into it. Life, in different shapes and forms, might already exist elsewhere in the vast expanse of the universe as there is plenty of water in the cosmos to fuel it with energy, memory, and structure. Even life as we know it here on Earth will move with us to other planets and galaxies, reviving lost species, evolving current ones, and spawning new life-forms better suited for the new environments.

On humanity's ark to the cosmos, we will take the seeds of every living being to be resurrected in new environments. The surprises of biodiversity in new environments as we plant life seeds in new planets will create species that never existed on our Earth. Today we look with awe at the magic of nature, yet the future will be filled with wonders beyond our current imaginations. The beauty of life and its creatures will be something no eyes have seen, no ears have heard, and no living human has imagined.

You ask, "What is the future of humanity?"

Humanity is the expo-agent of life, and it will fulfill its function of evolving and expanding exponentially in the universe, spreading life with it across the galaxies. If an outside observer was watching the evolution of Homo sapiens, they would have concluded that this new species would be a disaster to life and not worthy of living based on the behavior of our early predecessors.

It's understandable if an observer of our short history would be pessimistic of our future, or would even conclude that humanity is a failed experiment of nature. But past and present cannot predict the future of creatures with the powers of choice, infinite desires, and limitless creativity.

If iSH were to look down on humanity, iSH would see a child with incredible potentiality that is capable of evolving and expanding exponentially to become a co-creator of life. And just like human parents remain filled with hope and love as they watch their babies fall and get up as they learn to walk and experiment with breaking dishes, writing on walls, and even destroying irreplaceable pieces of art, iSH sees in humanity today an infant of potentiality that grew to become a child of exploration on its way to become an adult of creation. If observers of the past and present were to question iSH's will to grant choice to humans, iSH would simply respond, "I know what you know not."

In the future, humanity will show skeptics that we are worthy of iSH's trust. Humanity will embrace challenges, overcome obstacles, repair damages, and march forward to a better future, where every human child is provided with the resources they need to grow to their potential, where Earth is revered as the land of our roots as we branch out in the universe, where we view our ethnic diversity and unique individuality as living organisms and cells in one body, where we realize that every human is a needed neuron in the universal brain of consciousness, and where every challenge we overcome together expands our collective brain with new synaptic connections. This future will be infused with ingenuity with creations like bioengineering, artificial intelligence, and robotics; new discoveries like sources of abundant energy that don't harm nature but propel us through the stars; and with a common existential purpose focused on unleashing human potentiality and cherishing individual uniqueness while connecting on shared Purposehoods in order to spread life to the rest of the universe.

You ask, "What should we do to solve our current challenges as we move to the bright future ahead?"

The solution is straightforward. It is personal transformation. When you change yourself, you will automatically change your family, workplace, communities, and the nature that surrounds you. The world changes and the bright future is created with every personal transformation.

Your personal transformation starts by knowing that everything in existence has an existential purpose. And you, my friend, have a unique Purposehood that is essential for all your extensions to live theirs. Your transformation journey commences by having clarity of your Purposehood, choosing empowering beliefs, developing positive habits such as the five daily practices, and unleashing your potentiality with the five streams.

We need to first change ourselves, influence our extensions, and connect with those who have been transformed to build together the future we collectively desire.

Together, we need to create a Purposehood movement with people from all backgrounds, talents, and professions, united with the view that every person is an asset that must be cultivated, and with a vision to unleash the potentiality of every human.

This movement of champions, volunteers, influencers, and coaches from around the globe will help remove the obstacles preventing people from clearly seeing their guiding stars, and provide potentiality nourishment to our neglected children, adults, and elders. These apostles of purpose will visit schools, hospitals, prisons, refugee camps, nursing homes, businesses, and places of worship to help individuals and organizations find their guiding stars and understand the unique roles life needs them to play.

We need to create meetups and gatherings, workshops, coaching organizations, learning institutions, research groups of various specialists, community and wellness centers, addiction recovery treatments, inspirational art, music, and movies and technology platforms to make it easy to practice and connect with others through shared Purposehoods.

In every town and locality, we need a Purposehood community with a coordination committee to assist in arranging local forums, events, and organizing volunteers to help their communities and rejuvenate their neighbor's seeds of potentiality.

I call on you to join or start a Purposehood community in your family, neighborhood, workplace, and with your friends so we may all create a better future together as one movement, on one Earth, in one direction, moving in the vast ocean of existence toward humanity's destiny. Little streams can join to form a roaring river that reshapes the landscape and resurrects life in barren lands as it flows toward the ocean. Start with yourself, inspire your extensions, and join others on Purposehood.org so we may experience joy together as we take the beautiful, exciting, and challenging journey toward the amazing future we all will create. *Together, let's create a movement with the goal of helping every person discover and live their Purposehood. Let's unleash the potentiality of every human. Let's connect in groups and communities around shared Purposehoods. Let's aim to reach at least one billion people in the next 15 years. Together, we can do it.*

And you, my friend, are the doorway to the future of humanity. You have the choice, today, to find your guiding star and take the first step forward, removing the weeds of your limiting beliefs and planting the seeds of empowering ones.

Today, you can choose to grow with ease as you connect all your extensions with selfish-altruism.

Today, you can flip your pyramid from desires to values and follow the scent of happiness, success, and fulfillment, focusing on the role you are meant to play as a creator.

My friend, value your uniqueness and that of others, love without expectations of reciprocity, and be grateful to iSH, existence, the universe, life, humanity, your communities, your coworkers, your family, and yourself. They all made you who are you today so you may become what you want to be tomorrow.

You are the conductor of the symphony of life; listen to the music of existence with mindfulness, lead your orchestra with passion and compassion, be patient and strong, and believe in yourself, in your extensions, and in humanity.

My friend, may you be happy, successful, and fulfilled every day of your life, and may you grow with ease.

And a selfish request: Don't forget to send me a thought of love, kindness, or a prayer.

Appendix A: Glossary

Consumer: A person who is directionless and totally consumed with their selfish pursuits.

Creator: A person who focuses on creating a better future for all.

Day of Clarity: The day that you discover a safe and welcoming place where you can grow to your full potential.

Day of Awakening: The day when you realize that you are living in the jungle of life.

Destroyer: A person who chooses to direct their life for the benefit of some and the destruction of others.

Expo-Agent: A disruptive force that leads to exponential growth or decline in a system.

Five Extensions of Being: The self, family, work, communities, and nature—a greater "you" that determines your own survival and growth.

Five Streams of Potentiality: Belief, mindfulness, giving, wellness, and belonging—your nourishments for happiness, success, and fulfillment.

Garden of Eden: Any safe and welcoming place where you can grow to your full potential in the direction of your Purposehood with ease.

Genius: Your innate ability to become a creator.

Humanity's Purposehood: The Purposehood of humanity is determined by the need of life to evolve and expand exponentially across the universe.

iSH: Your deity, ultimate force of creation, or the nothingness beyond the moment of emergence of existence.

Jungle of Life: Life without direction lived in pursuit of infinite desires and constant fears.

Linear-Agent: A force that causes a gradual growth or decline in a system.

Martyr: A person who is misdirected and totally consumed with their altruistic pursuits.

Negative States of Living: Ways in which you live in constant tension.

Night of Destiny: The night you find your Purposehood Guiding Star.

Positive States of Living: Ways in which you live with ease.

Purposehood: The existential purpose of everything. For a human, it is the purpose of their life.

The Purposehood Method: A framework to design a life worth living with happiness, success, and fulfillment, offered through books, technology platform, courses, workshops, and retreats.

Purposehood of Everything Theory (PoET): A statement and formula to explain the existential purpose of everything.

Pyramid of Desires: In humans, 33 driving desires ranging from basic to essential, fundamental, and existential – all driven by specific desire traits.

Pyramid of Values: The values you hold with regard to the 33 desires. These values make you a creator, a consumer, a martyr, or a destroyer.

Potentiality: The ultimate potential of a being as intended by its creator.

Purposehood Guiding Star: A clarity of direction through a Purposehood Statement, empowering beliefs, and commitment to potentiality practice.

Purposehood Statement: A powerful statement of your worthiness to existence, created when you link what you want with what you want to do for the world.

Return On LifeTime (ROLT): LifeTime is the ultimate currency worthy of investment. ROLT is the key measurement of fulfillment and a way to expand your legacy in this life and the beyond.

Seed of Potentiality: The part of every human waiting to be nourished with happiness, success, and fulfillment.

Selfish-Altruism: Being selfish for altruistic reasons and altruistic for selfish reasons, creating a powerful synergy for Purposehood.

Semideum: A demigod, a superhero, a creator, a human with unleashed potentiality.

Appendix B:
Brooks of Potentiality

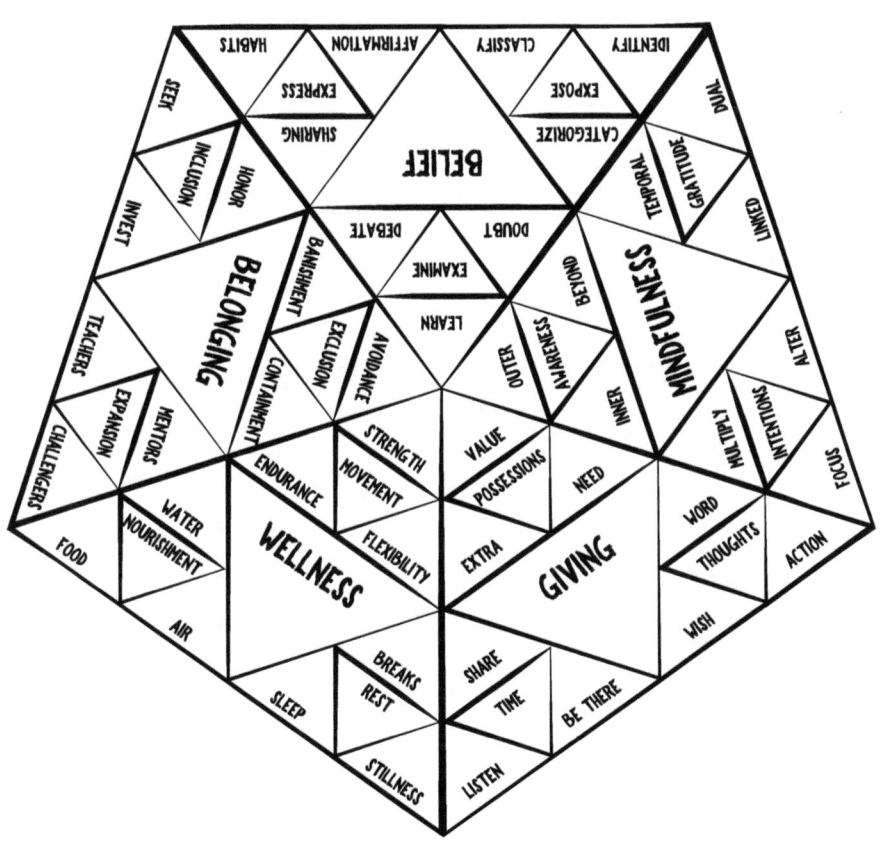

Appendix C:
The 33 Human Desires

Desire Traits	Betterment
	Excessiveness
	Haste
Basic Desires	Acceptance
	Accumulation
	Autonomy
	Curiosity
	Idealism
	Loyalty
	Movement
	Nourishment
	Order
	Parenting
	Power
	Rest
	Retaliation
	Sex
	Socializing
	Status

Essential Desires	Attraction
	Beautification
	Construction
	Domestication
	Exploitation
	Exploration
	Innovation
	Love
	Profiting
	Want
Fundamental Desires	Happiness
	Fulfillment
	Success
Existential Desire	Purposehood

Endnotes

1. "Branch Point," Wikipedia, last modified June 11, 2019, https://en.wikipedia.org/wiki/Branch_point.

2. Hedberg, Brulin, Alex, and Gustafson, 2011; Fahlman et al., 2009; Bigler, Neimeyer, and Brown, 2001; Harlow, Newcomb, and Bentler, 1986.

3. William Damon, *Greater Expectations: Overcoming the Culture of Indulgence in America's Homes and Schools* (New York: Free Press, 1995).

4. "Daily Life," The American Institute of Stress, accessed December 18, 2019, https://www.stress.org/daily-life.

5. "How Common Is PTSD?" National Center for PTSD, U.S. Department of Veterans Affairs, accessed April 12, 2020, https://www.ptsd.va.gov/understand/common/index.asp.

6. "Facts & Statistics," Anxiety and Depression Association of America (ADAA), accessed February 15, 2020, https://adaa.org/about-adaa/press-room/facts-statistics.

7. "Depression," World Health Organization, accessed February 15, 2020, https://www.who.int/news-room/fact-sheets/detail/depression.

8. "Suicide Statistics," American Foundation for Suicide Prevention, accessed April 16, 2019, https://afsp.org/about-suicide/suicide-statistics.

9. Neal J. Roese and Amy Summerville, "What We Regret Most... and Why," *Personality and Social Psychology Bulletin* 2005; 31(9): 1273–85, https://doi.org/10.1177/0146167205274693.

10. Bronnie Ware, "Regrets of the Dying," accessed December 12, 2019, http://www.bronnieware.com/blog/regrets-of-the-dying.

11. Boyle et al, 2009; Lyubomirsky, Tkach, and DiMatteo, 2005.

12. Patrick L. Hill and Nicholas A. Turiano, "Purpose in Life as a Predictor of Mortality Across Adulthood," *Psychological Science* 2014; 25(7): 1482–86, https://doi.org/10.1177/0956797614531799.

13. Carol D Ryff, Burton H Singer, and Gayle Dienberg Love, "Positive Health: Connecting Well-Being with Biology," Philosophical Transactions of the Royal Society B: Biological Sciences 2004; 359(1449): 1383–1394, https://www.ncbi.nlm.nih.gov/pmc/articles/PMC1693417.

14. Shirley Musich, Shaohung S Wang, Sandra Kraemer, Kevin Hawkins, and Ellen Wicker, "Purpose in Life and Positive Health Outcomes Among Older Adults," *Population Health Management* 2018 Apr 1; 21(2): 139–147, https://www.ncbi.nlm.nih.gov/pmc/articles/PMC5906725/.

15. Patricia A. Boyle, Aron S. Buchman, Lisa L. Barnes, et al, "Effect of a Purpose in Life on Risk of Incident Alzheimer Disease and Mild Cognitive Impairment in Community-Dwelling Older Persons," *Archives of General Psychiatry* 2010; 67(3): 304-310, https://jamanetwork.com/journals/jamapsychiatry/fullarticle/210648.

16. Arlener D. Turner, Christine E. Smith, and Jason C. Ong, "Is Purpose in Life Associated with Less Sleep Disturbance in Older Adults?" *Sleep Science and Practice* 1, 14 (2017), https://sleep.biomedcentral.com/articles/10.1186/s41606-017-0015-6.

17. B. Nygren, L. Aléx, E. Jonsén, Y. Gustafson, A. Norberg, and B. Lundman, "Resilience, Sense of Coherence, Purpose in Life and Self-Transcendence in Relation to Perceived Physical and Mental Health Among the Oldest Old," *Aging Mental Health* 9 (2005): 354–362.

18. A. Bowling and S. Iliffe, "Psychological Approach to Successful Ageing Predicts Future Quality of Life in Older Adults," *Health Quality Life Outcomes* 9 (2011): 13.

19. Bronk, 2013.

20. Csikszentmihalyi, 1990.

21. Lee, Cohen, Edgar, Laizner, and Gagnon, 2006.

22. William Breitbart, Barry Rosenfeld, Hayley Pessin, Allison Applebaum, Julia Kulikowski, and Wendy G. Lichtenthal, "Meaning-Centered Group Psychotherapy: An Effective Intervention for Improving Psychological Well-Being in Patients With Advanced Cancer," *Journal of Clinical Oncology* 2017; 33(7): 749–54, https://doi.org/10.1200/jco.2014.57.2198.

23. Dan Buettner, "9 Lessons from the World's Blue Zones on Living a Long, Healthy Life," World Economic Forum, accessed February 15, 2020, https://www.weforum.org/agenda/2017/06/changing-the-way-america-eats-moves-and-connects-one-town-at-a-time.

24. Carol D. Ryff, Burton H. Singer, and Gayle Dienberg Love, "Positive Health: Connecting Well-Being with Biology," *Philosophical Transactions of the Royal Society of London. Series B: Biological Sciences* 2004; 359(1449): 1383–94, https://doi.org/10.1098/rstb.2004.1521.

25. Patrick L. Hill and Nicholas A. Turiano, "Purpose in Life as a Predictor of Mortality Across Adulthood," *Psychological Science* 2014; 25(7): 1482–86, https://doi.org/10.1177/0956797614531799.

26. Hill, Burrow, and Sumner, 2013.

27. "What Makes a Good Life? Lessons from the Longest Study on Happiness," Harvard Second Generation Study, accessed February 15, 2020, https://www.adultdevelopmentstudy.org.

28. Bronk, 2013.

29. Fahlman et al, 2009; Bigler, Neimeyer, and Brown, 2001; Harlow, Newcomb, and Bentler, 1986.

30. Roos, Kirouac, Pearson, Fink, and Witkiewitz, 2015; Nicholson, Higgins, Turner, James, Stickle, and Pruitt, 1994; Harlow, Newcomb, and Bentler, 1986; Padelford, 1974.

31. Fahlman et al, 2009; Bigler, Neimeyer, and Brown, 2001; Harlow, Newcomb, and Bentler, 1986.

32. Inhelder Bärbel, Jean Piaget, and Anne Parsons, *An Essay on the Construction of Formal Operational Structures* (New York: Basic Books, 1961); Erik H. Erikson, *Identity: Youth and Crisis* (New York: W. W. Norton & Company, 1968).

33. Patrick L. Hill, Joshua J. Jackson, Brent W. Roberts, Daniel K. Lapsley, and Jay W. Brandenberger, "Change You Can Believe In," *Social Psychological and Personality Science* 2010; 2(2): 123–31, https://doi.org/10.1177/1948550610384510.

34. McAdams and Olson, 2010; Roberts et al, 2004.

35. Bleidorn et al, 2010.

36. Lodi-Smith and Roberts, 2007.

37. David S. Yeager, Marlone D. Henderson, David Paunesku, Gregory M. Walton, Sidney Dmello, Brian J. Spitzer, and Angela Lee Duckworth, "Boring but Important: A Self-Transcendent Purpose for Learning Fosters Academic Self-Regulation," *Journal of Personality and Social Psychology* 2014; 107(4): 559–80, https://doi.org/10.1037/a0037637.

38. Adolescent Moral Development Lab, "The Psychology of Purpose," accessed April 12, 2020, https://www.templeton.org/wp-content/uploads/2018/02/Psychology-of-Purpose-FINAL.pdf; Hill, Burrow, and Bronk, 2013; Pizzolato, Brown, and Kanny, 2011; Yeagar and Bundick, 2009; Damon, 2008; Benson, 2006; Benard, 1991.

39. Benson, 2008.

40. Dik and Duffy, 2012.

41. Dik and Duffy, 2009; Damon, 2008.

42. Ryff & Singer, 1998; Bonebright, Clay, & Ankenmann, 1989.

43. Jim Harter, "Employee Engagement on the Rise in the U.S.," Gallup, accessed February 6, 2020, https://news.gallup.com/poll/241649/employee-engagement-rise.aspx.

44. Amy Wrzesniewski and Jane E. Dutton, "Crafting a Job: Revisioning Employees as Active Crafters of Their Work," *The Academy of Management Review* 2001; 26(2): 179, https://doi.org/10.2307/259118.

45. "Nature Connectedness," Wikipedia, accessed November 24, 2019, https://en.wikipedia.org/wiki/Nature_connectedness.

46. Elizabeth K. Nisbet, John M. Zelenski, and Steven A. Murphy, "Happiness Is in Our Nature: Exploring Nature Relatedness as a Contributor to Subjective Well-Being," *Journal of Happiness Studies* 2010; 12(2): 303–22, https://doi.org/10.1007/s10902-010-9197-7.

47. Netta Weinstein, Andrew K. Przybylski, and Richard M. Ryan, "Can Nature Make Us More Caring? Effects of Immersion in Nature on Intrinsic Aspirations and Generosity," *Personality and Social Psychology Bulletin* 2009; 35(10): 1315–29, https://doi.org/10.1177/0146167209341649.

48. Andrew J. Howell, Holli-Anne Passmore, and Karen Buro, "Meaning in Nature: Meaning in Life as a Mediator of the Relationship Between Nature Connectedness and Well-Being," *Journal of Happiness Studies* 2012;14 (6): 1681–96, https://doi.org/10.1007/s10902-012-9403-x.

49. "How Americans Protect the Environment in Their Daily Lives," Pew Research Center Science & Society, accessed December 30, 2019, https://www.pewresearch.org/science/2016/10/04/everyday-environmentalism.

50. Martin E. Seligman and Mihaly Csikszentmihalyi, "Positive Psychology: An Introduction," *American Psychologist* 2000; 55(1): 5–14, https://doi.org/10.1037/0003-066X.55.1.5.

51. William Damon, Jenni Menon, and Kendall Cotton Bronk, "The Development of Purpose During Adolescence," *Applied Developmental Science* 2003; 7(3): 119–28, https://doi.org/10.1207/s1532480xads0703_2.

52. P. T. P. Wong, "Implicit Theories of Meaningful Life and the Development of the Personal Meaning Profile," in *The Human Quest for Meaning: A Handbook of Psychological Research and Clinical Applications*, eds. P. T. P. Wong and P. S. Fry (Mahwah, NJ: Lawrence Erlbaum Associates, Inc., 1998), 111–140.

53. Yukari Mitsuhashi, "Ikigai: A Japanese Concept to Improve Work and Life," BBC Worklife, last modified August 7, 2017, http://www.bbc.com/capital/story/20170807-ikigai-a-japanese-concept-to-improve-work-and-life.

54. "5 Whys," Wikipedia, accessed October 9, 2019, https://en.wikipedia.org/wiki/5_Whys.

55. "Pale Blue Dot," Wikipedia, accessed February 15, 2020, https://en.wikipedia.org/wiki/Pale_Blue_Dot.

56. "Competency 054: Characteristics of the Solar System and the Universe," BioEd Online, accessed April 12, 2020, http://www.bioedonline.org/online-courses/educator-certification/generalist-4-8/competency-054-characteristics-of-the-solar-system-and-the-universe.

57. Howard Gardner, *Frames of Mind: The Theory of Multiple Intelligences* (New York: Basic Books, 1983).

58. Chloe McIvor, "Learning by Experiment Is All in a Day's Play," Nature, last modified July 26, 2011, https://www.nature.com/news/2011/110726/full/news.2011.442.html.

59. Claire Cook, Noah D. Goodman, and Laura E. Schulz, "Where Science Starts: Spontaneous Experiments in Preschoolers' Exploratory Play," *Cognition* 2011; 120(3): 341–49, https://doi.org/10.1016/j.cognition.2011.03.003.

60. Puerto Williams is a pristine town of Tierra del Fuego in southern Chile.

61. "Self-Expansion Model," Wikipedia, accessed February 14, 2020, https://en.wikipedia.org/wiki/Self-expansion_model#Measuring_Inclusion_of_the_Other_in_the_Self.

62. Elliot Aronson. *Social Psychology* (Toronto: Pearson Prentice Hall, 2007).

63. "Prisoner's Dilemma," Wikipedia, accessed February 1, 2020, https://en.wikipedia.org/wiki/Prisoner's_dilemma.

64. "Burn-out an 'Occupational Phenomenon': International Classification of Diseases," World Health Organization, last modified May 28, 2019, https://www.who.int/mental_health/evidence/burn-out/en.

65. Jack Harris, "Quantum Physics: Scientific Surprises All Around Us," YouTube video, 56:49, "YaleUniversity," October 14, 2017, https://www.youtube.com/watch?v=4VFjWiQHpFI.

66. Scott T. Allison, "What Is Your Purpose in Life?" Psychology Today, last modified June 26, 2014, https://www.psychologytoday.com/us/blog/why-we-need-heroes/201406/what-is-your-purpose-in-life.

67. *The Matrix,* directed by Lana Wachowski and Lilly Wachowski, Burbank, CA: Warner Bros. Pictures, 1999.

68. Timothy D. Wilson, David A. Reinhard, Erin C. Westgate, Daniel T. Gilbert, Nicole Ellerbeck, Cheryl Hahn, Casey L. Brown, and Adi Shaked, "Just Think: The Challenges of the Disengaged Mind," *Science* 2014; 345(6192): 75–77, https://doi.org/10.1126/science.1250830.

69. "Brainstorming: Rules & Techniques for Idea Generation," IDEO U, accessed February 16, 2020, https://www.ideou.com/pages/brainstorming.

70. A friend said he didn't agree with this statement because he doesn't believe in the creation of the universe. I told him this statement is specific for everything that is created and should at least apply to anything he creates. It also applies to those who believe in a creator or a creating force.

71. "Attracting Pollinators," Science Learning Hub, accessed February 16, 2020, https://www.sciencelearn.org.nz/resources/80-attracting-pollinators.

72. "Flowers Evolve to Suit Birds and Bats," LiveScience, accessed February 16, 2020, https://www.livescience.com/1448-flowers-evolve-suit-birds-bats.html.

73. "The Nobel Prize in Literature 1950," The Nobel Prize, accessed February 16, 2020, https://www.nobelprize.org/prizes/literature/1950/russell/lecture.

74. "Maslow's Hierarchy of Needs," Wikipedia, accessed February 6, 2020, https://en.wikipedia.org/wiki/Maslow's_hierarchy_of_needs.

75. Steven Reiss, *Who Am I? The 16 Basic Desires That Motivate Our Actions and Define Our Personalities* (New York: The Berkley Publishing Group, 2002).

76. Henry A. Murray, *Explorations in Personality* (Oxford, England: Oxford University Press, 1938).

77. Alejandra Borunda, "This Young Whale Died with 88 Pounds of Plastic in Its Stomach," National Geographic, last modified March 18, 2019, https://www.nationalgeographic.com/environment/2019/03/whale-dies-88-pounds-plastic-philippines.

78. Laura Parker, "Microplastics Found in 90 Percent of Table Salt," National Geographic, last modified October 17, 2018, https://www.nationalgeographic.com/environment/2018/10/microplastics-found-90-percent-table-salt-sea-salt.

79. Barry Schwartz, *The Paradox of Choice: Why More Is Less* (New York: HarperCollins Publishers, 2004).

80. Aekyoung Kim and Sam J. Maglio, "Vanishing Time in the Pursuit of Happiness," *Psychonomic Bulletin & Review* 2018; 25(4): 1337–42, https://doi.org/10.3758/s13423-018-1436-7.

81. "Stanford Marshmallow Experiment," Wikipedia, accessed December 22, 2019, https://en.wikipedia.org/wiki/Stanford_marshmallow_experiment.

82. A genesis block is the first block of a block chain.

83. This is a practical process that any business, organization, and even a family can implement. It's explained thoroughly in "Life Design for Business" workshops, workbooks, and with certified coaches.

84. Donald D. Hoffman and Chetan Prakash, "Objects of Consciousness," Frontiers in Psychology, last modified June 17, 2014, https://www.frontiersin.org/articles/10.3389/fpsyg.2014.00577/full.

85. "Digital Physics," Wikipedia, accessed February 16, 2020, https://en.wikipedia.org/wiki/Digital_physics.

86. Colin Dwyer, "'Like A God,' Google A.I. Beats Human Champ of Notoriously Complex Go Game," NPR, last modified May 23, 2017, https://www.npr.org/sections/thetwo-way/2017/05/23/529673475/like-a-god-google-a-i-beats-human-champ-of-notoriously-complex-go-game.

87. Max Tegmark, *Our Mathematical Universe: My Quest for the Ultimate Nature of Reality* (New York: Vintage Books, 2014).

88. Rob Dunn, "The Top Ten Daily Consequences of Having Evolved," Smithsonian Magazine, last modified November 19, 2010, https://www.smithsonianmag.com/science-nature/the-top-ten-daily-consequences-of-having-evolved-72743121.

89. Eric B. Dent, "The Observation, Inquiry, and Measurement Challenges Surfaced by Complexity Theory," In *Managing the Complex: Philosophy, Theory and Practice*, ed. Kurt Richardson, available at http://faculty.uncfsu.edu/edent/Observation.pdf.

90. Cara Feinberg, "The Placebo Phenomenon," Harvard Magazine, last modified March 3, 2014, https://harvardmagazine.com/2013/01/the-placebo-phenomenon.

91. Richard Alleyne, "Welcome to the Information Age—174 Newspapers a Day," The Telegraph, last modified February 11, 2011, https://www.telegraph.co.uk/news/science/science-news/8316534/Welcome-to-the-information-age-174-newspapers-a-day.html.

92. Sofie L. Valk, Fynn-Mathis Trautwein, Boris C. Bernhardt, Anne Böckler, Philipp Kanske, Nicolas Guizard, D. Louis Collins, and Tania Singer, "Structural

Plasticity of the Social Brain: Differential Change after Socio-Affective and Cognitive Mental Training," Science Advances, last modified October 4, 2017, http://advances.sciencemag.org/content/3/10/e1700489.

93. Veronika Engert, Bethany E. Kok, Ioannis Papassotiriou, George P. Chrousos, and Tania Singer, "Specific Reduction in Cortisol Stress Reactivity after Social but Not Attention-Based Mental Training," Science Advances, last modified October 4, 2017, http://advances.sciencemag.org/content/3/10/e1700495.

94. Scott Bea, "Wanna Give? This Is Your Brain on a 'Helper's High'" Cleveland Clinic HealthEssentials, last modified November 15, 2016, http://health. clevelandclinic.org/2014/12/why-giving-is-good-for-your-health.

95. Arthur Brooks, "Why Giving Makes You Happy," The New York Sun, accessed February 16, 2020, http://www.nysun.com/opinion/why-giving-makes-you-happy/68700.

96. Studies by Paul Zak, the director of the Center for Neuroeconomics at Claremont University, found that people on an "oxytocin high" can potentially jumpstart a "virtuous circle, where one person's generous behavior triggers another's."

97. James H. Fowler and Nicholas A. Christakis, "Cooperative Behavior Cascades in Human Social Networks," *Proceedings of the National Academy of Sciences of the United States of America* 2010 2010; 107(12): 5334-5338; https://doi.org/10.1073/pnas.0913149107.

98. Isabel Pastor Guzman, "Are We What We Eat?" Brain World, accessed February 3, 2020, https://brainworldmagazine.com/are-we-what-we-eat.

99. Biagio D'Aniello, Gün Refik Semin, Alessandra Alterisio, Massimo Aria, and Anna Scandurra, "Interspecies Transmission of Emotional Information via Chemosignals: From Humans to Dogs (*Canis Lupus familiaris*)," *Animal Cognition* 21, no. 1 (July 2017): 67–78, https://doi.org/10.1007/s10071-017-1139-x.

100. "The Water in You: Water and the Human Body," United States Geological Survey, accessed February 16, 2020, https://www.usgs.gov/special-topic/water-science-school/science/water-you-water-and-human-body?qt-science_center_objects=0#qt-science_center_objects.

101. Gerald Pollack, *The Fourth Phase of Water: Beyond Solid, Liquid, and Vapor* (Seattle: Ebner and Sons Publishers, 2013).

102. "WHO Global Ambient Air Quality Database (update 2018)," World Health Organization, accessed April 12, 2020, https://www.who.int/airpollution/data/cities/en.

103. "More than 90% of the World's Children Breathe Toxic Air Every Day," World Health Organization, accessed February 16, 2020, https://www.who.int/news-room/detail/29-10-2018-more-than-90-of-the-world's-children-breathe-toxic-air-every-day.

104. "What Is YPO Forum?" YPO, accessed February 16, 2020, https://publicvideos.ypo.org/what-is-a-ypo-wpo-forum.

Index

NOTE: Page numbers in *italic* indicate figures. **Bold** page numbers indicate a figure.

Purposehood

You ask, "What can I do right now?"

1. Pass this copy of the book to someone who can benefit from it or gift them another copy.

2. Download the Purposehood app and start your daily practices. Soon, you will be able to do more as new features added to help you connect with others around shared Purposehoods.

3. Volunteer your talent on Purposehood.org to become a co-founder of the Purposehood movement.

4. Sign up for The Purposehood Method course to expand your knowledge, examine your life, network with others, and become a qualified Purposehood coach to help others discover and live their existential purposes.

Lightning Source UK Ltd.
Milton Keynes UK
UKHW020043060620
364543UK00014B/608/J